Social institutions are prevalent wherever individuals attempt to live and work together. To be a member of a community or society is to live within a set of social institutions. Many of our fundamental questions about social life entail an examination of the role played by these institutions. Why do we have so many? Why do they take one form in one society and quite a different form in another? How did they develop? And when and why do the forms of institutions change?

In *Institutions and Social Conflict*, Jack Knight addresses these questions in two ways. First, he offers a thorough critique of a wide range of theories of institutional change, from the classical accounts of Smith, Hume, Marx, and Weber to the contemporary approaches of evolutionary theory, the theory of social conventions, and the new institutionalism. Second, he develops a new theory of institutional change that emphasizes the distributional consequences of social institutions. His primary focus is on the spontaneous emergence of the network of informal conventions and norms that form the basis of society. This emergence is explained as a by-product of distributional conflict in which asymmetries of power in a society generate institutional solutions to that conflict. The secondary focus is on the stability of these informal rules and on the effects of introducing the state into the bargaining over formal institutions.

Knight draws his examples from an extensive variety of social institutions: measures of time and space; property rights; the family, gender, and race relations; forms of economic organization; community associations; political institutions; and international organizations and treaties. This book should be of interest to social scientists, political and social theorists, philosophers, legal theorists, and anyone else interested in questions of institutional change.

INSTITUTIONS AND SOCIAL CONFLICT

THE POLITICAL ECONOMY OF INSTITUTIONS AND DECISIONS

Editors
James E. Alt, *Harvard University*
Douglass C. North, *Washington University in St. Louis*

INSTITUTIONS AND SOCIAL CONFLICT

JACK KNIGHT

Washington University

CAMBRIDGE
UNIVERSITY PRESS

Published by the Press Syndicate of the University of Cambridge
The Pitt Building, Trumpington Street, Cambridge CB2 1RP
40 West 20th Street, New York, NY 10011-4211, USA
10 Stamford Road, Oakleigh, Victoria 3166, Australia

First published 1992

Printed in the United States of America

Library of Congress Cataloging-in-Publication Data
Knight, Jack, 1952–
Institutions and social conflict / Jack Knight.
    p.   cm. – (The Political economy of institutions and
                decisions)
Includes bibliographical references and index.
ISBN 0–521–42052–0 (hc). – ISBN 0–521–42189–6 (pb)
1. Social institutions. 2. Social conflict. 3. Organizational
        sociology.   I. Title.   II. Series.
                HM131.K617   1992
303.6–dc20   92–3575
                                                           CIP

A catalog record for this book is available from the British Library.

ISBN 0–521–42052–0 hardback
ISBN 0–521–42189–6 paperback

To my mother
and
To the memory of my father

Contents

Contents

Series editors' preface

The Cambridge series on the Political Economy of Institutions and Decisions is built around attempts to answer two central questions: How do institutions evolve in response to individual incentives, strategies, and choices? and, How do institutions affect the performance of political and economic systems? The scope of the series is comparative and historical rather than international or specifically American, and the focus is positive rather than normative.

This book takes the view that social institutions are informal and formal rules which constrain individual behavior. Knight argues that making rational choices about institutions requires that individuals form expectations about their own and others' future preferences. The institutions themselves can help ensure consistency of expectations across individuals, a precondition for institutional equilibrium or stability. Individuals then act to secure those institutions that create the "best" constraints in view of their expectations. Knight argues that what counts in making some chosen rules or arrangements "best" is their distributional consequences rather than their expected social or aggregate output. Thus, although maintaining a rational-choice framework, Knight drops the welfare-maximizing postulate of the economic theory of efficient institutions in favor of the assumption that politics is about distributional conflict, yet still shows how strategic action and bargaining play a role in the development and maintenance of these institutions.

By starting out from the likelihood that individual and collective benefits could point to divergent choices, Knight avoids resorting to arguments about natural selection and functionalism. Instead, for him there simply are no necessarily efficient and inefficient institutions, just outcomes entailing different distributions. His theory of the emergence and maintenance of institutions is an important contribution to several disciplines, including economics, sociology, and philosophy.

Preface

Institutions matter. That was the basis on which I began the research in graduate school for the dissertation on which this book is based. But how they mattered and their implications were, at that time, beyond me. I had been motivated by dissatisfaction with both sides of the micro–macro debate in the philosophy of social science. The fact that social outcomes were a product of both individual action and social structure seemed self-evident to me. All of the discussion that focused exclusively on one side or the other of this question seemed beside the point.

So I set out to learn everything I could about the different ways that social institutions were treated in the social sciences. Over time I decided that the way to explain the institutional effects on social life was to concentrate on the relationship between rational action and institutional constraints. But although I thought that the rational-choice approach offered a key to the relationship between action and structure, I was unwilling to accept what I thought to be the narrow (and wrongheaded) emphasis on collective benefits. This emphasis failed to capture many of the reasons that I thought institutions mattered. It ignored the politics inherent in social life and it limited the ways in which institutional development and change could be explained.

After spending too much time worrying about what other people had to say about the issue, I wrote a dissertation that tried to explain the rationality of social institutions in terms of their distributional effects. I can thank Jon Elster, Russell Hardin, and Adam Przeworski for giving me all the rope I needed to hang myself at that point. They were tough, skeptical, demanding, insightful, extraordinarily helpful in their advice, unrelenting and exhaustive in their criticism, and occasionally supportive. In the end, as is true of many dissertations, no one, including myself, was completely satisfied with the results. Everyone seemed to agree with my ideas but found my arguments and justifications in need of a lot of work.

Preface

So I left Chicago and went to St. Louis to straighten out the arguments. In the process I completely rewrote the manuscript. Now I think that my arguments about emergence and change, stability and conflict, information and sanctions, action and structure, and, most importantly, distribution and power are about right. At least they seem to hold up in the face of much of the same skepticism and challenges. Now I can offer a theory of institutional emergence, stability, and change that includes the essential features of the disagreements in the old micro–macro debates. It is grounded in the relationship between rational action and institutional structure, but it centers on the distributional conflict characterizing much of the macro-level analysis of those institutions. It justifies this emphasis both theoretically and empirically, with arguments that should both appeal to and annoy everybody. Some of them will be challenged by rational-choice theorists, and others will be questioned by macro-level critics of the approach. In the end I hope that the readers will at least follow the arguments to their conclusion and will find them, on the whole, persuasive.

There are many people that I would like to thank for their help in writing this book. At the University of Chicago, I benefited from discussions with Chris Achen, Robert Barros, Bruce Carruthers, Tom Christiano, Ingrid Creppel, Saguiv Hadari, Chris Holoman, Jennifer Holt-Dwyer, Mark Hornung, David Menefee-Libey, Duncan Snidal, Gina Soos, Kimberly Stanton, Michael Wallerstein, Margaret Weir, and Cui Zhiyuan, among others. At Washington University in St. Louis, I gained from conversations with Barry Ames, Kevin Corder, Gayle Corrigan, Jean Ensminger, Robert Foley, John Gilmour, Brad Hansen, Steve Lewis, William Lowry, Carol Mershon, Gary Miller, Kristina Neidringhaus, Andrew Rutten, Norman Schofield, Itai Sened, Serenella Sferza, Andrew Sobel, Rorie Spill, Stephen Stedman, and Julie Withers. While writing the book I also learned much from discussions with James Alt, John Ferejohn, Vic Goldberg, Margaret Levi, Terry Moe, and Kenneth Shepsle.

Some people deserve special mention (and possibly blame). From Chicago to France and several places in between, Professors Elster, Hardin, and Przeworski continued to engage and stimulate me long after their role as dissertation advisers had passed. In St. Louis, Douglass North challenged, encouraged, and motivated me far beyond the call of duty. Even when he thought my arguments (especially those that question his own work) were half-baked, he encouraged me to work them out and get them straight. Jim Johnson has been the finest intellectual companion and friend that one could ask for. We were in graduate school together and have stood by each other ever since. Even though he is now at Northwestern and I am in St. Louis, there is no sign that our intellectual debate has diminished in the least. This book would have been quite different without his suggestions, criticisms, and support.

Finally, I want to thank Gayle Corrigan, Kristina Neidringhaus, Rorie Spill, and Steve Lewis for their outstanding research assistance. And I would also like to thank Emily Loose and Katharita Lamoza at Cambridge University Press for their exceptional assistance. If Emily had not been persistent in her support of this project, I would still be writing it. And I am very glad that I am not.

1

Introduction

Social institutions are prevalent wherever individuals attempt to live and work together. From the simplest to the most complex, we produce them while conducting all aspects of our social life. From political decision making to economic production and exchange to the rules governing personal relationships, institutional arrangements establish the framework in which these social interactions take place. To be a member of a community or society is to live within a set of social institutions.

Consider their variety. At the most basic level of society, an array of social conventions, rules, and norms affects the ways in which we act in our everyday lives. Their influences on social life are substantial and numerous. They structure relations between the sexes and the ongoing affairs of family life; they set the standards of behavior among the members of a neighborhood or community; and they constitute an important source for the transmission of social knowledge and information from one generation to the next. In short, these informal conventions form the base on which a vast range of formal institutions organize and influence economic and political life. Economic organizations, from the small firm to the multinational corporation, are governed by institutional frameworks in the workplace and the boardroom. More generally, economic markets themselves are structured by institutions that include the systems of property rights defining economic exchanges. Political decision making, from the neighborhood association to the government of a nation, is framed by institutional rules and procedures. The very establishment of these political institutions is regulated in most countries by a constitution, probably the most all-encompassing form of institution found at the national level. Many of these economic and political institutions are buttressed by the force of law, itself a pervasive institution that in many important ways is the mere formalization of informal conventions and norms. Finally, an ever-growing set

1

of international conventions and norms, treaties, and rules influence everything from international trade to the rules of engagement in a war zone.

Many of our fundamental questions about social life entail an examination of the role played by these institutions. Why do we have so many? Why do they take one form in one society and quite a different form in another? What are the effects of these different arrangements? How did they develop? And when and why do the forms of institutions change? Many conflicting answers from a wide range of intellectual sources have been offered to these questions. The implications of how we answer them are numerous. From an explanatory perspective, social explanations of institutional development and change help us understand both the history of a society and its contemporary events. From a critical perspective, an understanding of institutional change allows us to determine whether our existing institutions further those goals by which they are usually justified. From a normative perspective, an understanding of how institutions evolve influences our ability to reform them.

Questions such as these are the main subject of this book. The primary focus is on the basic network of conventions, norms, rights, and rules on which a society is based. I shall analyze how this informal network develops and changes and what happens when this network is formalized as law backed by the enforcement of the state. I also shall consider this network's effects on the development of other formal institutional arrangements, both economic and political. To do this, first, I shall examine the various existing theories, delineate their common themes (even across diverse intellectual disciplines), and assess their merits. Second, I shall propose and develop an alternative theory of institutional emergence and change that captures important features of social life missing from the other accounts. Third, I shall consider the implications of different theories of institutional change for our understanding of existing social institutions and for our critical and normative judgments about those institutions.

Let us begin by defining a *social institution*. Social theory offers various definitions, ranging from that of formal organizations, which have explicit rules and forms of administration and enforcement, to that of any stabilized pattern of human relationships and actions (March and Simon, 1958; Taylor, 1982; Weber, 1978). Although each of these definitions singles out certain aspects of institutional detail, the simplest and most straightforward way to derive a working definition is to identify the common features of institutions in these various contexts. First, an institution is *a set of rules that structure social interactions in particular ways*. Second, for a set of rules to be an institution, *knowledge of these rules must be shared by the members of the relevant community or*

Introduction

society. This definition gives broad scope to what might be considered a social institution while at the same time excluding behavior often considered institutional. Thus, rules of thumb such as the maxims "pay my bills on the day I get my paycheck," "get an hour of exercise five days a week," and "get a physical once a year" are not institutions. Although such rules may help organize one's daily life, they are purely private constraints, idiosyncratic to the individual actor.

In subsequent chapters I shall explore and elaborate this conception of a social institution, but I shall mention briefly two related issues now. By so doing, I can clarify at the outset the scope of my analysis and also address two contemporary debates. First, an important implication of this broad definition is the implicit rejection of the law–society dichotomy underlying much of the analysis in legal anthropology and jurisprudence (Comaroff and Roberts, 1981; Starr and Collier, 1989). According to this distinction, the only institutions with lasting structural effects on social life are legal ones. Thus, societies that lack developed systems of legal enforcement are presumed to lack an institutional framework worthy of analysis. Although it is important to acknowledge a variance in the extent to which institutions require some external authority to ensure their enforcement, the dichotomy is a false one. Law and legal institutions rely on the state's enforcement powers to guarantee that social actors will abide by these rules and procedures. Other types of institutions, such as social conventions and international institutions, are self-enforcing in the sense that no external authority is available to guarantee that social actors will respect them. Whatever sanctions do exist in these cases are informal and decentralized. Between these two extremes of externally enforced and self-enforcing institutions are many institutions with some of the characteristics of both, institutions that are recognized and authorized in principle by some external authority such as the state but that are organized by the behavior of the particular actors involved. Note that each of these institutional forms can have significant and related effects on the structure of social interactions. The distinction between formal and informal sanctions is relevant primarily to the extent of those effects and their stability over time.

A second clarification pertains to the difference between an institution and an organization. Whereas institutions are sets of rules that structure interactions among actors, organizations are collective actors who might be subject to institutional constraint. Organizations generally have an internal structure, an institutional framework governing the interactions of those persons who constitute the organization. Accordingly, several collective entities can be conceptualized as both an institution and an organization, for example, a firm, a governmental bureaucracy, a church, or a university.

3

To underscore the importance of this distinction, consider the recent resurgence in the emphasis on political institutions. According to analyses of state institutions and bureaucracies, institutions are important because they are independent political actors with their own goals and interests (Evans, Rueschemeyer, and Skocpol, 1985; Katzenstein, 1978; Skowronek, 1982). State institutions are combined with other factors in macro-level explanations of political outcomes.[1] The power of these explanations rests in their elaboration of "state capacities" – the extent to which the state can implement its own goals in the face of opposing actors and adverse conditions (Nordlinger, 1981; Skocpol, 1985). The key theoretical point is that the greater the "state capacities" are, the more important the role of state institutions will be in the production of political outcomes.

This is helpful as far as it goes, but this is really a debate about the autonomy of the state: To what extent do state institutions have autonomous interests motivating their agents to act in independent ways?[2] As I have defined it, this is merely a debate about the effectiveness of state organizations as collective actors and not about the distinctiveness of social institutions. An inquiry in the spirit of my analysis would ask: What are the effects on "state capacities" caused by various state institutional arrangements? More generally, questions about the effectiveness of organizations as actors do not address what is distinctive about institutions for social explanations. This question can be addressed, as I shall suggest, only by considering the relationship between institutional rules and social action.

CLASSICAL ACCOUNTS OF INSTITUTIONAL CHANGE

Social and institutional change has long been a subject of concern to scholars of various intellectual traditions. Although the proposed explanations have been diverse, we can categorize them into two schools of thought characterized by their differing emphasis on the distinctive effects of social institutions. The first conception of development and change stresses the collective benefits of social institutions for the community as a whole. The second conception emphasizes the discriminating benefits of such institutions, the disproportionate advantages for some segments of a community produced by an institutional framework. The distinction is, broadly, one between coordination and conflict, between the coordination of interests and the competition among

---

1 See Levi, 1988, for a thorough and intelligent review of the burgeoning literature that seeks to "bring the state back in."
2 See Przeworski, 1990, for a general critique of theories on the autonomy of the state.

interests.[3] By reviewing some of the prominent proponents of these two conceptions, we can begin to see some of the implications of the different approaches and how the first conception has come to dominate contemporary thinking on these questions.

Consider first the coordination-for-collective-benefits conception of social institutions. Four central mechanisms for institutional change have developed in this tradition, mechanisms which still dominate contemporary discussions. One of these mechanisms, the contract, forms the basis for classical accounts of the intentional development of social institutions. Thomas Hobbes (1963) used the contract to explain the intentional design of the state's original political institutions. Those who lived in a pregovernment state of nature were said to have entered into a general social contract in which the nature and form of basic political institutions were established. Because the focus of my book is primarily the evolution of social institutions and only secondarily their intentional design and reform, the Hobbesian influence on contemporary accounts of the intentional design of political institutions will receive less attention. I shall return, however, to the question of the contract as a mechanism of intentional design in Chapter 6.

The classical accounts use three mechanisms to explain the evolution of social institutions: spontaneous emergence, exchange coordinated by the market, and social selection. Although these mechanisms do share common characteristics, they offer distinctive answers to questions of institutional development. Their basic logic can be found in the classical works of David Hume, Adam Smith, and Herbert Spencer.

Hume introduced the idea of the spontaneous emergence of norms of justice and property as a counterargument against two existing justifications of such institutions: (1) natural-rights accounts, such as John Locke's view of property, and (2) contractarian accounts such as Hobbes's view of the state (Hume, 1978: bk. III, pt. II, sec. II). To counteract these explanations emphasizing the intentional design of property rights, Hume used an evolutionary account that focused on the emergence of social conventions and norms as the unintended product of an ongoing process of social interaction. The problem, to which the conventions of justice and property are conceived as a solution, is a classic one: In a world of scarce resources, how does a community prevent others from interfering in the enjoyment of the benefits of one person's

---

3 The term *coordination* has come to have a technical meaning in the game-theoretic literature. A coordination game is a game in which there is more than one equilibrium that will benefit the actors if they can find a way to coordinate their strategies on the same one. Here I use the word more generally to describe both situations in which social actors intentionally coordinate their actions and situations in which the coordination is accomplished by a mechanism such as the market.

property? According to the spontaneous-emergence thesis, social actors resolve this problem over time in the process of being confronted by it in their repeated interactions with one another. In these recurring interactions, individuals come to realize that some rule of "just" division will be an improvement over anarchic transgressions of property claims. Through a process of trial and error the actors begin to recognize that certain patterns of behavior become the standard responses to questions of property division. How these patterns come to be established in the Humean account is unclear. But as people come to anticipate these patterns in the appropriate situation, they begin to expect that these rules will be followed in the future. Eventually a convention stabilizes, and the members of the community come to treat this rule as the appropriate and just form of behavior. From this, Hume concludes that norms of justice and property are therefore artificial and not the product of conscious design. A further implication is that the establishment of such norms is arbitrary and could just as easily have developed in substantially different forms. The key here for Hume is not the exact nature of the norm but, rather, that some norm is necessary for the collective benefit of the community as a whole.

This theme of spontaneous emergence is also prevalent in Adam Smith's account of the institutional development of capitalism, but it is supplemented by the concept of institutional development through exchange coordinated by the market. In analyzing Smith's work on morality and political economy, we find a social theory that synthesizes intentional and unintentional institutional design. The logic is the same in either case: the development of social institutions through an ongoing network of interactions among small subsets of the community. In regard to a community's normative order, Smith shared a view similar to Hume's, describing the spontaneous emergence of a system of basic sanctions to control the selfish behavior of individuals (Smith, 1969). Smith emphasized a similar learning through trial and error in which people establish both internal and external sanctions to restrain self-interested actions. These sanctions introduce a certain degree of impartiality in the behavior of social actors, moderating selfishness with a concern for what an "impartial spectator" in a community would consider appropriate behavior (pp. 161–2). Although the external sanctions appeal to the individual's desire for social approbation, the internal sanctions are the product of an internalization process necessary to satisfy the individual's desire for self-approbation. Thus, a two-tiered sanctioning mechanism evolves to constrain self-interested behavior, for the benefit of the community as a whole.

Within this normative order a variety of economic and political institutions are produced from the exchanges of individual actors in the mar-

6

Introduction

ket (Smith, 1976). This is the logic of the famous "invisible hand" argument. Through exchanges, individual actors devise patterns of behavior that allow them to exploit their gains from specialization and trade. The market coordinates in two ways these individual contracts for the benefit of the community as a whole. First, the pressures of the market prevent individual actors from using their bargaining power to produce institutional arrangements that would harm either other individuals or the whole community. Smith stresses the negative effects of economic power unconstrained by the market (IV.vii.c. 631–2). Second, the competitive pressures of the market encourage greater efficiency in the development of economic institutions (I.xi.b. 163–4). Over time, those institutions that are less efficient are squeezed out of the market by those who emulate more efficient contract exchanges. In these ways the market tends to produce collectively beneficial economic institutions.

Hume's and Smith's themes of spontaneous emergence and the market coordination of exchange are central to the classical tradition of collective benefits. A third theme, social selection, comes from a quite different intellectual tradition, but it also can be detected in the invisible-hand arguments. To identify the similarities, consider the logic of social selection as presented by Spencer (Spencer, 1969). Theories of social selection explain the development of social institutions according to the criterion of fitness. Social institutions arise and persist to the extent that they help societies survive in a competitive world. Social institutions are viewed in terms of their capacity to satisfy the functional needs of the community. The central elements of this evolutionary process are variation, selection, and inheritance. For Spencer the growth of a society follows a path of increasing structural differentiation, an ever-growing variety of institution forms. These social institutions have an important impact on a society's capacity to adapt functionally to changing circumstances. The pressures to adapt arise from the population's growth and the resulting competition among communities for available resources. This competition then becomes the mechanism for evolutionary selection: Only those societies whose institutions render them capable of growth and adaptation will survive. For Spencer this competition is ultimately manifested as war and struggle among societies, with those societies that grow in both number and abilities conquering those less able to adapt. The remaining societies pass on collectively beneficial institutional forms to future generations. Then the social-selection mechanism repeats itself through future competition. The division of labor in a society is the prototypical example of successful evolution.

Here we can see the similarity between Smith's market-coordination-of-exchange mechanism and Spencer's social-selection mechanism. Smith identified the division of labor as the product of individual

7

exchange tempered by market competition; that is, the market selects those institutional forms producing the most benefits for the community. The market is for Smith what competition among societies is for Spencer. Both theories emphasize the collective benefits produced by social institutions.

In contrast with this collective-benefits approach to social institutions, there is a second classical tradition that places greater emphasis on the discriminating effects of these institutions. According to this alternative approach, social institutions can be explained in terms of their beneficial effects on particular segments of the community. It suggests a central focus on the conflict of interests inherent in distributional questions. Yet despite all of its implications for a theory of conflict in institutional development and change, the second approach, the "discriminating effects" approach, remained much less elaborated than the first approach in terms of microfoundations and mechanisms for change. Two theorists reflect this emphasis on distributional questions: Karl Marx and Max Weber.

For Marx, social and institutional change was not a smooth path of increasing collective improvements but, rather, was a sequence of fluctuations between stability and substantial change, with each change shuffling those social groups who most benefited from the dominant institutional arrangements (Marx, 1986: 187–8). He offered two distinct theories to explain this change: historical materialism and class conflict.

The first theory proposed a societal-level dynamic of change driven by a functional relationship between the forces and the relations of production. When the relations of production (the existing institutions) no longer satisfied the functional requirements for the continued growth of the forces of production (the famous "fettering" of the forces-of-production argument), an institutional revolution would occur, creating new institutional relations more functionally suitable for continued economic growth. How this revolution would come about remained unanswered by the theory of historical materialism. The second theory elaborated an irreconcilable tension between the interests and capacities of different economic classes and suggested that this tension would be manifested in a fundamental social revolution. How this revolution would lead to new institutions functionally superior to the previously existing order remained unanswered by the theory of class conflict. Thus, although both theories rested on the view that social institutions discriminated in favor of the dominant social groups and could be explained in these terms, they remained alternative accounts of inevitable institutional change, failing to offer a synthesis that would explain the necessity of the change in the relations of production – the institutional founda-

8

tion of society – in terms of conflict among the classes.[4] Here the emphasis on distributional effects is important to the explanation of institutional maintenance, but it fails to enter adequately into an account of the mechanism of institutional change.

A similar attention to the bias inherent in social institutions is present in Weber's account of social and institutional change. His major works can be characterized as an attempt to show why social institutions favoring some social groups survive, whereas those favoring other segments of the community either fail to arise or perish.[5] His classic account of the rise to dominance of the Protestant ethic and the resulting institutions of modern capitalism is his most concise and systematic account of the competition inherent in institutional change (Weber, 1989). Although Weber recognizes the important distributional effects of these institutional changes and even explains their maintenance in terms of dominant interests, these effects fail to enter fundamentally into his theory of change. Weber's theory is a classic account of the systematic adaptation of behavior to changes in the economic and social environment. Initially a subset of economic entrepreneurs found it in their interests (broadly defined to include nonmaterial interests) to alter their economic behavior. Such behavior was found to be advantageous (defined more narrowly in terms of material interests) in light of changing economic conditions and was, therefore, emulated by others. After a period of transition, market conditions forced others to comport with the new forms of economic behavior. Here Weber's theory adopts aspects of Smith's notion of the competitive pressures of the market: The new forms of behavior become a necessity and not a choice. Note that the mechanism initiating the change seems to be accidental and that serendipitous, nonmaterial interests produce a strategy dynamically superior to those dictated by material interests in the market. In the end Weber offers a theory of social change that fails to elaborate a mechanism for change that adequately incorporates the fundamental insight of the importance of conflict and distributional effects.

CONTEMPORARY THEORIES OF INSTITUTIONAL CHANGE

In contemporary analyses the problem of institutionalization has been conceptualized as a problem of collective action. The role of institutions

4 For a detailed analysis of the alternative theories of social change in Marx's writings, see Elster, 1985.
5 See, for example, Weber's programatic statement of the study of change at the beginning of *Economy and Society*, 1978: 39–40. This statement has led some writers to describe Weber erroneously as an adherent of a social-selection theory of institutional evolution; see, for example, Langton, 1982. A careful review of this statement will show that it in no way implies an acceptance of the standard social-selection thesis.

is to resolve recurring problems in society (Schotter, 1981); institutions are constraints that help individuals avoid the negative "emerging effects" of collective action (Boudon, 1981); institutions enable social actors to work together to produce beneficial social goals (Elster, 1989a); and institutions reconcile rationality at the individual level with rationality at the collective level (Bates, 1988). The possible citations are endless. Given the heightened sensitivity to problems of collective action and collective decision making in the years since the publication of the seminal works by Arrow (1951) and Olson (1965), this emphasis on institutions as a solution to collective problems is understandable.

This contemporary focus is reminiscent of the classical tradition of coordination and collective benefits. The fact that this tradition had better-developed microfoundations of institutional change makes the contemporary dominance of theories of institutions as collective or public goods even more understandable. In some ways the contemporary discussion of institutional change is merely a continuation of the tradition represented here by Hume and Smith. This is also true of the conception of the fundamental role of institutions in social life as well as the mechanisms for institutional change.

To illustrate this, let me suggest a way of categorizing contemporary theories of social institutions, according to two criteria: (1) the institutional effects invoked to explain maintenance and stability and (2) the mechanism for institutional change. First, institutional maintenance and stability are explained in contemporary accounts by their ability to produce collective goods or benefits for the relevant group or community. The collective benefits may be efficiency (in regard to the allocation or employment of resources), social optimality (in regard to the maximization of social benefits), minimization of transaction costs, stability, or the satisfaction of some other functional need. Here we can distinguish "naive" and "sophisticated" variants of this collective-benefits explanation. The naive variant assumes that social institutions produce efficient or socially optimal outcomes. The sophisticated variant allows for the possibility that suboptimal institutions may develop and persist, but it retains the conception of collective benefits and seeks to explain these inefficiencies in the context of failures or weaknesses within the community. However, in either variant the continued ability of an institution to provide one of these collective benefits is invoked to explain its ongoing stability.

Second, theories of institutional change can be distinguished by the form of the change on which they focus. Evolutionary theories generally rely on one of the mechanisms foreshadowed by classical theory: spontaneous emergence, market-coordinated exchange, or social selection. Theories of intentional design usually adopt a contractarian ap-

10

Constituti

proach, defining institutions as the intentional product of either (1) an enforceable exchange of resources or benefits among private actors or (2) political competition over the influence of public policymaking.[6] Complicating this conceptual distinction is the fact that a number of recent theories either explicitly or, more often, implicitly combine aspects of both approaches: intentional design at the micro level that is subject to some competitive selection process (either the market or some other competitive mechanism) at the macro level.

Throughout this book I shall examine in detail the explanations and arguments for several of these theories. Here I shall merely situate various contemporary accounts in this framework, reserving assessment and criticism for later discussions. Evolutionary accounts of social and institutional change use a collective-benefits emphasis to describe a wide range of institutional forms. Naive theories that focus on evolutionary development explain basic social conventions (Lewis, 1969), norms (Axelrod, 1986), law (Posner, 1980), property rights (Schotter, 1981), and various forms of social and economic organization (Brennan and Buchanan, 1985; Merton, 1968; Parsons, 1945; Williamson, 1975, 1985). Sophisticated evolutionary theories include explanations of social conventions and norms (Sugden, 1986, 1989), property rights (Barzel, 1989; Libecap, 1989; North, 1990), and some forms of economic organization (Coase, 1960; Nelson and Winter, 1982).

Some of these theories, especially those explanations of a community's network of conventions and norms, are based on the spontaneous-emergence logic, whose most influential contemporary formulation was devised by Hayek (1967). Hayek's theory of cultural evolution establishes the framework for these "spontaneous order" explanations. First is the invisible-hand mechanism: Social institutions are the unintended social consequence of individual action. Second is the arbitrariness of the resultant institutions: Because people lack the knowledge to design socially optimal institutions by themselves, the spontaneous order can take any one of a number of different forms. This also implies that the spontaneous order does not systematically favor any particular segment of the community. Third is a process of social selection: The collectively beneficial nature of the emerging order is determined by a competitive-selection mechanism. In his various works, Hayek offers differing ac-

---

6 Here the influence of the Hobbesian social-contract tradition can be seen in analyses of political institutions. An alternative source of influence, however, can be found in others as diverse as Smith and Marx. Although Hobbes is often cited in contemporary accounts as the one who formulated the basic question of why we design and comply with political institutions, his influence on the analysis of the contracting and design process is less well established.

counts of this selection mechanism, but among them is the Humean mechanism, which has been the basis for many recent formalizations of spontaneous order: learning by imitation (1967: 78).[7]

Other theories, mainly those seeking to explain property rights or other economic institutions, are based on the market-competition-as-selection-mechanism thesis that is most often attributed to Alchian (1950). A direct descendant of Smith's invisible-hand thesis, the Alchian logic relies on the market's competitive pressure to select socially beneficial forms of economic organization. In its purest form, the argument requires no particular intentionality on the part of individual economic actors; rather, the main purpose of the original article was to suggest that economic analysis need not rely on the claim that economic actors actually make the sophisticated utility-maximization calculations prevalent in rational-actor models. Thanks to the competitive pressure of the market, the resulting equilibrium consists of a socially efficient set of economic organizations whose behavior appears "as if" they were utility maximizers. The market selects out the most efficient forms of organization and production, thereby guaranteeing social efficiency even if the actors' intentions do not allow for it.

Many recent accounts that use the market-selection logic deviate from the pure evolutionary form and synthesize competitive selection with intentional attempts to create rights or forms of organization through market exchange. Prominent examples are those employing Coase's (1960) theory of transaction costs to explain the structure of economic exchange. A naive variant is provided by Williamson (1975, 1985), and a sophisticated variant by North (1990). Individual economic actors try to order their exchanges in such a way as to minimize the costs of these transactions. But for these private orderings to become institutionalized for the community as a whole, there must be some means of generalizing them. Here the competitive pressure of the market comes into play, selecting those orderings that best minimize costs.

Some of the theories ostensibly based on the spontaneous-emergence or market-coordinated exchange mechanisms in fact rely on less developed Spencerian notions of social selection. Other theories do explicitly adopt such an explanatory strategy. In studies of the law this evolutionary functionalism has a long history, gaining early modern acceptance in the work of Montesquieu (1989). Legal evolution is described as a response to a community's changing functional needs. This logic – the dominant explanation of theorists in the sociological tradition such as Parsons (1945) and Merton (1968) – has been used to explain legal de-

7 In addressing the evolution of nonmarket institutions, Hayek often suggested that a more classical social Darwinian natural-selection mechanism was in operation. See my discussion of the ambiguity in Hayek's philosophy of spontaneous order in Chapter 4.

velopments in both primitive (Posner, 1980) and modern (Ellickson, 1991) societies.[8]

Theories of intentional design have been employed mainly to explain the creation of political institutions. Here I separate the transaction costs–based theories, which synthesize intentional and evolutionary elements, from those theories completely based on intentional efforts to develop institutional arrangements.[9] Among the intentional accounts, the sophisticated variant of the collective benefits thesis is used to explain maintenance and development. Two strands can be detected. In the first the creation of basic political rules and institutions is attributed to competition among members of a "founding" body: either constitutions (Heckathorn and Maser, 1987; Riker, 1988; Tsebelis, 1990) or legislative rules and principles (Shepsle, 1986; Shepsle and Ordeshook, 1982). In the second strand the establishment of political institutions and rights is the responsibility of an established government. The nature of those rights is seen as the product of competition among state officials and private interest groups (Bates, 1989; Ensminger, 1992; North, 1990; Sened, 1990). Issues of distribution are explicitly acknowledged in these intentional theories, usually to explain the suboptimality of political institutions. But the interpretations given in these accounts maintain a primary focus on collective benefits and coordination. Implicit in these arguments is the idea that inefficiency and suboptimality are somehow the product of state intervention in the natural order of things.

RATIONALITY AND SOCIAL INSTITUTIONS

In this book I argue that the emphasis on collective benefits in theories of social institutions fails to capture crucial features of institutional development and change. I further argue that our explanations should invoke the distributional effects of such institutions and the conflict inherent in

8 Gordon (1984) suggests that evolutionary functionalism has been the dominant vision of modern jurisprudence since the sixteenth century, arguing that such an approach informed the traditions of both Smith and Marx. His analysis offers a detailed discussion of the implications of a functionalist perspective for the development of legal histories.

9 One important branch of intentional analysis is characterized by normative concerns. In economics this emphasis is represented by the literature on the incentive-compatibility and demand-revelation mechanisms: What types of rules will induce economic actors to choose optimal forms of behavior (Clarke, 1971; Groves and Loeb, 1975)? In political science such concerns are reflected in the examination of constitutional questions: What are the optimal constitutional rules and arrangements for limiting the independent actions of government officials (Brennan and Buchanan, 1985; Buchanan and Tullock, 1962)? Because the main emphasis of this research is normative and not explanatory, it is not a major focus of this book. To the extent that these works can be read as a claim that such rules either are the actual goal of political actors or are in fact the most stable form of economic or constitutional principles, then such claims enter into subsequent discussions.

13

Institutions and social conflict

those effects. This requires an investigation of those factors that determine how these distributional conflicts are resolved. To undertake such an investigation, I believe, is to analyze how the asymmetries of power in a society influence the evolution of social institutions.

The main weakness of previous theories that stress the importance of distributive questions has been the lack of microfoundations, or the mechanisms by which institutions emerge and change. To develop such a theory it is necessary to consider the nature of the relationship between social institutions and individual action. Standard theories regarding this relationship take the following general form: Social outcomes are the product of the interactions of individual social actors, and institutions matter because they affect the nature of this interaction. There are basically two competing theories of individual action that one might use to investigate this relationship: the theory of rational choice and the theory of norm-driven action.[10]

It is not my purpose here to resolve the controversy surrounding these competing theories. Exclusive reliance on either theory to describe social action seems to contradict common-sense evidence. It is reasonable to assume that both norms and rational calculation motivate action in different contexts. But to distinguish the exact circumstances in which one motivation predominates is beyond the scope of my project. Nonetheless, there are both theoretical and practical reasons for my reliance on the rational-choice approach in this book. The theoretical justification rests on the claim that most social outcomes (at least those social and political outcomes about which we are most concerned in the social sciences) are the product of conflict among actors with competing interests. The rational-choice theory of action is better able to capture the strategic aspects of that social conflict. The practical justification is that the conception of institutional effects derived from the theory of social norms is less successful in explaining these outcomes. Let me first support this later justification with a brief discussion of the conception of institutions implied by the theory of social norms. Then I will begin to develop the former justification by sketching the framework for my own analysis.

Individuals often act in accordance with the existing norms in a particular society. Such action may be considered either rational or irrational. By this I mean that the norm-generated action may result in the same type of action that would be predicted by an interest-maximizing calculation. If so, it might be considered rational; if not, it can be considered in some sense irrational. But this is a judgment that would be made by some external observer, for actions in accordance with norms are not the

10 See Elster, 1989a, for an extended discussion of the differences between these two theories of action.

14

same as actions in accordance with some rational calculus. Norm-driven behavior is, in its purest form, nonconsequentialist. When an individual acts pursuant to a social norm, that action is governed by a rule, and the individual will act according to the dictates of the rule even if it is not in his self-interest to do so.

Social institutions can affect norm-generated behavior by creating and maintaining these social norms. This conception of institutions was advocated by March and Olsen. In explaining why a normative conception is superior to that offered by a theory of rational action, they describe the relevant reasoning process:

> Although the process is certainly affected by considerations of the consequences of action, it is organized by different principles of action, a logic of appropriateness and a comparison of cases in terms of similarities and differences. The process maintains consistency in action primarily through the creation of typologies of similarity, rather than through a derivation of action from stable interests or wants. (1989: 26)

Here social institutions are best understood as those rules that establish and maintain the typologies of similarity and the logic of appropriateness. This is the language of roles: Institutional arrangements create roles that determine the appropriate behavior of anyone who might occupy that role. In this framework, institutions define what Parsons calls "legitimately expected behavior" (1945: 239).

Boudon (1981) describes this conception as the standard sociological view of social institutions; and he offers an extensive critique of the types of social explanations that follow from this conception. In the standard view, the characteristics and interests of the specific actors are not crucial to the explanation of the particular outcome. What is crucial is the nature of the role defined by the particular institutional arrangement. But such an approach has obvious weaknesses. It fails to explain behavior inconsistent with the defined institutional roles, and it fails to provide a unique explanation in those situations in which a social actor is confronted by conflicting roles.[11] As Boudon demonstrates through several examples from contemporary sociological research, such conflicts are the rule rather than the exception. Without an alternative theory of individual motivation and action, the sociological approach is forced to reach for ad hoc explanations of inconsistent or ill-defined actions.

This creates special problems for those who seek to explain institutional change from a norm-driven behavior perspective. Explanations of the origin and development of such institutions have relied mainly on a functionalist logic following Spencer. For Parsons, these roles can be defined in terms of the social system's functional needs. Institutional

---

11 Barry, 1978, provides a compelling critique of the difficulties that such an approach encounters when it is used to explain political outcomes in democratic regimes.

structures channel behavior according to socially beneficial goals. To occupy a role is to act in a "legitimately expected" and socially beneficial way. The development of such institutions is thus explained by the capacity of these roles to satisfy functional needs. How and why these particular rules evolve is left unspecified.

To their credit March and Olsen seem to reject this standard functional explanation but fail, nonetheless, to offer any substantive alternative (1989: 56ff.). They reject the idea that social institutions are optimal solutions to social problems and suggest that an "institutional theory of politics" must allow for problems of suboptimality and inefficiency. However, to the extent that they explain the origin of these problems, they rely mainly on the limited capacities of the actors who develop these institutional arrangements, limitations such as the inability to foresee the future or to assimilate all of the information necessary to make rational decisions. Such a reliance follows naturally from their emphasis on institutions as norms of appropriateness. For March and Olson, this conception correctly places "the individual as member of community" in the center of our conception of political and social life. Because the community as a whole assumes the central focus in such a conception, explanations of institutional change are located in the process of improving the effects of these institutions on the community's collective functions or needs. Therefore, although such explanations stress the importance of individual action for institutional creation, they also demonstrate the limitation of the norm-driven approach for understanding the conflict over different institutional forms.[12]

If social outcomes are the product of social conflict, then we need to understand the nature of that conflict. Social conflict implies the interaction among intentional actors who have competing interests in those outcomes. Rational-choice theory, as a subset of intentional explanations, provides a basis for understanding such conflict. According to this theory, individuals act in pursuit of various goals and interests and

---

12 It is probably best to anticipate a potential criticism of the analysis offered in this book. The explanation of the spontaneous emergence of social norms developed in subsequent chapters is grounded in a theory of strategic action. This implies that the origin of self-enforcing rules, which come to be treated by social actors as norms and are defined in the text as nonconsequentialist rules of appropriate behavior, can be explained as the outcome of a process of self-interested consequentialist behavior. Although I defend this explanation for the emergence of norms in Chapter 5, I should acknowledge that although it shows how the rules can come to be self-enforcing in a community, it does not resolve the question of why some individuals come to treat the rules as standards of appropriate behavior, regardless of their consequences. Unfortunately, this is not a problem unique to the arguments presented here. For a more general discussion of the problem, see Elster, 1989a. Nonetheless, the choice of rational action over norm-generated behavior as a basis for a theory of institutional change can be defended on the grounds that the former takes us further than the latter does in understanding the basic emergence of informal conventions and rules.

16

choose their actions in order to satisfy those interests most efficiently. Whereas rational-choice approaches are usually associated with self-interested desires and goals, the analysis need not be limited to the type common in economic analysis. All we need to assume is that individuals act intentionally and optimally toward some specific goal. Through their actions, individuals produce social outcomes.[13]

Actors choose their strategies under various circumstances. In some situations individuals regard the rest of their environment, including the actions of others, as given. They calculate their optimal strategy within the constraints of fixed parameters. Such is the logic of market behavior in neoclassical economics. But actors are often confronted by situations characterized by an interdependence between other actors and themselves. Elster (1986) distinguishes three kinds of interdependencies that may exist in strategic situations: (1) The reward of each depends on the rewards of all; (2) the reward of each depends on the choice of all; and (3) the choice of each depends on the choice of all. Under these circumstances individuals must choose strategically by incorporating the expectations of the actions of others into their own decision making. Actors involved in strategic conflict must be aware that social outcomes are the product of their mutual choices and that their choices will affect the choices of others.

Social institutions are an important resource in forming these expectations. In the rational-choice framework, social institutions affect the calculus used by rational actors to assess their potential strategies and to select their rational choice of action. These effects alter the chosen strategies and affect the outcomes of conflict. They change these outcomes by altering what is rational for social actors to do. Institutional rules do this by providing two types of information: (1) the nature of sanctions for noncompliance and (2) the probable future actions of others. A key to their effectiveness is that they are socially shared: The knowledge of their existence and applicability is shared by the members of the relevant group or community. The fact that the rules are known to be generally applicable guides not only our own future actions, but also our expectations about the future actions of others with whom we interact.

The rational-choice approach to institutional analysis has been criticized from several perspectives. Although most of the critics share the view that institutions are products of collective action, they reject the rationalist conclusions. The fundamental challenge questions the narrowness of a focus on the rationality of social actors, asserting that some aspects of institutional effects cannot be captured by such a focus. Four

---

13 See Elster, 1986, and Hardin, 1987, for analyses of the various issues involved in using rational-choice explanations. Also, see Levi, 1988, for an informative review of efforts to use such explanations in the social sciences.

of these criticisms are worth considering. First, the approach fails to take account of the changing nature of preferences. Second, its treatment of social institutions as part of a world of autonomous individuals motivated by self-interest cannot encompass two important features of society: (1) Institutions reflect the cumulative historical experience of a community, and (2) institutions provide a cohesion that represents the commonality of social experience. Third, the rational-choice account of social institutions does not explain suboptimality and inefficiency (March and Olsen, 1989: 38ff.). Fourth, there is a general lack of attention to power relationships affecting the maintenance and development of those institutions (Oberschall and Leifer, 1986; Zald, 1987). The continuing focus of these critics on the assumption of individual rationality suggests that there is something inherent in the reliance on this assumption that prevents the incorporation of these features.

But such suggestions are misplaced. There is nothing inherent in the approach to preclude the consideration of these issues. Of these four criticisms, only the first – of the changing nature of preferences – causes serious concern. Any theory based on the relationship between rational action and social institutions can readily incorporate questions of historical experience, commonality of experience, or suboptimality. Although March and Olsen accurately criticize much of the existing work in the rational-choice tradition for its excessive attention to optimality and efficiency, they are mistaken to conclude that this is an inherent flaw in the approach. The problems of suboptimality are one of the main themes of the second chapter of this book, and an explanation of how social institutions contribute to social cohesion and a sense of community in a world of autonomous individuals is offered in the third chapter. More significantly, the explicit incorporation into a rational-choice framework of a community's power relationships allows me to explain in the fourth and fifth chapters how social institutions embody the historical experiences of a society.

Criticism of the assumption of stable preferences, however, is widespread, frequent, and often appropriate. For a static analysis, the assumption seems a reasonable oversimplification. At any particular time we can reasonably assume, for example, that my preferences are fixed. But for a dynamic analysis such as a theory of institutional change, the assumption of stability can be problematic. To see this, consider the following problem: At time t, how can I rationally create institutions that will affect my future at time $t + 1$ if I do not know what my future preferences for institutions will be? As I discuss in subsequent chapters, this is less of a problem for evolutionary accounts than it is for intentional design. It is not so critical as to obviate the use of a rational-choice perspective in developing a theory of institutional emergence and change. But it is a problem to which I shall return.

What should an adequate theory of emergence and change provide? First, it should explain the mechanism by which an institution initially develops. This entails answering two questions: (1) Through what process does a rule become the socially shared standard in a community? and (2) Why does the rule take the particular form that it does? Second, it should explain how the established rule changes. This requires answering these questions: (1) How and why was the stability of the existing rule undermined? and (2) How was the new rule established? Here the question of the new rule's establishment returns us to the two questions pertaining to the explanation of initial development.

In the following chapters I challenge the dominant contemporary accounts of coordination and collective benefits and offer answers to these questions in terms of the distributive effects of social institutions. To do so I present a study of the rationality of social institutions that places greater emphasis on the role of *strategic* action in both the development and the maintenance of these institutions. My primary focus is on the evolution of the informal network of social conventions, norms, rules, and rights that forms the basis of society. My secondary focus is on intentional design: both the attempts to reform existing rules and conventions and the efforts to construct new social institutions within this network.

My primary emphasis on distribution suggests a shift in the underlying logic of institutional development: Rather than conceiving of social institutions as the product of efforts to constrain social actors as a collectivity, *social institutions are conceived of as a product of the efforts of some to constrain the actions of others with whom they interact.* Here my explanation of institutional emergence concentrates on the conflict over social expectations and on the credibility of efforts to establish them. Similarly, the distributional emphasis focuses questions of institutional maintenance and stability on the ongoing tension over distributional benefits and the continuing efficacy of such institutional constraints.

The main consequence of this analysis is that *the ongoing development of social institutions is not best explained as a Pareto-superior response to collective goals or benefits but, rather, as a by-product of conflicts over distributional gains.* In order to avoid unnecessary confusion, let me underscore here that the claim that explanations of social institutions

19

should invoke distributional effects does not imply that such institutions do not provide some measure of collective benefits. Rather, it implies that such benefits are merely by-products of distributional conflict and that they are not, therefore, the principal element of explanations grounded in rational action.

In the next two chapters I present the basic argument in favor of a distributive conception of social institutions. In Chapter 2 I show why distribution and not collective benefits should be the primary focus of institutional analysis. This is an argument grounded in (1) the underlying logic of strategic-actor models and (2) empirical evidence concerning the effects of social institutions. In Chapter 3 I analyze the ways in which institutional rules constrain strategic behavior and structure social interactions. In this discussion I suggest a way of thinking about the relationship between strategic decision making and the socially shared knowledge, manifest in social institutions, that binds together the various actors in a society. In these two chapters I begin examining the conditions under which social actors are able to develop and maintain institutions that give them disproportionate distributional benefits.

In Chapters 4 and 5 I analyze existing evolutionary theories of institutional development and propose a bargaining theory of institutional emergence and change, suggesting that only this approach can capture the inherent conflict in the development and maintenance of social institutions. Through examples drawn from a range of social conventions, norms, and rights, I elaborate the mechanism by which such rules emerge spontaneously, but in such a way as to favor systematically a community's particular subsets. I discuss the importance of relative bargaining power, the sources of relevant asymmetries of power in a community, and the conditions under which such asymmetries can be exploited.

In Chapter 6 I address issues related to institutional maintenance, stability, and change. Here my focus shifts to include formal social institutions. Among the issues I examine are the stability of self-enforcing rules, the effects of introducing the state as an external-enforcement mechanism, the importance of transaction costs for the formalization of institutional rules, and the conditions under which intentional change will succeed. In the concluding chapter I assess the implications of both an emphasis on distribution and a bargaining theory of change for our basic understanding of the role of institutions in social life.

2

The primary importance of distributional conflict

In giving an explanation of a social institution, either of its maintenance and stability or of its development, we focus initially on the impact of that institution on a particular aspect of social life: the difference that the existence of the institution makes for social interactions. This "impact" may be called an effect, a benefit, a satisfaction of a need, or whatever, depending on the type of explanation offered. The persuasiveness of the explanation, however, depends on more than a description of an "impact"; it depends on the elaboration of a mechanism that connects the impact to some cause, intention, functional adaptation, or whatever: how the particular institution developed and why it took the form that it did. Here we connect the what with the how and why. Because my interest is in the development of theories that combine rational action with institutional structures, my attention here is on mechanisms that connect the benefits of social institutions with the intentions of social actors. The basic argument of this chapter is that although social institutions may have a number of discernible benefits, some do better than others in providing the how and why.

In the first section I briefly discuss the benefits provided by a variety of social institutions. These examples are offered to highlight the relationship between the collective and distributive benefits of these institutions. In doing so I begin to illustrate the practical problem of focusing primarily on collective benefits. In the next section I discuss the theoretical questions related to rational-action models and institutional development and change more systematically, analyzing a number of existing theories that focus primarily on the collective benefits of these institutions. Here I argue that explanations of social institutions grounded in rational-action theory must give primary emphasis to distributive effects. This emphasis directs our attention to why and how social actors seek to establish particular institutional forms. In the last section I consider the implications for a social explanation of two sets of problems that

21

confront social actors who seek to establish institutions: uncertainty and cost (both transaction costs and the costs of collective action).

THE BENEFITS OF SOCIAL INSTITUTIONS

The focus on the provision of collective benefits is grounded in the central importance of social institutions in our lives. Without social institutions, the myriad of interactions constituting social life would be more difficult, if not impossible. The fact that the existence of these institutions makes possible these interactions understandably leads us to look at their impact on the collective interests of society. To see this we need only examine the importance of a variety of institutions for social, political, and economic affairs.

Measures of time and space

We take for granted many of these rules and measures, but conventions of time and space provide the context in which we live our lives. Consider, for instance, measures of time. Time, as designated by such measures as the day, the week, and the year, serves as a referent for planning our affairs and coordinating them with the actions of others. As societies have become more complex and the benefits of collective behavior in the economic and political realms multiplied, the need for a temporal referent to structure this behavior has increased (Zerubavel, 1985). The week, with its division of time into periods of work, rest, and, for many, religious observance, offers a method of coordinating activities that produce benefits for each member of the community.

A similar account can be given for the conventions by which we define and structure space and other physical objects. Here we can refer specifically to systems of weights and measures, the criteria by which we categorize and compare land, resources, crops, goods, and the like. Without common criteria, we would be unable to enter into many of the forms of cooperation and exchange necessary to benefit fully from these products and resources. The history of the development of such systems of measure demonstrates that as exchange and trade became more prominent aspects of economic life, the pressures for a common criterion of measure increased as well (Kula, 1986; Sydenham, 1979).

Property rights

The rights to property in a society are defined by rules that designate their appropriate use, control, and right to transfer. These rules may take the form of either informal rules and conventions or formal laws enforced by the state. The designation of these rights facilitates a wide

22

The primary importance of distributional conflict

range of social interactions, from economic exchange to the peaceful resolution of disputes involving property. Basic economic exchange requires some initial definition of rights so that the participants in the exchange will know what they can exchange and what they are getting in return. Without these initial definitions the stability of exchange would be threatened, and the potential gains from trade might be lost (Coase, 1960). To the extent that the members of a society are able to participate and benefit in these economic exchanges, established rules of property accrue to the benefit of the society as a whole. Similarly, rules are often established to anticipate disputes arising from problems with the division of property that frequently arise in a community, problems such as bankruptcy and intestate succession (Eisenberg, 1976). Here the rule has the effect of establishing a criterion for dispute resolution that prevents the potential disputants from diminishing the value of the property in the course of their distributional conflict.

Marriage and other rules governing the family

The family is the basic unit of association in most societies; and an extensive set of rules and procedures has developed to define both the relationship between the family and the community in which it lives and the relationship among the members of the family. These rules have important effects on the social relationships within a community: They define what constitutes a family unit; they define a social division of labor within a family; they establish rights between adult family members and between parents and children; and they establish the duties and responsibilities of family members vis-à-vis the outside community (Moore, 1989). This clarification of social relations can benefit the general community in many ways. To the extent that the members of a community are concerned with reproducing themselves through future generations, well-defined duties and responsibilities in regard to children can simplify the task of providing welfare and security. To the extent that the continuing social security and welfare of adults and, more importantly, the elderly is a product of cooperative behavior among members of the extended family, similar rules can stabilize and facilitate the satisfaction of those needs. These rules tell people for whom they are responsible and on whom they can rely in satisfying security and welfare needs (Comaroff and Roberts, 1981).

The organization of economic production and distribution

In most societies, economic gains result from cooperation in production and exchange. In less-developed economies, such gains may result from

23

Institutions and social conflict

the coordination of agricultural activities, cooperation in tool production or cattle development, or the long-term pooling of resources as a form of community insurance (Bates, 1989). In more-developed economies, these gains arise from the division of labor and specialization of productive activities (North, 1990). These collective activities are organized by institutionalizing procedures for production and distribution. Consider the modern firm: Production techniques and procedures are established by rules governing every aspect of the firm's activity. Without some stable procedures, many of the gains from cooperative production would be lost in the chaos of informal efforts to coordinate the division of labor. Concomitant with the rise of collective economic activity is the increasing complexity of distributive questions: How are the gains from collective action to be divided? In the case of the modern firm these distributive questions have been resolved within the institutional framework of bargaining between labor and management. In a manner similar to some of the rules of property division, this framework can structure distributional bargaining in such a way as to make it less likely that the gains from collective production will be lost in the conflict over their distribution.

Political institutions of the state

Just as economic actors can benefit from collective activity, social actors can benefit from the activities of a centralized government authority. The benefits of such activities as the production of public goods and the enforcement of property rights are well documented. Governments are organized according to a network of political institutions that facilitate collective decision making and coordinate the activities of government officials. Two examples from democratic societies are illustrative: Electoral laws offer an institutional method of translating the preferences of individual voters into governmental policy through the election of legislative representatives (Rae, 1967). The institutions of the legislature provide a framework within which representatives can conduct the business of lawmaking; the established rules and procedures allow representatives to develop the long-term relationships and coalitions from which policy is made (Weingast and Marshall, 1988). Without these fixed procedures, the process of political decision making would be more difficult and more costly.

Summary

This sketch of various social institutions gives us a sense of the difference that these institutions make in social life. Institutions make life easier; in

24

a world of social interdependence, they provide a means of living and working together. They allow social actors to produce, by acting with others, benefits that they would fail to achieve by acting alone. In some contexts, these benefits are called *gains from trade;* in others, *gains from cooperation;* in still others, *advantages of coordination.* The stability of these institutions and the knowledge of that stability shared by the members of a group or community enable the types of behavior necessary to achieve these benefits. It is not surprising that these collective benefits form the basis of an answer to the question of what difference social institutions make.

But this is an incomplete sketch. For although we need stable institutions to achieve the benefits of acting together, these institutions can take many forms. In most cases there are a number of ways to institutionalize the rights, duties, responsibilities, procedures, methods of action, appropriate strategies, and the like so that the additional benefits of collective action or social coordination can be realized. Consider the following examples. Some of our measures of time, such as the year or the day, have an underlying astronomical basis, but others, such as the week, are merely conventional. Even the measures of the year and the day have been subject to variation in criteria and interpretation (Rifkin, 1987: 76–8; Whitrow, 1988: 4). In order to coordinate behavior in a community we need a common criterion of time such as the week, but it need not be seven days in duration. Historically, weeks of varying lengths have structured the economic and social lives of different communities (Zerubavel, 1985). Similarly, although a community needs a common set of measures for land and other resources to facilitate commerce, many different sets of measures can, and have, served as that criterion (Kula, 1986: 98–122; Thompson, 1928: 596, 736).

Rules of property division, in the form of either informal convention or formal law, also take various forms. For example, the criteria for resolving such problems as bankruptcy or intestate succession have differed historically among nations and among communities within a single nation (Dalhuisen, 1968; Lloyd, 1877). The common characteristic of these rules is that they have established a stable criterion on which social actors can anticipate the future and act accordingly. But they have differed substantially in the exact method of distribution. Property rights have also entered into the network of institutions defining relationships within the family. They have been particularly important to defining the differing social and economic responsibilities between husbands and wives (Sen, 1990). Here, too, the collective benefits gained from a clear and precise delineation of duties and responsibilities have taken many forms. One way of characterizing these differences is in their treatment of women: To what extent are the rules gender neutral, and to what extent are wives treated in the same manner as their husbands are (Carr and Walsh, 1977: 564; Salmon, 1986: chap. 7)?

As we move from these underlying conventions and norms to those institutions usually characterized by a more intentional form of development, we can find a similar diversity. The basic organization of economic production can have a number of different institutional forms (Elster and Moene, 1988), as can the rules and procedures established for resolving issues related to working conditions and distribution (Clegg, 1976). The institutionalization of the state's political activities differs across a wide range of electoral and administrative forms (Lijphart, 1984).

The main point here is that there is generally more than one way to structure social institutions in order to produce gains from cooperation, coordination, or exchange. And the major distinguishing feature of these different institutional forms is their distributional consequences. Although they all can produce gains from acting collectively, they distribute these additional benefits differently. The establishment of conventions of measurement can significantly affect the distribution of economic and political benefits in a community; and the method of defining property rights can affect the distribution of economic benefits. The network of conventions and formal rules defining relationships in the family can substantially alter the relationship between the sexes and the enjoyment of the various benefits of social life. The structuring of the various economic and political institutions that constitute the framework of social life can dramatically influence the fundamental distribution of economic and political success and failure in a community. And all of this also provides the structure and stability necessary for social actors to produce gains from cooperative behavior.

The practical implications for explanations of institutional development, maintenance, and change are straightforward. Such explanations must do more than demonstrate that social institutions exist because they benefit us. For example, it is not enough to say that particular property rights can be explained by the fact that they enhance the efficiency of economic exchange. Several different sets of property rights can do this. Our theories thus must explain why one institutional form developed, as opposed to another, when a number of different ones will produce the basic benefits; that is, why one set of property rights evolved and another did not.[1]

One response to this criticism of theories based on collective benefits takes the following form: We can explain the development of a partic-

---

1 Note that these examples are manifestations of the problem of multiple equilibria in rational-choice models. Any of several institutional forms constitutes an equilibrium outcome. The question is, Why one equilibrium over another? This formulation of the problem is developed in Chapters 3 and 5.

ular social institution by the fact that it does a better job than do competing institutional forms of providing these collective benefits. For example, certain property rights are more efficient; they do a better job of minimizing costs; they are Pareto superior to other alternatives; and so forth. This is the implicit logic of many of the explanations to be discussed in this book. For these explanations to be acceptable, however, they need to demonstrate why the collective benefits are the key element of the explanation. To do so they should elaborate a mechanism that either connects collective benefits to the actors' intentions or shows how collective benefits are produced despite the actors' intentions. Here we turn from the practical problems of explanation to more theoretical issues.

RATIONALITY AND INSTITUTIONAL BENEFITS

Rational-choice accounts of social institutions are in principle dedicated to explanations based on the intentions and motivations of social actors (Davidson, 1980; Elster, 1986). This implies a particular focus on institutional development and change. If institutional rules are intended to influence future action, these rules should embody the substantive effects that their producers desire. Here it is important to clarify the difference between intended and unintended consequences. If social institutions are the product of human interaction, the substantive content of institutional rules should embody the goals and motivations underlying those interactions. Just as the provisions of a contract reflect the intentions of the parties to that contract, institutional rules should reflect the intended effects desired by those who produce them. This does not mean that institutional effects will duplicate the exact preferences of any particular actor or group; in fact, this will seldom be the case. Rather, the final form of institutional rules is a product of the conflict of interests among the relevant actors. This final product is grounded, however, in the intentions and motivations of the conflicting actors.

If these institutions either fail to produce these effects or produce unintended consequences that counteract the desired effects, it will be necessary to look to other mechanisms by which these unintended effects are produced. We need to explain the intervening factor that produced the unintended effect; otherwise, explanations of institutional effects that rely on unintended consequences can lapse into unspecified functionalism.

In relying on intentional explanations to analyze institutional effects on social outcomes, we commit ourselves to concentrating initially on the substantive content of these rules and only later on their unintended effects. In Chapter 1 I suggested that relying on the concept of rational

27

action did not commit us to a narrow, "self-interest" view of individual preferences. Though this is true, I now propose that we restrict our assumption about preferences to one of individual self-interest (what, following Hardin, 1982, I will call *narrow rationality*). This restriction is justified on several grounds. First, by adopting a narrow perspective on the motivations underlying social institutions, we can use our conclusions as a baseline to compare explanations that relax this assumption. If we understand what the nature of social institutions would be in a world of narrowly rational social actors, we can then focus on the changes that might result if these actors adopted more other-regarding preferences. Second, the assumption of narrow rationality allows us to emphasize the conflict that characterizes many aspects of social life. The third, and probably the most important, justification is that this perspective serves as the basis for other analyses of the rationality of social institutions.

If we want to explain the development and maintenance of social institutions in terms of the relevant actors' preferences, we will need to specify what rational actors want the substantive content of such rules to be in the context of diverse distributional forms. For the dominant contemporary account of social institutions to be sustained, the strategic actors' main concern must be the collective benefits provided by these institutions. The question therefore is whether strategic actors would give priority to collective goals over distributional advantage in the development of social institutions. If they are motivated by the narrow self-interest assumed by standard analyses, the answer will be no.

To see this, consider the following analysis. The existing theoretical literature is based mainly on three social goals: social efficiency, Pareto optimality, and stability. These concepts are theoretical measures of the types of gain from coordinated action produced by social institutions. Contemporary arguments explain social institutions in terms of the provision of these goals: Social institutions constrain actors (either society as a whole or subgroups) as a way of achieving these collective benefits. We therefore need to determine the compatibility of these goals with the assumption of narrow rationality. I begin by analyzing the ways in which social efficiency has formed the cornerstone of contemporary explanations of the existence of social institutions. Then I turn to Pareto optimality and stability and discuss the relationship of these concepts to the rationality of institutional development and change.

Social efficiency

By *social efficiency* I am referring to what Coleman (1988: 71) defines as *allocative efficiency*: the maximum productive use of resources. In this

28

sense, efficient social institutions are those that maximize social welfare or utility. Technically, this measure raises several conceptual problems for comparative institutional analysis. First, this concept assumes that there is some way for us to make interpersonal comparisons of utility among social actors in order to aggregate individual utilities and maximize collective welfare. The problems with this assumption are well known (Hardin, 1988: 169–78). The simplest way of thinking about the problem is to remember that the utility functions employed in rational-choice explanations are inherently subjective. The criterion by which I measure my utility is based on my own evaluation of alternatives, and so it is unique to me. The assumption of interpersonal utility comparisons entails a transferable utility requiring a shared criterion of value. Given the idiosyncratic criteria of subjective utility functions, the requirement of transferability has not been fulfilled, and so interpersonal comparisons cannot be made.

Second, the measurement in terms of utility can be problematic when employed as a means of comparing the relative efficiency of different institutional arrangements. Eggertsson points out that changes brought about by reallocating property rights can produce new indifference curves and a new criterion to assess efficiency. He suggests that such a change "affects both the production capacity of the economy and the distribution of wealth, and creates, in a market economy, a new basis for the valuation of commodities. Therefore, from the viewpoint of positive economics, it is impossible to evaluate the impact of changes in property rights on social welfare" (1990: 100–1). Here the problem comes when determining changes in aggregate utility after changes in the nature of a particular social institution. To make such an assessment we must have a criterion of aggregate utility that remains consistent both before and after the institutional change. If the institutional change to be examined also affects changes in the underlying context in which social outcomes are to be evaluated (e.g., if our preferences for social outcomes vary with the level of resources at our disposal), our underlying preference rankings may change, thereby altering the criterion for aggregate utility. Thus, the pre-change and post-change criteria may differ, thwarting efforts both to compare utility changes and to attribute such changes to specific alterations in social institutions.

Both of these problems call into question a comparison of different institutional forms in terms of utility. Although these conceptual problems in themselves tend to undercut claims about the relative efficiency of different institutional forms, I want to set these problems aside, assume that relative comparisons are possible, and assess the relationship between this efficiency concept and narrow rationality. For this purpose we can think about social efficiency as measuring how well institutional arrangements allow us to enjoy gains from coordinated behavior. All we need here is the rather simple assumption that social actors can roughly determine the relative gains of different institutional forms. Thus, socially efficient institutions would be those rules that produce the greatest collective gain.

In studies of institutional development, social efficiency has been used to explain the existence of such institutions as the basic network of conventions and norms in a society, property rights, law, and various forms of political and economic organization. Here we need to distinguish naive from sophisticated accounts. Whereas the naive explanations point merely to the provision of increased collective benefits, the more sophisticated accounts investigate how and under what circumstances institutions offer these benefits.

Consider, for an example of a naive account, the economic-analysis-of-law perspective, which employs social efficiency as a criterion to explain the substantive content of many areas of the law.[2] In describing the logic of this perspective, Posner asserted that "common law (i.e., judge-made) rules are often best explained as efforts, whether or not conscious, to bring about either Pareto or Kaldor–Hicks efficient outcomes"[3] (1987: 5). In this approach the maximization of social efficiency takes both an explanatory and a normative role. Legal rules and principles are both explained by and justified according to their ability to establish incentives to maximize welfare.

Consider, for example, rules that govern liability for unintentional torts (Landes and Posner, 1987). There are three basic forms of the liability rule: strict liability, negligence, and no-fault. The first places absolute responsibility on the tortfeasor, regardless of whether the tort could have been avoided; the second abrogates liability when the tort could not have been avoided with reasonable due care; and the third does away with the issue by placing responsibility for compensation on the victim's own insurance provider. The economic-analysis-of-law approach explains the existence of a particular liability rule in terms of the rule's effects on the incentives to take precautions against tortious behavior. If a strict liability criterion would do the best job of creating incentives for efficient precautions in a products liability case, that criterion would be

2 The seminal work in this area is by Posner (1986). The burgeoning literature can be found in the various volumes of the *Journal of Law and Economics* and the *Journal of Legal Studies*. For a discussion of the strengths and weaknesses of this approach, see, for example, Coleman, 1988, and Coleman and Paul, 1984.
3 It is not clear what Posner means by the "unconscious" effort to bring about efficiency. Given his invocation in other contexts of a mechanism of natural selection, he may have in mind some evolutionary process unrelated to the intentions of judges or other actors.

30

predicted by the approach. Here the precautionary behavior induced by the liability rule increases the collective benefits gained by society from the production and exchange of goods.

The law-and-economics approach distinguishes between judge-made law and law produced through the political process. Although it leaves open the possibility that the latter type of law will fail to maximize social efficiency, this approach generally predicts a socially efficient common law. This distinguishes law-and-economics explanations from those grounded in Coase's theory (1960) of transaction costs. Transaction costs "consist of the costs of arranging a contract and monitoring and enforcing it ex post, as opposed to production costs, which are the costs of executing a contract" (Matthews, 1986: 906). According to this approach, the most socially efficient social institution is the one that minimizes these costs. As I shall point out later, some of these transaction-costs theories allow for the possibility that the most socially efficient social institutions will not be produced. But even these rest their explanations for the existence of social institutions on the fact that such institutions lower the collective costs of transactions. Two examples demonstrate how Coase's theory is used to explain the existence of economic institutions.

First, Williamson (1975, 1985) argues that efficiency considerations can explain various ways of organizing economic activities at the level of production. The logic of his analysis stresses the importance of minimizing transaction costs. Different economic transactions have different types of costs. Economic actors can organize their transactions in numerous ways: by means of firms, markets, or some combination of both. The choice of organizational form is dictated by the corresponding costs: Actors choose the form that minimizes costs. For example, firms with hierarchical forms of decision making and related procedures for monitoring work performance are preferred to more cooperative procedures, because the former do a better job of minimizing the costs of production.

Note that the idea that institutions are created according to the principle of cost minimization is grounded in the notion of individual efficiency. Although Williamson (1986) argues that the transaction-costs approach allows us to break out of the neoclassical conception of the firm as a unitary actor, he falls back on the idea that institutional decisions are made by individual utility maximizers (in this case, the owners of capital). But this leaves the principal's agents (the employees) with a rather unimportant role in the analysis. Williamson finds unacceptable the idea that forms of workplace organization are the object of conflict between the owners of capital and the workers. Although others have contended that hierarchical forms of organization are created to maintain asymmetric

31

power relationships rather than to minimize costs (Marglin, 1974; Stone, 1974), he rejects such arguments on the grounds that such organizational forms would not be chosen by the principals if they were not efficient.[4] Yet what is individually efficient for the principals may not be socially efficient for the firm. If we reconceive of the firm as a group (principals and agents) seeking to maximize their collective welfare, we may have to reexamine Williamson's efficiency justification for certain forms of workplace organization.

Before going further into the weakness of Williamson's analysis, however, we should take account of the positive contributions of the transaction-costs approach. To see this, consider the related approach offered by North (1981, 1990). North employs a similar cost-minimization criterion in his explanation of the historical development of property rights and other political and economic institutions. Here institutions are created by principals (either political rulers or the owners of economic resources) to govern relationships with other principals and with their agents (citizens, bureaucrats, employees, etc.). These principals are motivated to create institutional forms that will maximize their individual utility. In order to do so they choose institutional rules that minimize the costs of doing so:

As a first approximation we can say that property rights will be developed over resources and assets as a simple cost–benefit calculus of the costs of devising and enforcing such rights, as compared to the alternatives under the status quo. Changes in relative prices or relative scarcities of any kind lead to the creation of property rights when it becomes worthwhile to incur the costs of devising such rights. (North, 1990: 70)

A criticism of North's early theory (1981) is that it erroneously predicted the existence of socially efficient property rights and economic institutions.[5] His later account (1990) clarifies his theory and suggests three main causes of the inefficiency of social institutions. The first two relate to problems faced by the actors directly involved in the transaction. First, economic actors may not have the information and knowledge necessary to produce such institutions. They may want to create them, but either they lack the information necessary to do so, such as knowledge of the costs of monitoring long-term performance, or they have inadequate subjective models of social causation such that they fail to understand the effects of their efforts at institutionalization on the actions of others. Either of these problems can lead to the creation of socially inefficient institutions. Second, the costs of producing socially efficient institutions

4 See Goldberg, 1981, for a recent critique of these "radical" accounts of economic organization.
5 See Bowman, 1989, for an analysis of the importance of political factors for North's theory of institutional change.

may be prohibitive. That is, they may have the capacity to create rights that will do the best job of maximizing their collective welfare, but the costs of establishing and maintaining them offset the benefits of doing so. Here we should note a fundamental contribution of the transaction-costs approach to institutional change: Transaction costs serve here not to explain the existence of social institutions but, rather, to explain the constraints on efficient institutional development (I shall return to this point later).

The third cause of inefficiency involves, for North, the introduction of additional actors: the role of the state's political agents in enforcing rights. Enforcement is inefficient when "enforcement is undertaken by agents, whose own utility functions influence outcomes" (1990: 73). Because rulers may have interests that conflict with those of their subjects and because they choose rules that maximize their own interests, they may produce property rights schemes that do not maximize the collective welfare. Thus, the creation of socially efficient rights is thwarted by the contrary interests of political actors.

Here we arrive at the crux of the problem for explanations based on minimizing transaction costs or, for that matter, on maximizing social efficiency more generally. The possibility of a conflict between individual and collective interests is, contrary to North and the other transaction-costs theorists, much more widespread than are instances of state involvement. The reformulation of Williamson's conception of the firm as a group (managers and workers) seeking to maximize collective welfare offers only one example. The theoretical problem is what becomes of social efficiency when actors have conflicting interests.

The conflict between individual self-interest and social efficiency was clarified by Coleman (1984), among others. The logic of his argument can be applied to the choice of institutional rules, whether it be forms of organization in the workplace or property rights for society as a whole. Consider the outcomes represented in Figure 2.1. Say that outcome *A* is on the Pareto frontier, which represents those points that maximize the collective welfare of *X* and *Y*. How would each actor compare this outcome with outcomes *B* and *C*? *X* would prefer *C* to *A*, and *Y* would prefer *B* to *A* on the grounds that those outcomes would produce greater individual payoffs. Motivated by individual self-interest, the actors, faced with a choice of moving from either of these individually preferred outcomes to the more socially efficient one, would reject the move and opt for the less socially efficient alternative. Applying the logic to Williamson's analysis of the choice of economic organization in the workplace, owners of capital, acting rationally, would opt for less efficient forms of organization if these rules resulted in an increased relative share of profits. More generally, this demonstrates that self-interested

33

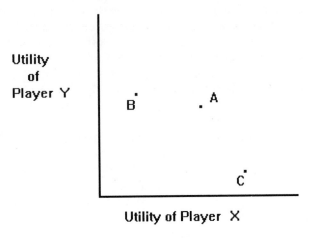

Figure 2.1. Social efficiency.

actors will prefer socially inefficient institutional rules if those rules give them greater individual utility.

For this reason I conclude that social efficiency cannot provide the substantive content of institutional rules. Rational self-interested actors will not be the initiators of such rules if they diminish their own utility. Therefore, rational-choice explanations of social institutions based on gains in social efficiency fail as long as they are grounded in the intentions of social actors.

Pareto optimality

The concepts of Pareto optimality and efficiency are often used to refer to the same features of social outcomes. Here I want to distinguish between the two in order to emphasize a different way of thinking about institutions. *Pareto-optimal* institutions have the following feature: Any change in the allocations produced by the institution benefits one actor only, at the expense of another. Institutions that are socially efficient are Pareto optimal, but the reverse need not hold. Institutions can be Pareto optimal without maximizing social welfare, as is the case when the only path to greater social welfare requires reducing the benefits to some members of the group (e.g., the move from C to A in Figure 2.1).

To clarify the importance of the criterion of Pareto optimality for the study of institutions, additional Paretian criteria must be introduced. An outcome will be Pareto superior to another if the welfare of at least one person can be improved by moving from the latter outcome to the former without adversely affecting the welfare of anyone else. An outcome will be Pareto inferior if there is another distribution Pareto superior to it. The logic of the Paretian criteria is that rational actors make Pareto-superior moves until they achieve a Pareto-optimal outcome.

This logic of Pareto improvement is at the heart of many studies of institutional development. Schotter (1981) employs it in his discussion of the evolution of economic institutions in the marketplace, and the growing literature on norms and conventions (Hechter, Opp, and Wippler, 1990; Lewis, 1969; Sugden, 1986) rests on similar arguments. It provides the motivation for all arguments emphasizing the importance of institutions for the resolution of recurring problems faced by social actors. The social outcomes produced by such interactions without institutions are suboptimal; that is, they are Pareto inferior to other alternatives. Therefore, the motivation behind the production of social institutions is to achieve the Pareto-optimal alternatives.

In his discussion of the creation of economic institutions, Schotter succinctly puts together the logic of the argument: How do some institutions develop to help us achieve Pareto-optimal outcomes? I will analyze Schotter's discussion of institutional creation in a later chapter, but an important feature of that discussion is relevant to the idea of Pareto optimality as the motivation behind such institutions. Institutions will be created only if they produce outcomes Pareto superior to those that would be achieved in a world without institutions. Otherwise, they serve no beneficial purpose. Given problems of limited information and communication, Schotter acknowledges that Pareto-optimal institutions may not develop.[6] Yet for Schotter, this is a problem of the capacity to achieve one's goals (due to an inability to assimilate information) and not a change in the underlying motivation for one's actions. Pareto superiority becomes the criterion by which institutional creation and change are assessed.

At first glance, the concept of Pareto superiority seems to be uncontroversial. Why would self-interested actors object to Pareto-superior improvements produced by introducing social institutions? Although no one would be adversely affected in regard to losing present benefits, objections might be raised when the future implications of the relative changes in benefits are taken into consideration. Two cases need to be identified. If I am the person most benefited by the new institution, then I will not object to the Pareto-superior move. But what if others are to benefit and I am to gain (or lose) nothing? Then I might object. One ground for an objection rests on the effects that a relative change in benefits might have on my and others' future interactions in other contexts.

6 Sugden (1986) also acknowledges the possibility that evolving social conventions will not be Pareto optimal.

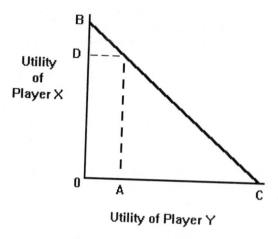

Figure 2.2. Pareto optimality.

For example, an increase in your present economic benefits might provide greater leverage in future political conflicts between us, producing inferior payoffs for me in the future. But a rejoinder could emphasize that such future changes that adversely affect me might be incorporated into the present welfare calculus.

Hardin (1984) proposed a second ground for an objection that is more devastating to the Pareto-superiority criterion. He points out that any present change affects those outcomes that will be judged Pareto superior in the future. Consider the relationship between players X and Y in Figure 2.2. If they start out at the origin, any move toward the Pareto frontier, BC, will be a Pareto-superior move. What then would X's reaction be to a proposed move to A? His benefits would not be affected; only Y's benefits would be improved. Yet X could rationally object to the move because of the changes it makes in what constitutes future Pareto-superior moves. Outcomes to the left of A are now ruled out; the maximum possible payoff available to X shrinks from B to D. If X has some future hope of achieving outcomes in the newly prohibited range and such future moves will be limited to Pareto improvements, he will object to the Pareto-superior move. This shows that "if I am narrowly rational, I can be indifferent to what you receive only if it does not potentially interact with what I can receive" (Hardin, 1984: 458).

This objection undercuts the claim that Pareto optimality is the underlying motivation for institutional creation. Social life is replete with instances in which my rewards interact with the rewards of others. Rational, self-interested actors who give substantive content to institutional rules do not opt for Pareto-superior alternatives if they can have adverse future consequences. It is true, as Schotter admits, that social institutions may not achieve Pareto-optimal outcomes, but it is mainly for reasons quite different from those on which he relies for this conclusion. Social institutions may fail to achieve Pareto-optimal outcomes because it is not in the interests of those who establish those institutions to do so. Pareto-optimal institutions are contingent on the particular path by which self-interested actors achieve institutional change.

Stability

Stability is a quality of social outcomes different from that of social efficiency and Pareto optimality.[7] Whereas the latter two concepts refer to the substantive nature of social outcomes, stability is a formal characteristic. Social institutions may be stable even if they are neither socially efficient nor Pareto optimal. One aspect of institutional stability, a static feature, is contingent on the achievement of equilibrium outcomes. If no one wants to deviate from the institutional rules – given that everyone else is complying with them – the institution will be in equilibrium, and it will be stable in the weak sense that no individual has an incentive to violate the rule. A stronger sense of stability means that there is no group of individuals with an incentive to form a coalition and either violate or change the rule.

A second aspect of institutional stability pertains to dynamic elements. An institution is dynamically stable if the following condition holds: If a few actors inadvertently deviate from the institutional rule, the other actors will prefer to remain in compliance, and the deviating actors will have an incentive to return to the prevailing institutional form. This is an issue mainly in cases of multiple institutional equilibria. Such dynamically stable institutions are more likely to be maintained over time because they are less subject to change.

The stability produced by institutional arrangements is a major focus of the public-choice literature. Some of the earliest results in this field centered on the instability of democratic outcomes: Except under severely restrictive conditions regarding the nature of individual preferences, the aggregation of such preferences is subject to cycles among the various collective outcomes (Ordeshook, 1986). Shepsle (1979) demonstrated that institutional rules could reduce this instability, and he introduced the notion of structurally induced equilibria to explain the existence of certain types of equilibria that would not emerge without the

---

7 Stability is a complex notion, and I can address in this chapter only a few of the ideas directly related to institutions. See Schwartz, 1986, for a presentation of the complexities inherent in the meaning of stability.

constraints that institutions place on feasible collective outcomes. Here institutional rules provide the much-needed stability for democratic institutions.

But one can easily see that the benefits from stability depend on the substantive nature of the outcomes. For example, if I live in a democratic society as a member of a segment of the population that never prevails on policy questions – what Barry (1982) labels a "permanent minority" – then the benefits of stable democratic institutions are less valued by me and others similarly situated. More generally, if I am consistently slighted in the outcomes produced by a stable institutional arrangement, stability will seem like a mixed blessing. On the one hand, institutional stability increases the reliability of the information used in formulating expectations about future behavior. On the other hand, the stability of inferior payoffs leads me to want to change the prevailing institutional arrangements. Given the potentially negative implications of stable institutional arrangements, it is easy to conclude that stability alone does not motivate the substantive content of institutional rules.

Summary

This analysis of the concepts of social efficiency, Pareto optimality, and stability leads to the following conclusion: The primary motivation for social institutions cannot be the achievement of collective goals. Such goals are inconsistent with the narrow rationality underlying these institutions. Rather, institutional rules are created by and communicated through the claims and actions of rational actors. To the extent that such rules can have substantive effects on social outcomes, the substantive content of those rules should reflect the self-interest that motivates these claims and actions. Rather than focusing on collective goals, self-interested actors want institutions that produce those social outcomes that are best for them as individual strategic actors.

This is not to say that social institutions do not produce benefits for all of the members of a group or community. Self-interested actors will not comply with social institutions if compliance does not give them greater benefits than does noncompliance. As the examples in the previous section suggest (and as I will show in the next chapter), compared with the lack of relevant institutions, stable social institutions do in fact provide such benefits. Thus, this insistence on the theoretical primacy of distribution does not deny the importance of gains from coordination or trade. The main point here is that such gains cannot serve as the basis for a social explanation; rather, these benefits are merely a by-product of the pursuit of individual gain. If we want to ground explanations in terms of the intentions and actions of rational actors, we must look to the distributional consequences of those institutions.

Theories of social institutions that emphasize these collective benefits cannot provide microfoundations for their explanations in terms of individual rational action. If they insist on grounding their explanations in collective benefits, they must describe the mechanism that transforms the effects of social institutions into collectively beneficial forms. That is, rational-choice theories that ignore the pursuit of distributional gain and concentrate on collective benefits must describe the mechanism that restricts self-interested behavior exclusively to mutually beneficial changes. Consider what this mechanism might be. It cannot be merely the existence of external enforcement, as is implied by many standard accounts. Such enforcement is created by strategic actors to ensure compliance with institutional rules. Because there is nothing about strategic rationality that guarantees social efficiency in the substantive content of social institutions, there is nothing in the existence of the enforcement mechanism that guarantees it. An external-enforcement mechanism is a means of securing binding claims, not a mechanism guaranteeing social efficiency.

Rather, the mechanism must be something outside the direct control of individual strategic actors. One such possibility is found in North's use (1981) of Alchian's argument (1950) concerning the efficiency of the market: The pressure of market competition serves as a selection mechanism for socially efficient economic institutions, forcing out firms that fail to perform in a utility-maximizing way.[8] But this argument suggests what a difficult problem one faces when describing such a mechanism. Here the mechanism is the competition produced by the existence of a large number of economic actors in close proximity to one another who are pursuing the same goal. To be applicable to the development of institutions more generally, we would have to find the conditions for a "market" for social institutions. The problem is that even if Alchian is correct about the workings of a perfectly competitive market, the requirements of (1) a large number of actors (2) employing a wide range of institutional forms (3) in close proximity to one another (4) in pursuit of the same goal are a difficult standard to meet in the development of most social institutions. I will consider the viability of such explanations of institutional development and change in Chapter 4.

8 Note again that the market is structured by institutional rules that are the product of human creation. Given this fact, we know that these rules also have distributional effects on social outcomes. This, in a sense, merely sets back by one step the question of institutional development and change. See Ensminger, 1992, for an illuminating account of the development of market institutions.

Without a similar mechanism, relying on such collective benefits to explain social institutions is reduced to functionalist musings: Social institutions exist to satisfy the functional needs of a group or society, even though they are not created with those needs in mind. Such arguments are reminiscent of the description offered by Posner of the economic-analysis-of-law approach: "I emphasize once again that, in suggesting that primitive people are economically rational, I am not making any statement about their conscious states. Rational behavior to an economist is a matter of consequences rather than intentions, and in that respect resembles the concept of functionality in traditional anthropology" (1980: 53). But an "explanation" based on positive consequences without a mechanism detailing their development is more an expression of faith than an explanation.[9]

A DISTRIBUTIVE CONCEPTION OF SOCIAL INSTITUTIONS

Social institutions affect the distribution of benefits from the numerous interactions that constitute social life. Although it is true that we need such institutions to reap the gains from these interactions, the forms of these benefiting institutions vary across time within a particular society and across communities and societies at any particular time. As I have suggested and will continue to emphasize throughout this book, what separates these distinct forms is their distributional consequences.

The importance of distributional consequences implies the following conception of social institutions: Institutions are not created to constrain groups or societies in an effort to avoid suboptimal outcomes but, rather, are the by-product of substantive conflicts over the distributions inherent in social outcomes. According to this conception, the main goal of those who develop institutional rules is to gain strategic advantage vis-à-vis other actors, and therefore, the substantive content of those rules should generally reflect distributional concerns. The resulting institutions may or may not be socially efficient: It depends on whether or not the institutional form that distributionally favors the actors capable of asserting their strategic advantage is socially efficient. Note that the inefficiency need not arise from any incapacity of the actors (due to either lack of information or faulty understanding) but, rather, from their self-interest, their pursuit of a less efficient alternative that gives them a greater individual gain.

The role of distribution in explanations of social institutions has recently received more attention. Libecap (1989) introduced distributional

9 For a discussion of the strengths of functional explanations, see Cohen, 1978, 1982a, and 1982b, and Hardin, 1980. The problems and weaknesses of such explanations are discussed in Elster, 1978, 1980, and 1982.

conflict into his explanation of efforts by economic actors to contract for rights over property. Bates (1989, 1990) emphasized the inefficiencies produced by distributional concerns in property rights and kinship systems. And Tsebelis (1990: 92–118) proposed a distinction between efficient and redistributive institutions in his analysis of the existence of differing forms of political and economic association. Although each of these efforts contributes to our understanding of institutional change (I will discuss them in more detail in subsequent sections), their analyses have been limited mainly to discussions of intentional design and the implications for inefficiency. Here I want to insist on the primacy of distributional consequences in all aspects of explaining social institutions, especially in explaining the spontaneous emergence of the informal conventions and norms on which societies are based.

North presents a challenge for those who seek to emphasize distributional questions: "To the extent that exploitation models are to be convincing they must demonstrate that the institutional framework does indeed produce the systematic uneven consequences implied by the theory" (1990: 178). Such distributive explanations must address two general questions: (1) Who does the institution systematically favor? and (2) How might those so favored have gained these benefits? This should direct our attention to those factors influencing the capacity of strategic actors to determine the substantive content of institutional rules, and this introduces questions of the asymmetries of power in a community.

Introducing power into analyses of social life raises complicated conceptual issues. Rational-choice accounts have generally avoided the concept and opted instead for analyses of problems arising among equals.[10] There is good reason to be wary of employing power asymmetries in our explanations, because they too often result in ex post rationalizations of social outcomes. That is, we attribute a power advantage after the fact to those who are successful in achieving their goals. For power to have an explanatory role in our analyses of social institutions, it must be something more than an ex post description of events; it must be something that we can identify ex ante.

The possible definitions of power are numerous.[11] Here I propose the following working definition: To exercise power over someone or some group is to affect by some means the alternatives available to that person or group. To use more formal language, power relates to the ability to affect one's feasible set. This can be accomplished in a number of ways. First, A can constrain B's feasible alternatives in such a way that it

---

10 Note that this is one of the main criticisms of rational-choice explanations of social institutions. See Oberschall and Leifer, 1986, and Zald, 1987.
11 See Lukes, 1974, and Morriss, 1987, for analyses of the competing definitions.

precludes choices that are in *B*'s interests. Second, *A* can expand *B*'s feasible set by adding alternatives that are in accord with *B*'s subjective interests but are contrary to *B*'s real interests. Third, *A* can fail to act in such a way that it prevents certain alternatives from becoming available in *B*'s feasible set. This failure can be a deliberate withholding of certain preferred alternatives, or it can merely be a failure to remove a constraint that prevents the possibility of making such choices. Fourth, *A* can alter *B*'s valuation of the available alternatives by threatening a retaliatory action that would make an available alternative less attractive. Fifth, *A* can change *B*'s understanding of the alternatives, by manipulating *B*'s preferences. And there are surely other ways in which one can adversely affect someone's freedom of action.

The key here for a strategic analysis of the emergence of social institutions is how some actors can affect the alternatives available to others in such a way as to get them to act in a way that they would not otherwise choose to do: how *A* can get *B* to adopt an institutional rule that distributionally favors *A* (when other alternatives would be better for *B*). If we are to attribute to *A* power over *B*, our analysis must concentrate on the conditions under which *A* adversely affects *B*'s freedom of action. This calls our attention to the differences among a community's individuals and groups that allow actors to achieve strategic advantage. Such differences are numerous, but I shall limit my analysis to asymmetries in the possession of resources used in the pursuit of substantive outcomes. Examples range from the resources employed in the use of violence, which North (1981) has documented, to levels of membership in various unions and political parties to the other alternatives available to actors in social interactions. Although some may raise questions about the ambiguity of this formulation, few would disagree, I think, with the premise that these asymmetries in resources capture an important characteristic of asymmetries of power. It is by analyzing these resource asymmetries that we obtain an important measure of asymmetries in power.[12]

Explanations of social institutions in terms of their distributional consequences are complicated by factors that can undercut the strategic advantage enjoyed by social actors. From an analytical perspective, the problem is that we may not find the level of distributional consequences that is predicted from the resource asymmetries in a community. The reason is that social actors may be confronted by barriers to the successful establishment of social institutions that can produce distributional advantages. Two such factors will be considered here – the costs of collec-

12 I have postponed further elaboration of the explanatory role of power asymmetries in a theory of institutional change until Chapters 4 and 5.

tive action and uncertainty.[13] I introduce these factors now to anticipate possible objections to my insisting on the primacy of distribution and power asymmetries in the emergence of social institutions. It is easiest to understand these objections by considering them from the perspective of an individual who is designing a social institution: What are the implications for designing and creating the institution most favorable to me?

Costs

The costs of institutional development can significantly affect the final form of institutional arrangements. By definition, rational actors will not create institutions if the costs of doing so exceed the benefits that they subsequently provide. This has been one of the central lessons of the transaction-costs literature. Such costs enter into the analysis in two ways. First, in regard to the effects on the establishment of rules for small groups, the emphasis has been mainly on the costs to individuals of drafting and enforcing contracts governing property rights and other forms of economic organization. These costs can explain why rights that would appear to produce greater gains from trade are rejected on grounds of the costliness of their enforcement. Second, in regard to the effects on the collective institutional action of the community as a whole, Eggertsson explains the inefficiency of state institutions as follows: "High (transaction) costs of collective action are the principal reason why the members of a community cannot agree on new rules that would increase the community's aggregate output" (1990: 214). The costs of overcoming the well-known problems associated with collective action prevent the establishment of more socially efficient laws.[14]

Although the transaction-costs literature centers on the collective benefits of these institutions, social actors who seek to establish distributionally favorable institutions face similar cost problems. The distributional consequences of such institutions highlight two additional aspects of the cost problem. As for the costs of enforcing institutional compliance, distributional bias divides social actors into those groups who reap the larger share of the benefits and those who prefer a more favorable institutional arrangement. This possibility of tension for institutional change

---

13 As noted in an earlier discussion of the classic texts, Smith emphasized a third factor that can inhibit the use of a strategic power advantage: market competition. The existence of competition can, in fact, diminish the value of asymmetries of resources in the development of social institutions. I have postponed discussion of the effects of competition on strategic power until Chapter 4 so that I can take it up in the context of a more comprehensive consideration of the general role of competition and the market in theories of institutional change.
14 The problems of collective action and free riding were made famous by Olson (1965). Accounts elaborating the issues associated with these problems include those by Hardin (1982) and Taylor (1987).

can increase the costs of enforcement and will, therefore, enter into the cost-benefit calculation of those who benefit disproportionately from the institution. If the costs are substantial, these actors may opt for an alternative rule that is less distributionally biased as a means of lessening the tension for change. As for the costs of collective action, distributional bias increases the costs for social actors who seek to bring about collective change. Not only do they have to incur the normal costs of any collective endeavor, but they also have to incur the additional costs introduced by those who benefit from the existing rules and who will fight efforts at redistributive change.

Yet the existence of these additional costs should not preclude the pursuit of distributional advantage in the establishment of social institutions; they are merely an additional factor to be considered by strategic actors in distributional conflict. Here we need to distinguish institutions that emerge spontaneously from those that are the product of intentional design. These costs of enforcement are an important aspect of explanations of intentional institutional design and change and, therefore, of institutional stability. For institutions that emerge over time, the establishment of institutional rules is an unintended consequence of repeated social interaction. Thus, any costs included in the actors' strategic considerations are limited to those included in the choice of action in those interactions.

Uncertainty

Uncertainty about the relationship between our actions and the outcomes they produce makes rational action difficult. If we do not know the exact relationship between the choice of an institutional rule and the subsequent effects of that rule, the quest for the institutionalization of strategic and distributional advantage will be hampered. The standard argument concerning the effects of uncertainty on institutional development was restated by Tsebelis (1990): Uncertainty causes social actors to design institutions based on the criterion of social efficiency and not on redistributive advantage, focusing on collective welfare and not on individual gain. The logic is that uncertain social actors hedge their bets and adopt a risk-averse institutional strategy: to create social institutions for the average social actor (thus seeking to maximize social efficiency).

In considering the implications of this standard account, we should note that social actors can be uncertain about many things in their efforts to design social institutions. For the moment we can set aside the principal uncertainty facing social actors – uncertainty about the actions of others with whom they interact. (This strategic uncertainty requires an extended discussion that I will postpone until the next chapter.)

44

The primary importance of distributional conflict

Here I shall concentrate on those types of uncertainty that an individual actor would confront if she were free to design any type of institutional rule she wanted. This will allow me to focus on the effects of uncertainty on an individual's unconstrained preferences over feasible institutional alternatives. Social actors can be uncertain about (1) the present institutional alternatives available to them, (2) the present consequences of their present institutional choices, (3) the future consequences of their present institutional choices, (4) the future institutional alternatives that will be available to them, and (5) their future preferences regarding future alternatives and outcomes. Each of these forms of uncertainty can influence efforts to institutionalize distributional advantage. But the implications for explanations of social institutions differ depending on whether the institutionalization is the product of intentional design or of an unintentional evolutionary process.

Uncertainty about present factors, either alternatives or consequences, influences the actions that lead to both intentional and unintentional institutional development. This is the basic problem of a lack of information about the consequences of institution formation emphasized by North (among others) in his work on economic institutions. Social actors may not be able to establish a distributional advantage if they do not understand how an institutional rule works. Here we might expect two types of behavior: either experimentation with different institutional forms in an effort to obtain more information about institutional effects or the establishment of rules that can easily be changed.

Uncertainty about either future consequences or future preferences regarding outcomes can significantly affect efforts at intentional institutional design but has little effect on unintentional evolutionary processes. Both forms of uncertainty complicate intentional design because they relate to the future effects of presently created institutions. If social actors are uncertain about future effects, how can they design institutions that ensure long-term distributional advantage? First, this uncertainty may include doubts about the continuing effects of these institutions. Say we establish a rule at t_1 that we know will distributionally favor the owners of capital. But we may not know whether future circumstances will be such that the rule will continue to favor owners of capital at t_{1+n}. This is another form of the problem of the lack of information about how to structure social institutions to meet our needs.

But there is a second, more vexing form of future uncertainty for social actors: uncertainty about their own future status in a community. This is a variation of Rawls's veil-of-ignorance decision problem (1971): What kinds of institutions do we want when we are uncertain about our own position in the community? Thinking back to our institutions established to favor capitalists at t_1, the problem is whether I will still be an owner

45

of capital at t_{1+n}. This is the type of uncertainty envisioned by Tsebelis's argument in favor of efficient institutions. Here the question of the effects of uncertainty about the future is tied up with questions of how much the future means to social actors (i.e., how much they discount the future).

The argument that uncertainty induces a greater concern about social efficiency seems to rest on the idea that uncertain actors forgo present distributional advantage in order to protect against the possibility of future harm (Brennan and Buchanan, 1985: 28-31). But this does not take sufficient account of the possibility that if we are uncertain about the future, we may discount its importance when calculating the utility of our present actions (Taylor, 1987). That is, the more that we discount the future, the more that we will base our present institutional choices on short-term distributional gain.

Even if the uncertainty does not produce serious discounting of the future, its constraint on the pursuit of distributional advantage may be overstated. If the actors are confronted by real uncertainty (meaning that they cannot predict the future with any reliable probability), we may expect the following behavior: whereas they deemphasize their efforts to achieve long-term distributional advantage (possibly relying on institutions that are easily changed), they resist efforts to establish institutions that disfavor them. The vast literature growing out of Rawls's theory of justice testifies to the interesting intellectual puzzle created by this problem. But this formulation of such extreme uncertainty abstracts too much from the choices faced by real-life social actors. There are many things about the future that people do know: Women will still be women; African Americans will still be African Americans; young people will grow old (or die); and so forth. Although people do not know with similar confidence that they will maintain their present economic and political status, they do know from experience that dramatic shifts in political and economic fortune are unlikely. Thus, social actors who seek long-term distributional advantage have substantial evidence about their future status in a community on which to base their actions. To the extent that social actors are confronted by this partial uncertainty, the literature on judgment under conditions of uncertainty states that we should expect them to base their expectations about their future status on their present evidence and so seek institutions that favor those people whom they expect to be in the future.[15]

Finally, uncertainty about future institutional alternatives deserves a brief mention. Such uncertainty has no real effect on intentional design.

15 See the studies by Kahneman, Slovic, and Tversky (1982) and by Arkes and Hammond (1986) for evidence of the ways in which social actors employ the experiential evidence available to them when choosing among uncertain alternatives.

Nelson and Winter distinguish this kind of uncertainty from some of the other types we considered:

> There is . . . a fundamental difference between a situation in which a decision maker is uncertain about the state of X and a situation in which the decision maker has not given any thought to whether X matters or not, between a situation in which a prethought event judged of low probability occurs and a situation in which something occurs that never has been thought about, between judging an action unlikely to succeed and never thinking about an action. The latter situations in each pair are not adequately modeled in terms of low probabilities. Rather, they are not in the decision maker's considerations at all. (1982: 67)

For those actors who seek to design an institution at t_1, unforeseen technologies and mechanisms that might be available for the creation of new institutions at t_{1+n} do not enter into their calculations. Nonetheless, a lack of knowledge of such future alternatives may appear to undercut my criticism of the Pareto-superiority criterion. Remember that my criticism there was that in strategic situations social actors may rationally reject Pareto-superior forms of institutional change if those changes preclude future changes that are distributionally superior for them. However, if they lack any knowledge of these superior changes – so the challenge to my criticism might go – why will they not accept any Pareto-superior move? Here, I think, my criticism is sustained by the mere fact that institutional change tends to preclude future alternatives; that is, institutional change is path dependent (North, 1990: 130). As long as social actors know that present changes in the way we do things can count out future alternatives, they can rationally resist Pareto-superior moves in strategic situations.

In summary, although costs and uncertainty can complicate the pursuit of strategic advantage in the development of social institutions and should, therefore, be incorporated into the analysis, they should not undercut the importance of distributional consequences in our explanations of these institutions. To understand how social conflict and power asymmetries can form the basis of a theory of institutional stability and change, it is necessary to investigate how social institutions affect the rationality of social action. This requires an examination of the effects of institutional rules on strategic decision making.

3

Institutions and strategic choice: information, sanctions, and social expectations

How do institutions affect the rationality of social actors? Answering this question is a prerequisite for understanding the emergence of social institutions. To see the context in which such an answer can be derived, we need to refer back to the conception of rational decision making sketched in Chapter 1. An individual actor, motivated by a desire to maximize his or her own set of goals, faces one of two possible decision-making environments. In the first, the parametric world, the rational actor calculates his optimal strategy by taking the rest of the environment as a given. This includes the choices of others with whom he interacts, as he assumes that their decisions are fixed and unaffected by his choices. But true parametric choices are generally limited to instances of perfect market competition and are not, I will argue, the relevant environment for most social and political interactions. The dominant environment for social interactions is, rather, that of strategic interdependence.

Note the three forms of interdependence characteristic of strategic interaction: (1) The rewards of each depend on the rewards of all; (2) the rewards of each depend on the choice of all; and (3) the choices of each depend on the choices of all (Elster, 1986: 7). The fact that social outcomes are the product of the interdependent choices of social actors has two implications for strategic decision making. First, in order to select a strategy that will maximize their own interests, rational actors must take into consideration the actions of others. Second, in making their decisions, rational actors must be aware that their choices will affect the choices of the other actors with whom they interact. Therein lies the main problem for strategic decision making: Strategic actors must formulate expectations about what other actors are going to do.

This is the key to understanding the effects of institutions on strategic choice: the formation of *social* expectations. To aid in understanding the arguments supporting this idea, I shall outline the central points of this

48

chapter: Social institutions affect strategic decision making by establishing social expectations, and they do so through two mechanisms: the provision of information and sanctions. Through these mechanisms social actors learn the information necessary to formulate expectations about the actions of those with whom they interact. With these expectations they choose the strategies that they think will maximize their individual benefits. In this way institutions affect strategic choice and, therefore, social outcomes.

Thus the distributional effects of social institutions are a function of the social expectations produced by those institutions. In any single social interaction the task of a strategic actor is to establish those expectations that will produce his desired distributional outcome, to constrain those with whom he interacts in such a way as to compel them by the force of their expectations to choose that strategy that will lead to the outcome he prefers. The expectations established by social institutions are effective because of the very fact that they are social: (1) Knowledge of them is shared by the members of the community, and (2) they are presumed to be generally applicable to all engaged in similar interactions. Consequently, the fundamental goal of institutional development is to establish social rules that produce favorable expectations, rules that, through those expectations, constrain the actions of those with whom they interact.

In this chapter I develop this conception of social institutions through an analysis of the relationship between strategic decision making and institutional rules. The analysis is organized as follows: In the first section I briefly elaborate on the problem of strategic choice. In the second section I focus on the two mechanisms by which institutions affect strategic decision making: information provision and sanctions. In doing so I clarify the distinction between self-enforcing and externally enforced institutions. Whereas self-enforcing institutions rely mainly on the strategic acuity of social actors, externally enforced institutions introduce additional actors as enforcers who can alter the nature of social interactions. Here I bring together this analysis with the previous conclusions about the primacy of distributional conflict to complete a distributive conception of social institutions. In the third section I consider some implications of this conception for our understanding of the context in which social interactions take place. The emphasis is on three main issues: the significance of conceptualizing institutions as social rules, the effects of the ambiguity of rules on the reliability of expectations, and the relationship between institutions and ideology. This focus allows me to address criticisms of the strategic approach to social institutions that claim that the approach cannot adequately deal with such issues as community, history, and meaning.

Table 3.1. *Simple coordination*

Player A	Player B	
	L	R
L	3,3	0,0
R	0,0	1,1

THE COMPLEXITY OF STRATEGIC DECISION MAKING

Consider first a world without institutions. Given their ubiquity in the real world, it may seem strange to start this analysis without them, but in doing so we can better examine the structure of social interactions and the complexity of the problem facing a strategic decision maker. To understand the effects of social institutions, we need first to see the task facing an actor seeking to achieve his or her goals in a strategic world. Throughout this analysis I primarily use simple 2 × 2 games to illustrate the structure of these interactions. Although such games inevitably leave out much that is relevant to understanding specific social situations, the implications drawn from these games can easily be generalized to more complex cases.[1]

The severity of the decision-making problem facing a social actor varies with the structure of the strategic interaction. In some situations, formulating expectations is not a problem. There are no difficulties in either cases of trivial coordination or cases characterized by dominant strategies. In the first case (Table 3.1) two actors agree to meet at some future time. Although they have failed to establish the details of their meeting, one location stands out as the most beneficial alternative for their rendezvous. Regardless of why this particular location is the most beneficial (perhaps it can be reached at the least cost to the actors), its greater reward serves to coordinate the expectations about the actions of the other party.

In the second case (Table 3.2), a dominant strategy is one in which the payoffs gained from choosing that strategy are greater than the payoffs to be gained from one's other choices, for every possible choice that can be made by one's opponent (Luce and Raiffa, 1957: 77–79). If an actor has a dominant strategy, he will choose that strategy without reference to his expectations about the actions of others. If an actor realizes that his opponent has such a strategy, his expectations about his opponent's

---

1 The standard review of 2 × 2 games is that by Rapoport and Guyer (1966). They discuss seventy-eight different ordinal 2 × 2 games, which they suggest cover all the possible interdependencies in a two-person strategic relationship.

Table 3.2. *Examples of dominant strategies*

Player A	One dominant strategy Player B		Two dominant strategies Player B	
	L	R	L	R
L	1,1	2,3	1,1	2,4
R	3,4	4,2	3,2	4,3

choice will be readily formulated. In the left-hand section of Table 3.2, only player *A* has a dominant strategy: to play *R*. Although player *B* lacks a similar strategy, she can use her knowledge of *A*'s dominant strategy in formulating her own choice. Given her expectation that *A* will play *R*, she compares the payoffs available to her from the two strategies. The optimal strategy is to play *L*, producing the 3,4 outcome. In the right-hand section of Table 3.2 both players have dominant strategies: to play *R*. In this case, neither player has to worry about the strategic choice of her opponent, because the dominant strategies will produce the 4,3 outcome. In both of these cases, the existence of the dominant strategy minimizes the problem of expectation formation.

Yet these instances of trivial coordination and dominant strategies are few in comparison with other forms of social interaction in which the problem of formulating expectations seriously impedes an actor seeking to achieve his desired goals. The source of the difficulty rests in questions about the existence of equilibrium outcomes.[2] The principal problem pertains to social situations in which there are multiple equilibria. These situations are characterized by the existence of more than one possible outcome that, if arrived at, would constitute an equilibrium for the actors in the interaction. Examples are plentiful in social life, with pure-coordination problems representing one type. Refer back to the trivial-coordination case discussed earlier. The two actors still have the problem of meeting at a future date, but we now complicate the example by increasing the number of locations that offer the highest payoffs to coordination. As represented by Table 3.3 the effort to coordinate is now no longer trivial, as neither location is more prominent than the other, and

---

2 An equilibrium outcome is characterized by the following condition: "No single player would have obtained a larger payoff had she used an alternative strategy, given the strategies of the other players" (Friedman, 1986: 3). Kreps calls our attention to an additional equilibrium condition, which usually remains implicit in most definitions: "The equilibrium actions of the [actors] are consistent with the conjectures that each [actor] is supposed to hold" (1990: 330). This latter condition emphasizes the importance of expectations (conjectures) for the stability of equilibria.

Table 3.3. *Pure-coordination problem*

Player A	Player B	
	L	R
L	3,3	0,0
R	0,0	3,3

there is a real problem in determining which location the different actors will choose. Because both outcomes are equally attractive, unless the two players can agree on a choice of strategies, each must find some way to form an expectation of what the other will do.[3]

Somewhat similar in structure to the pure-coordination cases are those cases characterized by a mixture of coordination and conflict. These mixed-motive cases, whose structure is represented in Table 3.4, have multiple equilibria that, unlike the pure-coordination cases, differ in their payoffs for the various players. Because of these distributional differences, the actors differ in their preference ranking of the available equilibria. For example, player A prefers outcome 4,2 to 2,4, whereas player B's preferences are just the opposite. Although both prefer coordination on one of the two equilibria, as opposed to the nonequilibrium alternatives, they disagree on which outcome should be achieved. Once again, for each player the value of the choices to be made depends on the other player's decision. As in the pure-coordination case, the structure of the interaction does not enable us to formulate expectations about the other actors' strategies.

A final problem for strategic decision making involves situations in which no equilibrium outcome exists. Examples can be drawn from the social- and public-choice literature on the lack of equilibria in committee and legislative decision making (Ordeshook, 1986: 243–302; Shepsle, 1979: 27–59). This research has demonstrated that given certain reasonable assumptions about the preferences of committee members, unrestricted committee voting procedures can fail to produce equilibrium collective decisions. This lack of equilibrium can lead to continuous cycles among possible voting outcomes, with no outcome being immune to the possibility of change produced by changes in the votes of some committee members. The simplest example of this problem is the Condorcet Paradox (Ordeshook, 1986: 56–9). Consider the preference orderings of

3 See Schelling (1960) for a discussion of various solutions to this coordination problem. I discuss in detail his proposed solutions in Chapter 4.

Table 3.4. *Mixed-motive game*

Player A	Player B	
	L	R
L	1,1	2,4
R	4,2	1,1

Table 3.5. *Voting cycles*

Voter 1	A	>	B	>	C
Voter 2	B	>	C	>	A
Voter 3	C	>	A	>	B

three voters regarding the three alternative outcomes presented in Table 3.5. If the actors must choose their outcome collectively by voting, a cycle will be produced in which $A > B > C > A$, and so on. The paradox rests on the fact that individual voters' transitive preference orderings produce an intransitive collective preference ordering. In more general contexts, given the instability caused by the lack of an equilibrium outcome, voters are unable to develop the expectations about the votes of the other committee members necessary for determining the effects of their own decisions.

This uncertainty about the actions of others presents serious obstacles to strategic decision making. It introduces considerable uncertainty for the rational actor who seeks to maximize his own goals and interests. Whether the actors are in interactions that are purely conflictual or those that require cooperation in the pursuit of mutual advantage, the problem is the same. Put simply, without some means of resolving this uncertainty, strategic action is impossible, because the actors are unable to assess rationally the outcomes associated with their choice of strategies. This is the problem of strategic interaction in a world without institutions.

INSTITUTIONS AND SOCIAL EXPECTATIONS

If we introduce social institutions into the analysis, we can see how this problem of uncertainty can be partially alleviated. In Chapter 1, I offered a broad conception of institutions that was intended to emphasize the wide range of institutional forms affecting social life. A more precise conception of institutions now is necessary, however, which uses those characteristics common to this wide range of institutions:

Social institutions are sets of rules that structure social interactions in particular ways. These rules (1) provide information about how people are expected to act in particular situations, (2) can be recognized by those who are members of the relevant group as the rules to which others conform in these situations, and (3) structure the strategic choices of actors in such a way as to produce equilibrium outcomes.

This definition highlights those features of social institutions most relevant to an analysis of the relationship between social action and institutional structure.

We turn now to the main question: How do institutions structure social interactions? A short answer is, by establishing rules to guide future action with which social actors comply in making their strategic choices. This implies that if institutions are to succeed in structuring our interactions, they must have some mechanism that ensures compliance with them. Institutions structure social interactions and ensure compliance by a combination of (1) information provided about the choices of other actors and (2) the threat of sanctions imposed by other actors in the event of noncompliance. The nature of the compliance mechanism differs between self-enforcing and externally enforced institutions. Information about the future actions of those with whom we interact is relevant to all institutions, as it directly alleviates some of the uncertainty present in social interactions. The threat of sanctions is relevant primarily to those institutions that in some way are characterized by external enforcement.[4] But informal sanctions may also be established to punish noncompliance even in the case of self-enforcing institutions.

A third effect of social institutions is associated with the externally enforced variety. Because some social institutions constitute the game that will be played by the social actors, in so doing they help define the payoffs themselves. Democratic electoral systems are one example. Although there are many ways of resolving the conflict over political power and the control of the state, political actors may limit themselves to democratic means. Through such limitations they submit to an electoral contest whose outcome is defined by the institutional rules of the game, for example, the procedure by which votes are translated into parliamentary seats (Rae, 1967: 87–114). This last effect is not directly related to compliance but, rather, to the definition of the social outcomes themselves.

---

4 In this analysis I often use the term *third-party enforcer* to refer to any external agent who has the power to sanction noncompliance or to affect the outcomes of social interactions in other ways. This term follows from the use of 2 × 2 games as a means of representing social interactions. I use it merely for convenience and not to imply that all social interactions can be reduced to the two-actor case.

But to the extent that present outcomes influence an actor's willingness to submit to future elections, this additional effect of social institutions is indirectly relevant to questions of compliance.

The effects of information and sanctions

To develop these claims further, we must now incorporate institutions into the analysis of social interactions. To do so requires us first to analyze the mechanism by which information structures strategic action. This structuring hinges on the relationship between the information provided by institutions and the expectations necessary to make strategic choices. In a world of strategic interdependence, this relationship is essential to producing social outcomes.

In order to analyze the different information environments in which rational decision making takes place, consider the example of a farmer who seeks to maximize his gain from planting (Elster, 1986: 5–6). The relevant decision concerns his choice of seed. If the farmer knows the exact relationship between the choice of seed and the amount of grain he will reap at the end of the season, his choice will be one of certainty: He will choose the type of seed that will produce the largest crop. If, however, he does not know the exact relationship between the choice of seed and the size of the crop, the decision-making process will become more complicated.[5] Now each of the farmer's choices may produce one of several possible outcomes. Say that the productive quality of the seeds is contingent on the weather during the growing season: Seed A is more productive in a dry season, and seed B is more productive in a rainy one. These different sets of circumstances are generally labeled *states of nature*. The task for the farmer is to establish probability estimates for these states of nature, each estimate reflecting the likelihood that a particular type of weather will dominate during the season. The rational choice of action is then defined by an expected-utility calculus. Each action has an expected utility attached to it: the sum of the payoffs of the various outcomes weighted by the estimated probability that it will be realized. Based on this calculus, the farmer should choose the seed that is expected to produce the largest crop, given the probabilities of the different forms of weather.

If the farmer knows the true probabilities for these states of nature, then the calculation is a straightforward decision under risk. If, however, he does not know the true probabilities, he must make a subjective

---

5 The general analysis of decision making under conditions of risk and uncertainty employs a framework developed initially in decision theory and then adapted (with limitations) to game theory. See, for example, Gardenfors and Sahlin, 1988; Harsanyi, 1977; and Luce and Raiffa, 1957.

probability estimate of the uncertain states of nature in order to calculate the expected utility of his choices. Decision theorists suggest that the problem can be resolved by using a Bayesian estimation procedure.[6] According to this procedure, the farmer bases his probability estimations on his own previous experience with the weather and the additional evidence that he can obtain from the experience of others.

Decision making under uncertainty is analogous to the problem of strategic indeterminacy. The problem here is one of establishing expectations about the actions of the other players in the game. If we change our formulation so that the benefits to the farmer depend on his ability to sell his crop to others, his choices of action will include the choice of seed and the choice of how to market his crops. Given the necessity of choosing the best way of selling his crops, the external circumstances affecting his expected utility will include the possible actions of other actors. Here the farmer's task is to determine probabilities regarding the choices of the other actors (Luce and Raiffa, 1957). He must form these expectations before he can choose rationally among the strategies in his feasible set of alternatives.

The problem of expectation formation is rendered more complex by the interdependent nature of strategic choice. Say that the farmer's problem is to choose the proper day to take his crops to the town square, the day on which most of the potential buyers will also come to town. The farmer must formulate expectations about the actions of potential buyers before making his own choice, but his choice will affect the choice made by the buyers (assuming that they are concerned about going to town on a day when there is a good selection of crops), thereby also affecting the farmer's original expectations about the buyers, and so on. Note the possibility of an infinite regress in expectation formation, which can be avoided only in those cases in which the expectations of the players come to rest at an equilibrium; only in such cases can we say that the players' expectations are rational.[7]

Here institutions can enter the strategic calculation, by providing information about the choices of the other players. If an institutional equilibrium exists – and by this I mean that the institution structures the actors' choices in regard to achieving an equilibrium outcome – then the actors have a rational basis for formulating expectations about the actions of others. The information provided by the institution will help the

6 For a clear exposition of the logic of Bayesian decision theory, see Jeffrey, 1983, and for an assessment of the strengths and weaknesses of the Bayesian approach, see Gardenfors and Sahlin, 1988.

7 Binmore (1987) and Bicchieri (1988) analyze the conditions necessary for equilibrium-expectation formation.

Table 3.6. *Multiple-equilibria game*

Farmer	Buyer				
	1	2	3	4	5
1	5,5	3,5	1,1	1,1	1,1
2	3,2	4,6	1,1	1,1	1,1
3	1,1	1,1	7,4	4,3	5,3
4	1,1	1,1	4,3	6,5	4,3
5	1,1	1,1	6,2	3,2	6,3

actors formulate the expectations necessary to make a decision that maximizes their payoffs, given the actions of the other actors. Thus, the exact mechanism of institutional structuring involves the way in which the information affects the probabilities attached to the actions of others.

Consider the following two-person game, which represents the days in which both farmers and buyers can come to the town square (see Table 3.6).[8] Both actors have five identical pure strategies, representing the five days on which they can go to town. The problem is that these strategies can produce five possible equilibrium outcomes. Both the farmer and the buyer benefit from going to the square on the same day, but without more information the players will not know how to maximize their payoffs.[9] What if, however, an institutional rule existed that declared that in situations like the one in the example, actors would go to the square only on days 1 and 2. For a moment, consider a world without third-party enforcers. Assume that the rule is self-enforcing (an assumption that must eventually be justified) and that there is no formal external sanction for violating the rule.

What is the rational thing for the farmer to do? He clearly prefers one of the equilibrium outcomes that can be achieved only by going to town on one of the days prohibited by the rule. Should he violate the rule and choose one of these strategies? He must make a decision based on what he thinks the buyer will choose to do. The rule suggests to him that the buyer will choose either day 1 or 2. If he considers the information to be a reliable prediction of the buyer's future action, the farmer will attach high values to the probabilities of the first two days and low (approaching

---

8 This two-person example is an oversimplification of the actual multiperson decision problem facing farmers and buyers. But the main issues in a situation involving a large number of actors can easily be illustrated with this simple example.
9 Here I am ruling out mixed strategies in order to simplify the analysis. But if we did allow for them, the basic analysis of institutional effects would not change.

zero) values to the other probabilities.[10] His expected utility will then be maximized by choosing either day 1 or 2. In this example, the farmer will choose day 2 once he incorporates the additional fact that day 2 is the better strategy for the buyer to choose in the truncated game. The resulting outcome (4,6) is an equilibrium offering a payoff to the farmer that he cannot improve as long as the buyer maintains his same strategy.[11]

Note that the results would have been different if the rule had authorized the exclusive use of the square on days 3 through 5. Then all the equilibria would have favored the farmer. As long as the information provided by the rule were reliable, the buyer's feasible set would have been constrained so as to limit his preferred strategies to days 3 to 5. Without more information the actors would still have problems formulating determinate expectations in the truncated game.

The rule in force in the farmer–buyer case is an example of the importance of time measures in coordinating social activities. The establishment of the week and its division into days of work and rest can be seen as an institutional solution to the problem of how social actors can gain from coordinated behavior (Weber, 1952: 151; Zerubavel, 1985: 10).[12] More generally, this is the logic of the compliance mechanism for all self-enforcing institutions, from the conventions that are present in many aspects of social life to national constitutions to various forms of international treaties and organizations. These institutions structure social interactions through the information that they provide concerning the future action of others, thereby decreasing the uncertainty faced by the players in the game. The information provided by the institutional rules alters the expectations that we attach to the possible strategies of the other actors with whom we are involved in these interactions. This distribution of probabilities that we formulate for the actions of others affects our feasible set and limits the strategies that will produce our preferred outcomes.

But note that as in the second formulation of this rule, it may not eliminate all of the uncertainty in this situation. Although institutions may restrict the range of strategies available to the actors, only in the limiting

---

10 I leave open the possibility that he will not attach zero probability to the prohibited strategies because he may take account of the possibility that the buyer may, for some reason, violate the rule. How he would go about establishing the probability of the violation is a separate question.

11 Although the fact that he was adversely affected by the rule may give him a reason for wanting to change it, the rational decision was to comply with the rule in the absence of the ability to do so. I discuss this problem in Chapters 5 and 6.

12 Schotter (1981: 31–5) similarly emphasizes this problem of economic coordination as a source of the development of the week. In Chapter 4 I take up Schotter's explanation of how the problem is resolved.

case will they restrict the set to one alternative. This is always a possibility in the case of social institutions, regardless of their form of enforcement. How much the alternatives are limited depends on various factors related to the subject matter of the rule and the conditions at the time of its creation. The institution may establish the general parameters for the interaction (by excluding some strategies) but allow for considerable flexibility in the choice of strategies within that framework. For example, democratic electoral institutions rule out certain strategies for gaining state power (revolution, military coup, other nondemocratic procedures) but allow for a range of strategies for acquiring power by democratic means. In these cases, preserving a range of available strategies is a conscious decision by those who create the rules.

Although the provision of information is the main force for compliance in these institutions, informal sanctions often develop as well, lending additional force to these constraints. But note that what I am arguing here is that with complete information, actors comply with these institutional rules even without the additional sanctions. One might therefore ask whether if these institutions are truly self-enforcing, why we would see such violations. Two possibilities come to mind. First, there could be slippage in the socially shared knowledge of these institutional rules, which could be caused by a lack of knowledge of these rules on the part of members of the community. Or it could be caused by differences in the interpretation of the rules' content. In such cases we would anticipate instances of noncompliance that might provoke criticism. Second, when institutional rules affect the distribution of the benefits of social outcomes, it is likely that some actors will want to change these institutional arrangements. Their efforts to change such rules will begin with individual or collective violations that will be resisted by those who benefit from the rules.

The former explanation would entail a general sanction against rule violations, while the latter explanation would entail a specific sanction against noncompliance with particular institutional rules. While setting aside for now the question of the rationality of these informal sanctions, it is sufficient for the purposes of the present discussion to point out that the principal effect of informal sanctions is to diminish the value of noncompliant behavior, a mechanism similar to that characteristic of externally enforced institutions.

Externally enforced institutional rules add another mechanism to ensure compliance: the threat of sanction from a third-party enforcer. Although the potential actions of these enforcers are numerous, they can be reduced to mainly two effects on the expected-utility calculus of strategic actors. First, they involve sanctions against the use of particular strategies. Second, they directly establish the relative payoffs for certain types

59

Table 3.7. *Prisoner's Dilemma game*

Player A	Player B	
	C	D
C	3,3	1,4
D	4,1	2,2

of outcomes. In these ways, they both alter the actors' own assessments of the specific outcomes and provide additional information to be used in formulating expectations about others. Although the altered assessments can directly influence compliance with rules, the additional information only indirectly relates to this question.

First, the enforcement of sanctions by third-party enforcers is a common feature of many social institutions; for example, state enforcement of sanctions against prohibited actions is a common element of laws and legal systems.[13] These sanctions are employed in order to discourage the choice of certain strategies. Consider the laws against simple theft: The logic of the decision to steal can be modeled as a Prisoner's Dilemma game of the individual against society (Table 3.7) (Taylor, 1982). The cooperative strategy is to respect the property rights of others, whereas defection from it is the decision to steal. If we limit our analysis to a one-time interaction in a society of discrete individuals, theft is the dominant strategy for each person. But the social outcome is a world of anarchy and deception in which no one is safe from the possibility of being the victim, an outcome deemed by all to be inferior to universal cooperation.[14] Therefore, laws against theft are enacted to discourage such behavior. To be successful, the sanctions must be sufficiently large to reduce the benefits of theft to the point that it is no longer the dominant and preferred strategy.

13 There is considerable debate over the fundamental character of law. For seminal contributions to the debate, see Dworkin, 1977, 1985; Fuller, 1969; and Hart, 1961. Many of the issues related to this debate are outside the scope of this book. Here I merely focus on those aspects of a legal system necessary for developing this conception of externally enforced institutions. To the extent that sanctions are stressed as a fundamental feature of these institutions, they are also assumed to be part of the fundamental character of law.

14 This issue is more complicated than as I present it here. As we now know, if the Prisoner's Dilemma problem is formulated as an iterated game, theft may no longer be the best strategy for a rational actor to choose (Axelrod, 1984; Taylor, 1987). My only point here is to use the example to introduce the effects of external sanctions. I have postponed my investigation of the possibilities of the stability of self-enforcing compliance through repeated interactions until Chapters 5 and 6.

Although laws against theft seem to work to the benefit of all members of society when applied to all citizens, the enforcement of sanctions need not have such a universal effect. Consider the laws governing collective bargaining. Rules that prohibit workers from striking under various conditions can be found in many industrial societies, and sanctions against such actions can range from substantial fines levied against a labor union to the imprisonment of union leaders (IDE, 1981; ILO, 1981). The goal, of course, is to reduce the utility of this bargaining strategy in the negotiations with management. Such sanctions can have a significant effect on the outcomes of the bargaining process (Shaked and Sutton, 1984: 1351–64).

In the strategic decision-making calculus, these sanctions serve as costs of employing a particular strategy. Suppose that an actor knows the expected value of a potential strategic choice, given the choices of the other actors. If an externally enforced rule is introduced that penalizes that strategy, the actor must take into account the potential costs when assessing the utility of that choice. Note, however, that if there is some possibility that the sanction will not be used in her particular case (e.g., either problems in monitoring noncompliance or a policy of selective enforcement that is biased in favor of particular groups), the cost should be weighted by that probability. The more likely it is that the sanction will be enforced, the higher the weighted probability will be. Considering in this way sanctions that are externally enforced allows us to vary somewhat the form of that enforcement. For example, in labor–management bargaining, there are several rules that differ across countries in their enforcement mechanism. That is, the rule may be enforced as a law imposed by the state, as a clause in an enforceable contract, or as part of an informal bargaining framework. In contrasting the first two forms of enforcement, we should take account of the differences in the probabilities that the state and the other contractual party will impose costs for noncompliance.[15]

This threat of potential sanctions against strategic choices affects decision making in two ways. The potential costs make the prohibited strategies less attractive to those who face those sanctions. If the costs are sufficiently large and the enforcement is sufficiently probable, we may have to revise the preference ordering of our strategies. What was once an optimal strategy for us may become an unacceptable alternative. The

---

15 Macauley (1963) documents many instances in which business contracts, when violated, were not enforced. He suggests that the parties did not enforce them because of the complex nature of their ongoing relationships. On the one hand, they might have other means of achieving satisfaction for their losses; and on the other hand, they may have feared the adverse long-term effects on their business relationship of enforcing the sanctions.

strike that might have proved successful in a collective bargaining impasse becomes less valuable when the costs of sanctions against the union and workers are added to the strategic calculation. And note that the same logic holds in regard to the actions of others. The knowledge that sanctions may be imposed on the strategies of others is additional information about the probability of those others employing the sanctioned strategies. In deciding on its own negotiation strategy, a firm need not anticipate a burdensome strike if there are strong sanctions against such a union strategy.

When we reflect on the ubiquity of law (externally enforced social institutions) in our social lives, the central importance of sanctions for institutional compliance should seem well accepted. But sanctions, surprisingly, have not been the main focus of most social scientific accounts of political and legal institutions. For example, Rapoport suggests that the effects of rules are limited to what I earlier labeled as a third type of effect, effects that are relevant to those situations in which the institutional framework constitutes the game that will resolve the strategic conflict:

> Rules are important only to the extent that they allow the outcomes resulting from the choices of the participants to be unambiguously specified. Once these choices have been listed and the outcomes resulting from the participants' choices have been ordered according to the preference of each participant, the rules according to which the game is played are no longer of any consequence. Any other game with possibly quite different rules but leading to the same relations among the choices and outcomes is considered equivalent to the game in question. (1966: 18)

Here, although the actors participate in and influence the outcomes, the final payoffs depend on some determination by the external enforcer. Whereas in the other examples of institutional effects, we could imagine the interaction without an institutional framework, in most of these cases, no such institution-free resolution is possible. Dispute-resolution procedures are one such kind of institution. Courts, arbitration procedures, and informal mediators establish institutional frameworks in which the third-party enforcer takes an active role in producing the final outcome and accompanying payoffs (Auerbach, 1983).

A second category of such effects – which at first glance may seem quite different from these dispute-resolution procedures – is voting procedures. The analogy is not precise, but there are important similarities relevant to this conception of social institutions. If we conceive of the third-party enforcer as a vote counter who resolves disputes among voters with conflicting preferences, then we can see the effects of these rules on the actors' strategic calculation. The most straightforward examples can be found in committees. One of the earliest lessons drawn from public-choice studies of voting in committees is that the way we count votes makes a great deal of difference in the outcome.[16] In simple cases of sincere voting (voting according to one's true preferences), the same individual preference profiles can lead to different collective outcomes when aggregated by different counting procedures. The role of the vote counter is to translate the votes cast into the payoffs to the various voters. When we allow for the possibility of sophisticated voting (voting contrary to one's true preferences), the knowledge of the effects of a particular counting procedure can lead to strategic behavior among committee members.

Shifting from the simple case of committee voting to the more complicated voting found in elections, we discover that the effects of the externally enforced voting procedures are basically the same. The main difference comes with the introduction of additional strategic actors, mainly politicians and political parties. Elections can be modeled as a strategic contest among the parties, a game in which they choose policy positions to attract voters (Enelow and Hinich, 1984). The division of votes is a product of the parties' interdependent choices. But this division of votes can be translated into seats by a number of different formulas. The electoral rule tells the parties and the voters how this translation will take place.

The upshot of this process is that even though the game between the political parties produces outcomes in the form of votes, the external enforcement of the rules transforms them into outcomes in the form of seats. For each outcome that can be produced by the joint choices of the parties, the rules dictate payoffs in the form of seats. Because we assume that the parties want political control, the payoffs generated by the externally enforced rules constitute the outcomes that will eventually go into the party leaders' expected-utility calculus. Strategies will be chosen according to the rewards gained from the accumulation of votes. And with different electoral institutions, the rewards may be different for the same number of voters (Rae, 1967: 87–114). Furthermore, because the payoffs available to one's opponents are always important to determining the strategies they will choose, knowledge of the translation procedures is additional information about the expected actions of other parties and voters.

The point of this discussion is to emphasize how strategic actors incorporate the effects of externally enforced institutional rules in two distinct ways. Sanctions are treated as the costs of implementing particular strategies. They usually produce changes in the ordering of strategies in

16 See Black, 1958, for one of the earliest and now classic studies of this phenomenon. Although his interpretation of the implications of these effects is quite controversial, Riker (1982) offers a simple, yet thorough, review of the major findings in this area.

one's feasible set of alternatives. But there are cases in which the sanctions are not enforced or even instances in which the sanctions are not sufficient to prohibit choosing that strategy. In such cases the externally enforced rules do not significantly affect the strategic outcome. On the other hand, institutional rules defining the relative payoffs to the actors always affect the strategic calculus. These rules are part of the technology necessary for the production of the outcome. The interaction cannot be resolved without the intervention of external enforcement. Knowledge of the methods used to establish payoffs is central to strategic decision making in these contexts.

The distributive conception and institutional constraint

Now I can bring together the emphasis on distributional consequences and the effects of rules on strategic decision making. Put simply, if self-interested actors want institutional arrangements that favor them as individuals, they will prefer institutional rules that constrain the actions of others with whom they interact. That is, they will want to structure the choices of others in such a way as to produce social outcomes that give them the distributional advantage. Take the simple model of the multiple-equilibria problem shown in Table 3.4. Player *A* prefers an institutional arrangement that will produce the 4,2 outcome. To produce such an institution she will have to establish the following substantive guide to future action: In situations such as those shown in Table 3.4, actors who find themselves situated as player *A* play *R*, and actors situated as player *B* play *L*. Such a rule restricts player *B* to the *L* alternative. The key to successful institutional development and change rests on the ability of social actors to make compliance with such constraints strategically rational.

Strategic actors can constrain the actions of others through various types of institutions, but they are faced with the fact that social institutions constrain the choices of all actors in some ways. This fact may help explain why standard conceptions of social institutions focus on constraining all of the members of the relevant group or society. But such a conception mistakes an effect for the motivation for developing these institutions. Strategic actors want to constrain themselves only in those situations in which they feel it necessary to secure the strategic advantage.

It is easy to show that given the constraining effects of different types of institutions, strategic actors would generally favor self-enforcing institutions that produce favorable distributional outcomes. But these institutions, as we shall see, can be difficult to maintain in larger societies, and thus they are forced to turn to externally enforced institutions that entail more complex forms of interest conflict. To begin to see how social actors constrain the actions of others and make their compliance strategically rational, consider the following examples: The mechanism of enforcement for self-enforcing institutions rests mainly on our expectations regarding other actors. We decide what is best for us to do by formulating our expectations about the actions of those with whom we are involved. If we want to use self-enforcing institutions to constrain the actions of others, we must do so by affecting their future expectations. In order to influence future expectations, we must constrain ourselves, by committing to a future course of action. In the multiple-equilibria example, if the rule that player A prefers is to be self-enforcing, she (and other A players) must find a way to commit to the R strategy. If A players can make this commitment credible, the rational action for B players will be to follow the rule and play L. There are many ways of establishing the credibility of these commitments, but they share the common feature that they require us to restrict our own actions.

Our ability to establish our own future course of action is one of the important factors determining the viability of self-enforcing institutions. However, there are many situations in which such a commitment is not possible without introducing a third party who can sanction us if we fail to do what we have promised to do. This is the additional mechanism for enforcement characteristic of externally enforced institutions. Such institutions are required to structure many forms of social interactions: when there is no self-enforcing equilibrium, when the stability of the equilibrium is open to challenge by a coalition of actors, when the equilibrium outcome is suboptimal for all of the actors in the situation (e.g., in the static Prisoner's Dilemma situation). External enforcement may also be necessary for those institutions that might be self-enforcing if only the information were complete. Although there can be strategic advantages to limiting ourselves through the introduction of these third-party enforcers, there also can be problems. By granting power to external enforcers, we open up the possibility of additional sources of conflict. These enforcers will have interests of their own, interests that may conflict with those who originally develop the institution.

North's analysis (1981) of the conflict between the state and owners of economic resources offers one example. Although the owners of resources need the state to provide externally enforced mechanisms to structure their own interactions, the principals of the state have their own interests in accumulating revenues. This creates a situation in which the institutional rules that would further the interests of economic actors differ from those that would further the interests of state actors. In seeking to constrain the actions of others, the economic actors find it necessary to accept the enforcing power of a third party who may have interests different from their own. This potential conflict of interest is a problem inherent in all externally enforced social institutions, and it complicates efforts to establish social institutions that will produce clear distributional benefits.

IMPLICATIONS FOR A THEORY OF SOCIAL INSTITUTIONS

This distributive conception of social institutions provides a framework for understanding the context in which social interactions occur. Much of the criticism of explanations based on the logic of strategic decision making has emphasized the inadequate way in which the approach treats the environment in which choices are made. Here I have offered a way of thinking about the relationship between strategic choice and that social environment. My analysis so far has emphasized how institutions affect strategic choice when the rules are clear. However, there are many situations in which institutions affect social action in a more complex way. In this section I will consider three implications of this conception of social institutions that will advance our understanding of the environment in which social interactions occur. Each implication is closely related to questions of institutional emergence and change, and our discussion of them will allow us to see how a strategic approach can incorporate features of such concepts as community, meaning, and history – concepts that critics of the strategic approach stress in their claims about the inadequacy of the approach.

Institutions as social rules

To conceive of social institutions as sets of rules is to exclude alternative definitions. In a review of the literature on the study of institutions, Ostrom (1986) suggested that there are three main contenders: rules concerning behavior, regularities in behavior, and political structure. Because of its exclusive emphasis on the macro-level characteristics of a political system (e.g., size and degree of competition; see Dahl and Tufte, 1973), the third alternative can be rejected on the grounds that it is too narrow for our purposes. The second alternative, regularities in behavior, was advocated by Schotter (1981), who traced this conception back through several important studies of social institutions (Hayek, 1978; Menger, 1963; Ullman-Margalit, 1978).[17] In order to show the implica-

17 Schotter may have modified his view on this point. In a later essay (1986), he suggests that institutions are rules established by regularities in behavior. This would be more in line with aspects of the conception that I develop here. Regardless of whether Schotter has changed his own position, his 1986 essay offers several other examples of those who equate institutions with regularities in behavior.

tions of adopting a rule, as opposed to a regularity conception, we need to analyze more closely the characteristics of those rules that become institutionalized for the community or society as a whole. In doing so, I hope to show why a rules conception includes those features of a social institution that are absent in the regularities conception.

The debates about the nature of rules and rule systems have been complex and long-standing. Here I want merely to state a few characteristics important to this analysis, features that I consider to be less controversial and basically consistent with most accounts. Put simply, *rules are guides to future courses of action.* These guides can generally be formulated through verbal expressions. They may regulate existing forms of action or constitute new forms of action or practice (Rawls, 1955).[18] They are often taken to be merely prescriptions, but they may in fact "penalize, prohibit, require, obligate, prescribe, inform, guide, empower, permit, license, enable, facilitate, entitle, command, define, designate, constitute, distribute, describe, exempt, and identify" future courses of action (Marshall, 1983: 188). This varied list of possible effects suggests that when offering a general definition of a rule, it is unwise to be more specific than "a guide to future action." The greater specification comes in delimiting those rules that have been institutionalized for the community or society as a whole and in describing the mechanism by which compliance to such rules is achieved.

In characterizing those rules that become social institutions, it is instructive to distinguish them from both rules of thumb and regularities in behavior. In discussing the role of rules in the law, Marshall emphasizes the importance of generality in defining what constitutes a rule:

> Rules clearly cannot be particular and must in some sense be general; but what the requirement of generality amounts to is not easy to say. . . . Order and predictability flow, it is hoped, from generality and the assumption that like cases are treated alike. But it is not clear what restrictions this imposes on the formulation of something that can be called a rule. . . . What is necessary is that a rule deals with a class of *cases* (whether persons, objects, or occasions) and that the

18 This analytical distinction between "regulative" and "constitutive" rules is commonly used to distinguish rules that are used to aid action in particular situations from those defining the proper course of action in specific contexts. The standard approach is to treat only the later "constitutive" rules as features of institutions; see, for example, Hollis, 1987. To the extent that "regulative" rules are idiosyncratic rules of thumb, my conception of social institutions would exclude them. As I suggest below, a crucial feature of institutions is that they are rules shared by the members of the community. And some of these institutional rules have more of the features of regulating behavior than of constituting it. Compare a rule that defines a unique course of action from one that, though restricting certain strategies, leaves open a range of strategic alternatives. In defining social institutions a strict regulative–constitutive distinction is inappropriate (Rawls, 1955). A more suitable distinction is one between personal rules that are maintained by individuals to regulate their own behavior and social rules of either a regulative or a constitutive nature that are maintained by the group.

necessary degree of generality, whatever it is, can be acquired in any of these dimensions. (1983: 183–4, emphasis in original)

We can adapt Marshall's notion of generality to make the necessary distinctions among social institutions, rules of thumb, and behavioral regularities.

One of the main features of institutional rules is that they are socially shared: The knowledge of their existence and applicability is shared by the members of the relevant groups or community. This separates institutional rules from rules of thumb. As opposed to rules that are idiosyncratic for individual actors, for a rule to be a social institution it must be recognized as generally applicable to all persons in the community. This does not mean that the rule is required to treat every actor similarly, as would a criminal law prohibiting rape or murder. Rather, it means that the rule is known to be applicable to all members of the community when they engage in interactions covered by the relevant rule. An example of the latter rule is bankruptcy laws that differentiate among types of creditors in the provisions governing the division of a bankrupt's surviving assets (Dalhuisen, 1968). Although the law treats creditors differently, all creditors are presumed to be familiar with the provisions generally applicable to those who lend money, skills, or resources to debtors.

The fact that the rule is socially shared does not mean that it is preferred or embraced by all members of a community. To illustrate, consider institutional arrangements established to enforce apartheid in South Africa. An important subset of these rules regulates commercial relations between whites and blacks. They offer advantages to whites while restricting the activities of blacks. Obviously, these rules do not treat everyone similarly, but they do generally treat all members of the same race similarly. Most blacks and some of the whites may not like the rules, but they share the knowledge that the rules are applicable to all whites and blacks in South Africa who choose to engage in commercial activities. This system is fundamentally different from a rule of thumb that might be employed by a racist in other countries: Don't do business with blacks unless you can take advantage of them. Here it is not a general rule for the community but, rather, one invoked by an individual to guide his or her own behavior. Although this idiosyncratic rule may result in an inferior outcome for particular blacks, it is not an outcome that those blacks would have necessarily anticipated, given their reasonable expectations going into the interaction.

Two additional characteristics of institutional rules, which reflect their general applicability across both objects and occasions, distinguish institutional rules from mere regularities in behavior. Searle highlighted these features in his analysis of language:

68

Two of the marks of rule-governed as opposed to merely regular behavior are that we generally recognize deviations from the pattern as somehow wrong or defective and that the rule unlike the past regularity automatically covers new cases. Confronted with a case he has never seen before, the agent knows what to do. (1969: 42)

I will consider these in reverse order: first, showing that the generality of cases reinforces the forward-looking nature of institutional rules and, second, showing that expectations, created by the socially shared and forward-looking nature of rules, produce the judgment that deviations are wrong and should be corrected. This latter issue opens up questions related to informal sanctions against noncompliance with social institutions.

To say that institutional rules are forward looking is to underscore that they are used to guide our action in future cases that are similar to past interactions. Consider, for example, rules governing the measurement of land. In the Middle Ages, standard measures of the basic unit of agricultural land evolved according to one of three criteria: (1) the labor time necessary for plowing, (2) the amount of seed required for planting, or (3) the amount of area necessary for the subsistence of the landholder's family (Kula, 1986: 29–39). In a community, social interactions involving land were governed by a general rule based on one of these criteria. If a person lived in a community that had a rule based on labor time, then when he engaged in interactions involving land unfamiliar to him, he could reasonably expect that those with whom he was interacting would use the same measure. This notion of general applicability is central to the idea of following a rule:

To follow a rule, or more universally, to be committed to a system of rules as operative for guiding behavior, is to accept the principle that like cases should be treated alike. That is to say, I am following a rule if and only if I treat all cases that fall under the rule as the rule dictates I should treat them. (Ingram, 1985: 361)

Regularities in behavior need not produce this notion of generality, as they lack the forward-looking quality of rules. Regularities refer back to past patterns of behavior. The fact that an individual in the past has used a measurement based on labor time does not mean that he will find that measure appropriate to future interactions. Say that he had adopted a private policy of measuring land in terms of labor time. Owing to the varying quality of different plots of land, this measure may produce unfavorable outcomes for him in future interactions (Kula, 1986: 32). Then, if he fails to measure the land in terms of labor time in a new interaction, an outside observer could conclude that his past behavior was based on a regularity and not on a general rule of measure.

More importantly, this land measurement example illustrates what is most important about the rule-versus-regularity distinction in strategic situations: The general applicability of rules guides not only our own future action but also our expectations about the future actions of others with whom we interact. Knowledge of the forward-looking nature of such rules affects my expectations about future interactions with others. A labor-time measurement rule informs other actors about my potential future action when I interact with them regarding unfamiliar pieces of land. The distinction between rules and behavioral regularities is crucial when we consider the role of expectation in future situations in which an important feature of the past has changed.

Consider two scenarios in which questions of future generality come into play. The first concerns new actors who have not previously interacted with one another. Take as an example a hypothetical situation of collective bargaining between a local union and a firm.[19] Say that union representation has been part of the workers' bargaining process for a long time. The process, however, has been very informal; although the structure has been governed by a few general procedures, the substance of the bargaining process has followed a number of understandings between representatives of the workers and management. The union has had a long-standing policy not to strike over wages and benefits. This has been merely a regularity in their behavior; there is no rule forbidding a strike. Now, just before a new round of negotiations, the workers choose new bargaining representation. The question for management is, Does the long-standing no-strike strategy apply to the new negotiations? If there had been a general rule prohibiting strikes over wages and benefits, management could, with some confidence, apply the no-strike provision to the new representatives, as the generality of the rule would hold across new actors. Such is not the case, however, for a regularity in behavior. Regularities attach to the past actions of specific individuals, and unless the new representatives could in some way be connected to the actions of the previous bargaining team, the no-strike regularity could not be applied to the new negotiations.

The second scenario involves new issues that must be addressed by actors who have had previous experience with one another. Returning to the collective-bargaining example, say that we have the same informal procedures and that the union has just presented its demands for improved working conditions, including changes in the nature of production. These demands for new working conditions come as a surprise to management, because they have never before been the subject of bargain-

---

19 For an extended discussion of the structure of collective bargaining at the level of the firm, see Chamberlain and Kuhn 1986.

ing. One of the questions for management is, Does the no-strike policy apply to these new issues? The fact that the union's past history of not striking was based merely on a regularity developed in negotiations regarding wages and benefits makes it difficult to determine whether the regularity will apply in this case. If, on the other hand, there had been a general rule prohibiting strikes, the question of applicability could be more readily resolved for all parties. As new issues were placed on the bargaining agenda, the rule would be applied openly and explicitly. Although there might have been disagreements as to the interpretation of the rule's applicability, the existence of the rule would lead to a discussion of the differing interpretations.

Central to what makes rules more general and forward looking than mere behavioral regularities is the assumption that people will in fact comply with these rules. One important source of compliance is the informal sanctioning that can occur in a community. The second feature of institutional rules that Searle mentioned can contribute to this informal sanctioning: the judgment that deviations are wrong or defective. This is a judgment that people make about rules that they would have no reason to make about regularities in behavior.

This judgment also follows from the expectations created by institutional rules. Socially shared rules create the expectation that all of the members of the community will follow them in future situations. Landholders expect others to employ the standard measurement for agricultural land in those communities in which such a rule is generally in force. When someone tries to use a different measure, the other members of the community conclude that such individuals were either mistaken or devious (Kula, 1986: 133–8). Likewise, management expects union representatives to conform to no-strike rules when they are in force. When the workers decide to strike anyway, the management negotiators conclude that the workers are wrong to do so. In his discussion of legal rules, Hart (1961: 56) suggests that this "critical reflective attitude" is what really distinguishes rule-governed action from regularities in behavior. Two important questions arise from the existence of this critical reflective attitude: (1) What are the motivations for and the practical implications of this critical judgment? and (2) Must all of the members of the community share this attitude?

The motivation for this critical judgment must arise from the disappointment of the expectations produced by the institutional rule. If the firm mistakenly acted because of an inference drawn from a past regularity in the union's behavior, the management may be upset by the results produced by the strike, but it cannot reasonably believe that the workers had violated some shared expectations about acceptable behavior in collective-bargaining situations. If the no-strike rule were part of

71

the institutional framework of the bargaining process, such a judgment could be made. But this raises the question of how such a judgment can be justified. There are two possible responses. First, social actors may want, for rationally self-interested reasons, the expectations created by rules to be fulfilled. Remember that the failure to formulate correct expectations about the actions of others can result in social outcomes other than those that we prefer and set out to achieve. In such cases, actors may, for self-interested reasons, criticize noncompliers for causing them to lose valued outcomes. Second, social norms against noncompliance may develop around institutional rules. A general social norm favoring the fulfillment of expectations created by institutional rules may arise and produce a critical attitude toward rule violators. In such cases, the judgment is not tied to self-interested motivations in a particular social interaction but, rather, to a general criticism of those who violate any social institution.[20]

The distinction between these two responses can be illustrated by considering the practical implications of these critical judgments for institutional rules. Such critical judgments are often coupled with a desire to correct the violation. Landholders want to make sure that the same standards of measurement are complied with in the future. Management wants to make sure that the union will comply with the no-strike rule in subsequent negotiations. To achieve this future compliance, sanctions may be employed, sanctions directed not against the violation of a particular rule but, rather, against the general act of violating rules. And this raises the question of why such sanctions would be invoked.

Note that this is not a circular argument returning us to the question of what motivates a critical judgment. The critical attitude may exist independent of the motivation to invoke sanctions. Instead, the question of general sanctions against rule violators introduces a collective-action problem: Although such general sanctions may be collectively beneficial, why would any individual incur the costs of sanctioning such violations? If the attitude is generated by a general norm against rule violation, we may be able to explain the sanctioning as an act pursuant to that general norm. Although this may be the actual description of some sanctioning behavior, it is not at this point a promising source for a systematic explanation of sanctioning. If the attitude is generated by a general self-interested desire for expectations to be fulfilled, we will need to explain why actors would see it in their interest to invoke sanctions. In the case of interactions involving small numbers of actors, such as collective bargaining at the local firm level, it may be in the interest of either the union

---

20 Much of the general literature concerning norms of cooperation (Axelrod, 1984; Taylor, 1987; Ullman-Margalit, 1978) can be interpreted as efforts to explain such a general norm against noncompliance of social rules.

or the firm to impose sanctions to ensure stable expectations in future negotiations. When we generalize to the large-number cases, the search for actors who have such interests is more difficult. Although other actors may want me to comply with the standard-measurement rule, it is an open question as to whether any individual actor would find it in his or her interest to sanction my noncompliance. Explaining such sanctions is not really a problem in the case of externally enforced institutions: An external enforcer is established and paid to impose sanctions when institutional rules are violated. The explanatory problem is significant in the case of self-enforcing institutions. The possible explanations are open to challenge, but I will present a few in my discussion of stability.

One final question related to this critical reflective attitude: Does every member of a community or society need to have it in order for a standard of action to be a rule? Hart suggested that unanimous acceptance was not necessary and that minority rejection of the rule as a critical standard was possible, whereas Marshall argued that much more than a majority was necessary for the standard to be described as a social rule. Hart has the better argument here. All that is necessary is that a sufficient number of actors adopt the critical attitude to guarantee that the rule can be maintained, that the sanctions (either formal or informal) can be preserved. What that exact number is depends on the particular circumstances of the case. Here we must distinguish between the critical reflective attitude and the socially shared knowledge of the existence of the rule. On the one hand, not everyone needs to share the critical attitude toward the rule. Given the distributive bias that I argue is inherent in most social institutions, it would indeed be surprising if everyone adopted such an attitude. To doubt such unanimity, one need merely reflect on the institutionalization of apartheid in South Africa. Nonetheless, many instances of adopting such an attitude in the face of similarly biased state institutions have been proposed (see, e.g., Levi, 1988; North, 1981). If, however, those who have the power to change such rules fail to adopt such an attitude, we can anticipate future changes in the rules. On the other hand, a far greater number must share in the knowledge of the rule's existence. If the knowledge of the rule's existence is not shared by most of the members of the relevant community or society, then compliance with the rule will be open to serious question. This turns our attention to questions related to the interpretation of rules and the reliability of expectations.

Institutional rules and the reliability of expectations

If social actors are to use the information provided by institutional rules to establish expectations about the behavior of others, they must be confident of the reliability of this information. The importance of reliability can be demonstrated by noting how institutional rules are treated by strategic actors. This conception of social institutions, with its emphasis on information provision, sanctioning, and the interests and motivations of strategic actors, may appear to be reducible to individual actions and preferences. This is a common criticism of rational-choice accounts of institutional rules (McKelvey and Ordeshook, 1984) and is in fact a position advocated by some who adopt a radical form of methodological individualism.[21] But this position misunderstands how institutional rules are treated by individual strategic actors. I take the conception of social institutions offered here to be consistent with a broad view of methodological individualism.[22] Institutions are clearly the product of human action. To the extent that the tenets of methodological individualism require explanations to be grounded in the microfoundations of individual action, this conception of social institutions is not inconsistent. Nonetheless, it does emphasize that institutional rules have a special collective quality about them. They are rules and information external in some sense to any particular actor, but they are shared by the various members of the community. Unlike rules of thumb that each actor may create on his own in order to improve the quality of his actions, these institutional rules gain their efficacy through their social, shared character.

Most important, in the context of an isolated decision to act, social actors take as a given the information about the actions of others; that is, as opposed to calculating the subjective probability of others' actions, they use the information provided by institutions as their estimates of those actions. Social actors rely on the information provided by rules to establish their own expectations. Consider the conventions and norms defining and governing the social and economic activities within the family. Papenak (1990: 169–80) offers an example of how these rules affect family life in southern Asia. As in societies throughout the world, these norms and conventions are structured in such a way as to favor male family members in the distribution of family income. Some of the rules restrict the ways in which women can participate in the economic life of the community, limiting their range of activities to the home or to

21 Levy (1985) suggests that this is a plausible interpretation of Hayek's position.
22 The debate over methodological individualism has been long and often tedious. Early aspects of the debate are recounted by Gellner, 1956, Lukes, 1968, Mandelbaum, 1955, and Watkins, 1957. A more recent debate was that between Cohen (1978, 1982a, 1982b) and Elster (1978, 1980, 1982) over the merits of methodological individualism as a guide for social explanation. The issues raised in that debate were then addressed by Przeworski (1986) among others. In the latter essay, the relationship between rational action and institutions is explicitly raised as a potential problem for rational-choice explanations. See also Grafstein, 1988, for a discussion of the relative merits of individualistic and holistic conceptions of institutions.

activities in the community that complement those of men, what Papenak calls "family status-production work." Other rules – the most extreme of which are the traditions of purdah or veiling – serve to reinforce
the asymmetries of power in decision making in both the family and the
community at large. If we look at these rules from the perspective of
women preparing to enter into a marriage and new family life, we can see
that she anticipates her relationship with her husband by referring to
these underlying norms and conventions and without referring to the
specific characteristics of her husband-to-be. Her expectations about a
future life of subservience to the male members of her family can be
based on the actions of the average husband in her society.

To see the logic of this process, simply reconsider the multiple-
equilibria case shown in Table 3.4. We know the preferences of both
players: Player *A* prefers the *SW* outcome to the *NE* one; player *B*, just
the opposite. Yet the situation as such cannot be resolved. The additional
information provided by institutional rules applies to the issue of which
outcome we can expect the players to pursue. Because rules can be generalized, the information does not attach to specific individuals but,
rather, refers to anyone, the "typical" actor, who is in the position of
player *A* or *B*. In either event, the institutional rules cannot be reduced to
the preferences of individuals.

Given social actors' reliance on institutions, the concern with the reliability of this information is understandable. Will the other actors with
whom they interact recognize the same institutional rules as being applicable? And if so, will they comply with those rules? If the information
does not reliably predict the behavior of others, strategic actors will make
choices based on inaccurate estimates, and the resulting social outcomes
will differ from those anticipated by the actors. Here the question of reliability refers to issues of compliance and of coordinating expectations.

The standard analytical approach to this problem is to assume it away,
to assume that the rules are common knowledge in a community (Lewis,
1969: 52–60; Schotter, 1981: 65). This implies that everyone knows the
applicability of the rules and that everyone knows that everyone knows,
and so on. The recognition requirement that I proposed earlier as part of
my definition of social institutions is analogous to this assumption. It
implies that successful social institutions produce reliable expectations
about the future actions of others. I pose the requirement somewhat differently, however, in order to better emphasize the factors used to assess
the predictions drawn from institutional information in the strategic
decision-making process. Three of these factors deserve special consideration: (1) the potential ambiguity in the interpretation of the rule,
(2) the external conditions, and (3) the types of information communicated by institutional rules.

Institutions and social conflict

First, ambiguity in the interpretation of institutional rules is related to the extent to which the rules are shared socially by members of the community. If the rules are not well understood by the community at large, they cannot reliably predict the future behavior of the actors in situations that the institutions are intended to structure. This is more likely to be a problem with newly established institutions than with long-standing ones. If a rule is open to multiple but related interpretations, the actors will be able to use this information, but they must do so with less certainty.[23]

Consider, for example, an international treaty such as the General Agreement on Tariffs and Trade (GATT), which creates rules and procedures governing the establishment of tariffs and trade preferences among nations. The treaty attempts to limit the extent to which individual nations promulgate trade preferences and discriminatory quantitative restrictions on imports (Gardner, 1980: 348–80). Many of the agreement's provisions are open to multiple interpretations, especially in regard to the fact that signatory nations were committed to comply with only those trade restrictions consistent with their own national trade laws (Gardner, 1980: 380). Because individual nations gauge their compliance according to their own interpretation of the rules, this possibility of multiple understandings undercuts the reliability of the transmitted information.

Second, changes in external conditions may change the probability that the information can predict future behavior. If the values of the various outcomes are contingent on external conditions subject to change, these outcomes may change, creating a situation in which the institutional rules may no longer induce optimal strategies. Some actors may realize this more quickly than others do and may seek to alter their anticipated behavior for strategic advantage. Actors thus must take into account such changes when evaluating the probabilities that others will comply with institutional rules.

Because violations of externally enforced institutions incur sanctions that may offset the advantages of choosing a strategy not anticipated by institutional rules, this problem of unanticipated action is more likely to occur within self-enforcing institutions. Returning to the GATT treaty example, a critical weakness of the treaty allows for the following scenario: If a nation anticipates changing economic conditions that will make the GATT-structured outcomes less advantageous than other more discriminatory strategies are, it may choose one that is inconsistent with

23 This problem of ambiguity in interpreting social rules emphasizes the importance of social meaning in the analysis of strategic decision making. This suggests an area of common concern for interpretivist and strategic theorists. Johnson, 1991, offers an excellent analysis of the interrelationship of the two approaches.

76

the treaty's provisions. If such an unanticipated strategy is chosen, those nations that do not anticipate the changing conditions and, therefore, select strategies within the "nondiscrimination" constraints of the existing treaty may be adversely affected by their reliance on the unreliable expectations of the defecting nation's strategy.

Third, institutional rules can communicate two types of information about future courses of action: (1) a present assertion by an actor of her future intention to act or (2) a record of past patterns of action that are recognizable and distinctive, either by present individuals or groups or by past generations of actors. At any particular time, institutional rules can be characterized by these ways of communicating information. Some exclusively rely on one form of communication, whereas others are a mixture of both.

Consider the following two forms of information: Present assertions by actors of their future intentions to act may take the form of institutional rules. The most familiar example of this is a contract between two parties.[24] The basic interaction is a possible exchange of goods or services. Unless both parts of the exchange will occur simultaneously, the relationship between the actors will extend into the future. The future aspects of the relationship introduce two types of uncertainty (Williamson, 1985). First, the external conditions relevant to the exchange may change in the future. For example, even if an individual agrees on May 30 to build a house for a friend by August 15 in exchange for $50,000, the weather may turn unpredictably bad, and it may be impossible to complete the construction by the agreed-upon date. The changed conditions – the unseasonably bad weather – may not have been foreseen on May 30 when the construction was agreed to. Second, the fact that the exchange will not occur simultaneously opens up the possibility of future strategic behavior by the parties. On August 1, the friend informs the builder that he wants changes in the construction that must be completed on time or he will not pay for the house. Either he may really want the changes, or he may be trying merely to get the builder to revise the terms of his performance under the agreement. In either event, the August 1 announcement constitutes a change in the friend's promise under the original agreement.

The existence of uncertainty requires the participants in the exchange to draw up a contract that establishes rules to govern their future behavior and sanctions to guarantee compliance. Each makes a present assertion as to what his future behavior will be in the event of changes in

---

24 Atiyah, 1981, offers a readily accessible account of the relevant issues. For collections of essays that present wide-ranging views of the strategic aspects of contracting, consider Kronman and Posner, 1979, and Kairys, 1982. For a discussion of the relationship between game theory and the theory of contract, see Crawford, 1985.

either external conditions or the actions of the other party.[25] Generally, the parties bargain over these future terms and the sanctions for strategic behavior inconsistent with the rules of the contract. The extent to which these sanctions are deemed necessary may depend on the relationship between the parties: Sanctions may seem more important if this is a discrete, one-time exchange and less important if the exchange is part of an ongoing relationship. These agreed-upon rules provide information that will help predict the future behavior of the other actors to the contract. The information serves as a resource for future decisions that will further the actors' own interests in the exchange relationship.

Although the two-person exchange case may seem quite simple, it offers a clear example of how rules can communicate information about present assertions of future behavior. There are two additional types of rules that communicate present assertions. First, assertions by government officials or other third-party enforcers can be communicated by means of institutional rules. New rules and changes in interpretations of existing rules fall into this category. To cite a familiar example, states regularly announce changes in the interpretation of and enforcement procedures for tax laws. The new rules present valuable information about future state action, altering the strategic calculation of taxpayers in regard to their compliance (Levi, 1988).

Second, present assertions by others with whom we are involved can become institutional rules. A contract is one example, but I have in mind here other assertions that do not anticipate a reciprocal promise. Moments of either new institutional creation or significant institutional change fall into this category. Although instances of rebellion and revolutionary change seem to be the obvious examples, I argue in Chapter 5 that many more institutional rules are based, at least initially, on the communication of this type of information. Individuals or groups may assert a present intention to adopt a future course of action that can become an institutional rule. A well-documented example of such assertions can be found in the long-term cooperative relationship between workers and firms in Sweden. Beginning with the Saltsjobads agreement between the major national unions and the management association in 1938 that established an informal framework for nationwide collective bargaining, representatives of both labor and management formulated their long-term strategies through a set of assertions about future be-

---

25 MacNeil (1980) describes contracting as an act of "presentation," an act of bringing the future into the present. The idea is that the actors determine the future at the time that the contract is made. Given the fact that not all future contingencies can be foreseen, contracting is also an act of establishing rules of procedures through which these future contingencies will be resolved. This makes the present relevant to the future, but not as a moment for resolving all conflict.

havior that, once they had been confirmed by consistent patterns of behavior, became part of the informal institutional framework for subsequent rounds of negotiations (Martin and Ross, 1980: 43–48). Both sides came to rely on these assertions about such bargaining procedures as strikes and lockouts as a guide to future bargaining behavior (Rothstein, 1990). The key to the institutionalization of these rules, as it is in the contract and external-enforcement cases, is the credibility of the present assertion.[26]

The reliability of the information that we receive from institutional rules communicated by means of present assertions may differ depending on whether it is an assertion of an existing rule (that has its own record of past compliance) or of a new one. For an existing rule, the reliability should be enhanced if the assertion is consistent with the past pattern of behavior. For a new rule, reliability is tied to the efficacy of institutional development, which differs between self-enforcing and externally enforced rules. With externally enforced rules, reliability is less of a problem as long as the external enforcer has a record of enforcing similar rules. With self-enforcing rules, reliability is contingent on the credibility of the assertion: Is it truly in the interests of the rule-creating actor to accept the consequences of complying with the rule? If so, then the reliability of the new rule will be enhanced.

The second type of information communicated by institutions is a record of past patterns of action that are recognizable and distinctive. The past pattern of action may have arisen after an explicit assertion to act or without such explicit intention. The more distinctive it is as a pattern of behavior in the relevant context, the more likely it will be recognized by the group as an institutionalized rule. A necessary distinction here relates to the particular actors identified with the past pattern of behavior. These rules may offer information about a specific individual or group. For example, the leadership of an organization may have developed informal patterns of behavior to handle issues that are not covered by their explicit bylaws. Over time, these procedures can turn into informal rules recognized by the membership as standards governing future instances of these issues. This was the case with the ongoing relationship between Swedish labor and management in the post–Saltsjobad agreement period. As these informal patterns by the respective leadership persisted over time, they came to be relied on (Rothstein, 1990).

This represents an example of the concept of reputation in game theory. *Reputation* is a characteristic pattern of action that pertains to specific actors with whom we are involved in social interactions (Wilson,

---

26 The credibility of our assertions depends on the specific circumstances surrounding these interactions. See Schelling, 1960, for a discussion of some of the factors that make an assertion credible. I take up this question in greater detail in Chapter 5.

Institutions and social conflict

1985). But note that rules may also communicate patterns of behavior that extend across several generations. We recognize the pattern of behavior as a rule governing interactions in a particular context, but it does not apply to specific individuals. Social conventions and norms, such as the rules governing relationships between men and women in a family, are classic examples of such a rule. In general, long-standing institutional arrangements communicate this latter form of information. Questions of whether the rule is identified with particular actors and of whether it extends across generations pertain to the reliability of the information communicated. If the proper connections can be made between the past regularity and the present actors, then, all other things equal, reliability should be quite high. Factors affecting this include the clarity of the rule, the length of time the rule has been in effect, and the historical relationship between those who established the rule and present adherents.

All of the questions related to the reliability of expectations are affected by the size of the relevant community. Because reliability depends in large part on the capacity to assess both the knowledge and the credibility of those with whom we interact, smaller communities provide the relationships necessary to establish more informed judgments. As the size of the community increases, the problems raised by information quality become more pronounced. Larger communities are less likely to maintain the networks of ongoing relationships on which such judgments can be made. The effects of such problems threaten the efficacy of self-enforcing institutions.

Institutional rules and ideology

Ideological commitments have been offered as an explanation for institutional stagnation and inefficiency. North (1990: 111) emphasizes the importance of ideology to explain the inefficiency of property rights in developing societies, and Kula (1986: 111–12) similarly explains the persistence of measures of land and grain in precapitalist Europe. To analyze the possible effects of ideology, we need a way of thinking about the relationship between ideology and social institutions.

For this way of thinking we need a conception of ideology, of which there are many (Boudon: 1989). What is common to all competing accounts is the idea that a person's ideology is her beliefs and values, according to which she defines and evaluates the world in which she lives. What differs among the various conceptions is the characterization of the relationship between a person's ideology and an objective reality. One view (probably the dominant view in the social sciences), originating with Marx (1970), defines ideology as false beliefs. According to this view, ideology should be distinguished from true knowledge. A second

80

view, offered by Mannheim (1954), defines ideology as outdated ideas and beliefs. According to his view, ideology should be distinguished from values and beliefs about how the world should work in the future, what Mannheim called "utopian" ideas. A third view, generally associated with Geertz (1964), defines ideology merely as an individual's world-view, a cognitive map that one uses to interpret the world. According to this view, ideology should not be analyzed in terms of its veracity but in terms of its practical value for the individual.

Adopting completely any of these three views would limit the extent to which we could investigate the relationship between ideology and social institutions. For purposes of this analysis, I propose a variation of the Geertzian view: Ideology is the beliefs and values – the cognitive map – according to which social actors interpret and give meaning to the world. Although the practical value of a person's ideology is of central concern to her in her everyday social interactions, that value can be affected by both its veracity and its timeliness. Therefore, although we need not presume that an ideology is either false or outdated by definition, we leave open such possibilities.

With this conception we can establish a link between ideology and social institutions. If ideology consists in part of one's beliefs about how the world works, an important aspect of one's beliefs will be the ideas about how people act and how they are supposed to act. These ideas are a product of the expectations derived from institutional rules. Think back to Papenak's example (1990) of family conventions and norms in southern Asia. Both the men and women in these societies base their beliefs about gender relations and the family on their own experiences.[27] These experiences are structured by existing social institutions, and because of this structuring, members of both sexes draw their beliefs from experiences of social interactions that are guided by the expectations derived from existing conventions governing family life and accepted gender behavior. In this way a woman's ideological perspective regarding the proper role of women is formed in part by the existing conventions and norms of her society.

This relationship between beliefs and expectations establishes the link between ideology and social institutions. Ideology is a person's present worldview, a set of beliefs partly formed by the existing set of institutional arrangements in a community. The nature of this link allows me to underscore two points about explanations of social institutions

---

27 Of course, they also are influenced by a conscious socialization and education process in which their parents and others in the community participate. To acknowledge this is merely to restate the issue one generation removed: How did their parents acquire their ideology? To avoid an infinite regress, I would think it sufficient to say that established institutions play one important role in this process.

grounded in the strategic rationality of social actors. First, if we want to analyze the effects of ideology on institutional development and change, one of the important sources of that analysis will be the expectations established by existing institutions. To understand the effects of ideology on changes in marriage and family conventions in southern Asia, for example, we must focus on the durability of the existing conventions and norms.

Second, the explanatory importance of both ideology and social institutions rests on the socially shared nature of expectations and beliefs. Institutional rules transmit two types of information: the present assertions of intentions to act and the past regularities of behavior. In these ways, institutions link actions over time: The present and the past serve as focal points for the future. Thus, the history of a community, such as the history of relationships between the sexes, is embedded in its institutions and ideology and is transmitted through social expectations and beliefs. The fact that knowledge of this information is socially shared binds together the members of a community. By concentrating on these factors, theories of institutional development and change grounded in strategic rationality can incorporate important aspects of communal life, contrary to the claims of critics who contend that rational-choice explanations necessarily omit the effects of community and history. In fact, this conception of social institutions as information-transmitting rules offers a way to connect social action and community.

A FINAL CLARIFICATION

Finally, as a way of reinforcing some of the main points of this chapter, let me clarify an additional misconception found in explanations of social institutions, a misconception related to the information-provision role of institutional rules. Many explanations of institutional emergence and maintenance invoke the fact that social institutions supply information that stabilizes expectations (Hayek, 1978). But this reliance on information provision to explain an institution's existence is another example of confusing an institutional by-product with a reason for its development by rational actors. Such confusions can turn rational-choice accounts into unspecified functionalist ones.

Consider as a representative example the explanation of legislative institutions offered by Krehbiel (1988). The properties of legislative institutions are divided into two categories: distributional and informational. Distributional properties affect winning and losing; informational properties reduce uncertainty in decision making. Krehbiel suggests that "such reduction of uncertainty via sharing of information is essentially a public good within the legislature" (1988: 265–6). The relevant question here is whether the "public good" quality of information provision is sufficient to explain either the emergence or the maintenance of these institutions.

This is analogous to the discussion of the explanatory importance of stability in the previous chapter. Strategic actors do not create institutions merely to provide information that will stabilize expectations. Rather, they seek to stabilize expectations as a means of gaining benefits from social interactions. Thus, the pursuit of distributional gain can lead to the development of information-providing rules. Legislative rules do reduce uncertainty, but many different forms of those rules could accomplish this. The reduction of uncertainty is only a means of achieving distributional benefits. Rather, it is the distributional effect that must be invoked in rational-choice explanations. The mechanisms of information provision and sanctions are thereby secondary, albeit important, features of that explanation.

4

The spontaneous emergence of social institutions: contemporary theories of institutional change

Up to this point my analysis has focused on the effects of institutions on social life. My main argument has been that the primary force of institutional effects is distributional – the determination of the division of benefits that characterize social outcomes. Now, as we turn to questions about the origin of these institutions, we need to consider the implications of these distributional effects on explanations of institutional development and change. Given the importance of distributional effects, we would expect social actors to prefer and seek to establish those institutional arrangements that favor them in distributional terms. Therefore, our theories of institutional development and change should either invoke this pursuit of distributional advantage as a major source of explanation or explain why other factors counteract and override distributional concerns.

Contemporary theories of institutional change seek to understand both the conditions under which social institutions develop and the circumstances under which they change. In explaining the origin of institutions, such theories emphasize one of two processes: (1) spontaneous, or evolutionary, emergence or (2) intentional design. These theories primarily invoke the collective value of social institutions. If the earlier argument about the primacy of distribution is correct, these theories will need to elaborate mechanisms of change describing either how the pursuit of distributional advantage is offset by other factors oriented toward collective gain or how a selection mechanism favors the development of collectively beneficial social institutions.

In assessing the merits of these various theories, the central question is, Under what circumstances are the conditions that these mechanisms require satisfied? We can judge the value of any theory of institutional change in terms of how general it is, in terms of the breadth of the range of social institutions it can explain. The generality of any explanation

84

depends on the restrictiveness of the empirical conditions that must be satisfied for the theory to hold. As I will show in the following analyses, a major weakness of the existing theories of development and change is the restrictiveness of these conditions.

My principal concern in this book is to describe the development of and change in the informal network of conventions, norms, and rules forming the basis of social life. The importance of this network of self-enforcing institutions for the structuring of social life has already been emphasized. Note also that these informal rules form the basis for the intentional development of formal institutions: both as the prototype for formalizations of legal rules and as the context in which new formal institutions are established.[1] This focus on informal institutions means concentrating on spontaneous, or evolutionary, theories. Theories of spontaneous emergence try to explain the development of institutions in terms of decentralized mechanisms of institutionalization. The subsequent changes in these institutions are explained by either decentralized evolutionary processes or intentional attempts at reform.

My analysis over the next several chapters proceeds in three stages: (1) an assessment of existing evolutionary theories in light of the distributive conception of social institutions, (2) the development of an alternative theory that emphasizes the conflict over distributional gain, and (3) a consideration of the effects of efforts at intentional development and change. The first of these is the focus of this chapter. In the next section I set out the general structure and logic of evolutionary explanations. Then I use this framework to analyze contemporary theories of spontaneous emergence and evolutionary change. Three distinct accounts are considered: classical statements of cultural evolution, theories of the evolutionary emergence of social conventions, and market-based theories of exchange and selection through competition. My goals here are to show the restrictiveness of the empirical conditions required by these theories and to emphasize the inadequate way in which they address the issue of distributional effects.

THE LOGIC OF EVOLUTIONARY EXPLANATIONS

The idea that the existence of a society's informal institutions could be explained by a process of spontaneous emergence or evolution is an old

---

1 For most existing explanations of institutional development, the nature of the social institution generally dictates the particular process invoked: Formal institutions are developed by intentional design, whereas informal institutions evolve over time. One of the implications of my analysis, developed in Chapter 6, is that this sharp distinction has been overdrawn and that explanations of intentional design should take account of the existing network of informal institutions.

one. The underlying reasoning is that social, or cultural, evolution is analogous to biological evolution. Richerson and Boyd make the point as follows:

The idea that unifies all this work is that social learning or cultural transmission can be modeled as a system of inheritance: to understand the macroscopic patterns of cultural change we must understand the microscopic processes that increase the frequency of some culturally transmitted variants and reduce the frequency of others. (1987: 29)

Whether the models pursue the analogy explicitly (Boyd and Richerson, 1985; Faia, 1986) or adopt it implicitly as the logic underlying historical change (Alchian, 1950; Schotter, 1981), contemporary theories of institutional change conform to the basic features of the evolutionary process. Therefore, it is useful to begin this analysis of theories of spontaneous emergence and change by considering the requirements of an evolutionary explanation.

Evolutionary explanations generally are functional explanations that explain the features of a particular organism in terms of their ability to satisfy the functional needs of that organism. In a cultural context, an evolutionary explanation explains social institutions in terms of their ability to satisfy the functional needs of the members of that society. The functional criterion differs according to the explanation; for example, it is reproductive fitness in biological accounts, and some form of fitness or utility in cultural accounts. Change is explained in terms of adaptation to changes in external circumstances, that is, circumstances that affect fitness or utility.[2]

An evolutionary theory must account for and explain three essential features of the evolutionary process: (1) the existence of *variation* in the relevant traits, (2) some method of *inheritance* of the successful traits, and (3) the method of *selection* (Hirshleifer, 1977: 8). For example, say that we want to give an evolutionary explanation of institutions of land measurement. We must begin by demonstrating the variation in measures of land, a range of alternative criteria for land measurement. Next we must establish that the rules were passed on from one genera-

2 Some theories focus on explanations of particular features of an organism, and others pitch the explanation at the level of the overall set of institutions. Elster points out that the latter formulation incorporates two features of the evolutionary process lacking in narrower theories: "First, there is the omnipresent phenomenon of *pleiotropy*. A tendency to conform to a social norm might detract from genetic fitness and yet be retained by natural selection if it is the by-product of a gene whose main product is highly beneficial. Secondly, the general form allows for time lags. A social norm may be maladaptive today and yet have been adaptive at the stage in history when the human genome evolved and, for practical purposes, was fixed" (1989b, 114). As I will show later when analyzing classical statements of cultural evolution, although the latter formulation does allow for the inefficiency of particular institutional rules, it increases the complexity of the problem of developing empirical support for the theory.

tion to the next, some process by which future generations could learn the standard criterion for measuring land. Finally we must show how the existing rule of measurement was selected from the available alternatives, describing both the criterion of selection and the mechanism by which the selection takes place. In the process of satisfying each of these essential features, certain conceptual issues must be addressed. To demonstrate the relevance of these issues to theories of evolutionary institutional change, I shall use the land-measurement example and the framework presented by Boyd and Richerson (1985).

Variation

Evolutionary processes require variation in the range of alternatives that can be selected. In part this is self-evident, for if there were not a variety of rules of land measurement in a community at a particular time, there would be nothing to select. But the fact that a variety of alternatives do not exist in the present does not mean that there was not a variety of alternatives at some point in the past. In fact, evolutionary theory suggests that the selection process should eventually eliminate inferior (defined by some posited criterion) alternatives over time. What is crucial to the theory is that some variation in institutional alternatives can be established in the historical record. Two characteristics of the feasible alternatives are relevant to the analysis of evolutionary institutional change.

First, how are the variations generated? Theories of social selection can be distinguished by whether they limit selection to existing alternatives (explaining alternatives by chance) or whether they allow intentional innovation to be part of the selection process. The content of the selected criterion depends in large part on the available alternatives: Does the theory restrict the rules to chance variation, or does it allow those actors in land transactions to introduce new forms of measurement?

Second, how finely grained are the alternatives? Here the question is whether or not the alternatives are continuously distributed. By this I hope to capture the difference between finely grained rules characterized by only marginal differences among them and lumpy rules characterized by significant differences among them. Land-measurement rules can encompass either a variety of alternatives differing within a narrow range of finely grained units of measure or a few widely disparate alternatives recommending significantly different forms of measurement. I will argue later in this chapter that the character of the available alternatives can significantly affect both the mechanism of selection and, depending on the selection mechanism, the speed of evolutionary change.

87

Inheritance

The inheritance of social institutions requires both a means of transferring knowledge of these social rules and an appropriate unit of inheritance. Inheritance is the feature of evolutionary explanations that most contemporary theories of institutional change appear to take for granted, in part because there is a fairly standard way of addressing it. But one aspect of this inheritance process must be highlighted in order to resolve a lingering controversy in evolutionary theory: the unit of selection.

Knowledge of social rules is transmitted across generations by various means of learning and socialization. Boyd and Richerson (1985: 35) offer one of the most sophisticated accounts of this process, a dual-inheritance model of genetic and cultural transmission. For my purposes, we can concentrate exclusively on the latter, nongenetic form of inheritance. Boyd and Richerson define cultural transmission as a product of social learning: New generations learn existing rules and norms by means of imitation and reinforcement. Thus, I learn about land measurement and the various criteria concerning land through my experiences with family, friends, teachers, and so forth. Through these experiences I learn how existing institutions governed the social life of earlier generations.

Note that this social learning can be distinguished from the learning entailed in creating or selecting new institutions. This distinction is important to understanding the causes of evolutionary change. The former is merely the means by which the knowledge of existing institutional forms is transmitted, and the latter is one way in which new institutional forms might be selected in the evolutionary process. The fact that social institutions might be passed on from one generation to the next does not explain why one set of institutions exists, as opposed to another. Boyd and Richerson point out that "cultural transmission by itself does not cause any change in the frequency of the different behavioral variants . . . cultural transmission is a useful short cut to ordinary trial-and-error learning only if some force acts to increase the frequency of favorable cultural variants" (1985: 80). A successful evolutionary explanation of the emergence of land measures requires both inheritance and a selection mechanism that affects change.

If social institutions are inherited by means of social learning, then it would seem to follow that the individual is the appropriate unit of selection in these evolutionary accounts. Because people learn about measures of land and because learning is the means of inheriting land measurements, the evolutionary selection process (whatever it might be) should select from among the various land measures used by individuals in a particular society according to the benefits accruing to the *individuals* in that community. But there are opposing conceptions that contend that the appropriate unit of evolutionary selection is not the individual but is, rather, the group (Wilson and Sober, 1989). That is, an evolutionary selection process selects from among the land measures dominating in different communities according to the benefits accruing to the different *communities*. This choice between individual and group selection is central to the logic of evolutionary theories of institutional change. I raise this problem here to emphasize its relationship to the mechanism of inheritance, but it cannot be resolved until we have considered the alternative theories of selection.

Selection

The mechanism of selection is the key to explaining institutional change. Without some force altering the existing distribution of alternative institutional forms, evolutionary change cannot take place. Evolutionary explanations invoke a variety of selection mechanisms, which can be divided into three classes: random variation, decision-making forces, and natural selection (Richerson and Boyd, 1987: 30). Random processes of cultural evolution are analogous to the biological mechanisms of mutation and drift. Although I do not deny that randomness can play a role in the evolution of social institutions, I shall consider here the latter two classes of mechanisms because they are the ones stressed in contemporary theories of institutional change.

Mechanisms of individual decision making are based on people's capacity to learn about and adopt new institutional rules. The standard criterion for contemporary theories of institutional change is individual utility: New rules will be adopted if they increase utility.[3] Boyd and Richerson (1985: 10) distinguish between two forms of learning and selection based on the source of the rule variation. Direct biased transmission requires choosing rules from a range of preexisting alternatives; guided variation, on the other hand, is a trial-and-error approach allowing for the possibility that the actors will create new institutional alternatives.

---

3 I choose to avoid here the argument raised by Boyd and Richerson (1985) and Hirschleifer (1977), among others, that the criterion of utility and the concomitant pursuit of self-interest are traits that have evolved genetically because they maximize individual fitness. As I suggested in Chapter 1, my arguments in this book do not rest on a claim that self-interested action is evolutionarily superior to other forms of motivation. Rather, my claim is merely that for whatever reason, individual self-interest is an important motivation for social actors and that the assumption of self-interest is a valuable tool for building social theories. The question of the fitness value of self-interested behavior is relevant, however, to the unit-of-selection controversy discussed later.

Decision making can encompass a wide range of activities that might be the source of the learning process. Although the standard accounts concentrate on activities like individual invention, voluntary exchange, and coordination, it is important to keep in mind that there are many other forms of social interaction that might generate new rules. The rule resulting from this learning process may differ depending on the particular social interaction that generates it; for example, a land measure emerging from a set of voluntary exchanges may differ from a rule produced by bargaining or conflict. The general logic of evolutionary change through one of these decision-making mechanisms is as follows: Individuals in one generation use learning procedures to increase the frequency of using a particular criterion of land measurement, and then these newly learned measures are culturally transmitted to the next generation, thus increasing the frequency of using the new criterion in the next generation.

Such decision-making forces are distinct from mechanisms of natural selection. Whereas decision-making mechanisms depend on people's choices for change, natural-selection mechanisms produce change by a process independent of individuals' choices. The standard formulation of the natural-selection mechanism relies on selection based on fitness and survival criteria. Natural selection among available alternatives occurs when there is competitive pressure among the alternatives, pressure for whatever resource is necessary for the survival of the individuals in the group. If the competitive pressure is such that the available alternatives can no longer coexist, those least likely to contribute to the individual's continuing fitness will be selected out (Wilson and Sober, 1989: 339–40). In the case of land measurements, assume that various rules of measure are being employed by different groups in a community. The theory of natural selection suggests that if these different groups start to experience competitive pressure for scarce resources essential to their continued survival, a process of selection will ensue. Those groups whose rules allow them to succeed in the struggle for scarce resources survive. In this way natural selection eliminates those rules of land measurement used by the less successful groups.

Natural-selection theories can be classified according to the way they treat the question of how the variations arise among which selection takes place. In regard to cultural evolution, some theorists limit variation to random chance as a way of distinguishing natural selection from processes involving individual choice (Boyd and Richerson, 1985: 174). Other theorists synthesize aspects of individual decision making and natural selection along the lines of Alchian's market-selection argument (1950): People develop alternatives through learning processes, with the most efficient alternatives being selected out by means of a competitive process. What is common to both approaches is that the final selection of institutional form for transmission to future generations is governed by the natural-selection mechanism and not the decision-making process.

Individual versus group selection

These differences in the mechanisms of evolutionary change bring us back to the question of unit of selection. What is at issue in this debate for theories of institutional change? Given that evolutionary explanations invoke arguments regarding the optimization of some fundamental criterion (fitness, survival, utility), the question is what is optimized in the process of evolutionary institutional change. We can clarify what is at stake here by considering the phenomenon of altruistic behavior in communities. Studies of the evolution of altruistic behavior present the following results (Hirshleifer, 1977; Maynard-Smith, 1982): Within a single group, self-interested behavior is superior to altruism in terms of individual fitness; that is, individuals who act in their own self-interest give birth to a greater number of offspring, on average, than do those who act altruistically. But when we compare the growth rates of the different groups, we find that those with a higher percentage of altruists produce a higher average number of offspring than do groups with fewer altruists. Thus, even though self-interested behavior is favored within a group, groups seem to benefit from the existence of altruism. The question, therefore, is whether the evolutionary process optimizes fitness at the individual level to select self-interested behavior or whether it optimizes fitness at the group level to select some mix of self-interested and altruistic behavior.

For theories of evolutionary institutional change, the debate over unit of selection is reduced to two issues: (1) the locus of the pressure for change and (2) the mechanism of inheritance. In regard to the locus of pressure of change, the argument for individual selection is straightforward. Williams succinctly states the case for individual selection: "Every adaptation is calculated to maximize the reproductive success of the individual, relative to other individuals, regardless of what effect this maximization has on the population" (1966: 160). According to this account, the pressure for institutional change works at the level of the individual members of a society, selecting out those institutional forms that work best in a particular society.

The argument for group selection is more complex. Wilson (1983) and Wilson and Sober (1989) claim that under some conditions, groups have properties similar to those of an individual, and when those conditions hold, evolutionary pressure can affect change at the group level. According to their argument, in order for group selection to occur, a population must be divided into a set of functionally organized and mutually exclusive groups. For a group to be functionally organized, it must have the properties of an organism: "a form of life composed of mutually dependent parts that maintain various vital properties" (Wilson and Sober, 1989: 339). In such a case the fitness of the group is a function of the interdependent nature of the individuals within it. In addition, the fitness of the group must be independent of the fitness properties of any other members of the population outside the group (Wilson, 1983: 174).

When these conditions are met, the possibility of selection at the group level exists. For it to occur, the requirements of variation (that the groups vary in properties that affect group fitness) and inheritance (that these properties can be passed among generations) must also be met (Wilson and Sober, 1989: 342). For explanations of evolutionary institutional change, this argument suggests that the pressure for change can work at the level of functionally organized groups, selecting out those groups having superior forms of social institutions.

But this explanation does not address the tension between the pressures of individual and group selection illustrated by the altruism example. Wilson and Sober (1989: 342) contend that in a perfect group-selection model, an additional condition must be satisfied: There can be no differences in the fitness properties of the individuals who make up the group. Thus, for selection to work at the group level, there can be no selection working at the individual level. As Maynard-Smith points out, this is a stringent empirical requirement: "Are populations sufficiently isolated, and free of intragroup selection, to evolve complex group adaptations?" (1987: 130–1). Aware of the difficulty of satisfying this requirement, Wilson and Sober argue instead for a balancing standard:

Natural selection can act both within a unit (favoring some elements of the unit over others) and between units (favoring some units over others). When within-unit selection overwhelms between-group selection, the unit becomes a collection of organisms without itself having the properties of an organism, in the formal sense of the word. When between-unit selection overwhelms within-unit selection, the unit itself becomes an organism in the formal sense of the word. (1989: 343)

But this balancing standard is a difficult one to satisfy. When might between-unit selection overwhelm within-unit selection? Let us return to the altruism example. As the standard example is formulated, if between-unit selection dominates, evolutionary pressure will eliminate those groups with smaller numbers of altruists. Over time the variation in numbers of altruists among the remaining groups should decline. Without the pressure of group competition, within-unit pressure should come to dominate over time, and the altruists will be selected out in favor of the self-interested individuals. What then remains of group selection? There are two reasons that this scenario might not occur, but both seem to conflict with the group-selection model.

First, the members of the different groups might disperse and recombine in new groups, maintaining the variation in proportions of altruists in the population. By introducing a random element into the model, it guarantees that the variation necessary for between-unit selection will exist (Hirshleifer, 1977: 24). But such dispersal and reassortment tend to break up the group as a distinct unit of selection, introducing new interdependence among offspring of different groups and detouring from the direct chain of inheritance among generations of particular groups. Thus, it becomes difficult to sustain the claim that the evolutionary process works at the level of the group, as the value of fitness seems to be a property of those people who form the groups.

Second, contrary to the standard formulation, altruists can survive the pressure of within-unit selection by associating disproportionately with other altruists (Wade, 1978: 101). Axelrod (1984) demonstrated that cooperative behavior could survive in the face of the predatory behavior of self-interested actors as long as the altruists interacted with other altruists for a sufficiently high percentage of the time, making cooperation a long-term viable strategy. But note that the pressure for change is at the level of the individual actor. The only group features relevant to this analysis are the initial proportion and spatial distribution of altruists in the population. Without a stronger case for the likelihood that between-group selection will dominate within-unit selection, the argument that the locus of pressure for evolutionary change can be at the group level has a weak foundation.

This argument is further weakened by the method of inheritance. Maynard-Smith (1987: 121–2) distinguishes a "unit of selection" from a "unit of evolution." An opponent of group-selection arguments, he uses this distinction to insist that even if the conditions for group selection can be met, groups cannot be the unit of evolution because they lack the capacity for inheritance. Sober (1987: 136) argues, on the other hand, that although natural selection at the group level requires heritability, this inheritance need not take place at the group level: The benefits of group membership can pass through the individual members of the group to their offspring. But unless the offspring of a group from one generation constitute a distinct group in the next generation, the integrity of the group as a unit of selection will be undermined. As I suggested earlier, evolutionary theories of institutional change that rest on social learning as the method of inheritance focus on the individual as the unit of inheritance. It is hard to imagine what inheritance at the group level would be in a theory of social institutions.

EVOLUTIONARY THEORIES OF INSTITUTIONAL CHANGE

This framework for understanding the structure of evolutionary explanations is a useful way of classifying contemporary theories of institutional change. There are three basic approaches. First are contemporary formulations of the classical evolutionary account in which the evolution of social institutions is explained as the product of some form of natural selection. Second are theories of social convention in which institutional emergence is explained as the unintended consequence of decisions made by individual actors. Third are theories that synthesize aspects of the first two approaches, the most significant of which are market-based accounts combining the mechanisms of individual choice through exchange and selection through competition. In the following analysis I shall concentrate mainly on the latter two theories, spending only enough time on classical natural selection to show why it fails to explain adequately the emergence of informal institutions.

Classical evolutionary accounts

Classical evolutionary explanations for the development of society are pervasive. Whether in sociology (Coleman, 1990; Faia, 1986), economics (Hirshleifer, 1977), anthropology (Boyd and Richerson, 1985), law (Posner, 1980) or social philosophy (Hayek, 1967), the logic remains the same: Social institutions evolve to meet a society's functional needs. We have institutions because we need them; they persist because they continue to satisfy our needs. The various accounts differ in their level of generality, but the primary focus on selection based on societal fitness is constant. There are, however, two weaknesses in this approach: (1) the conceptual confusion in the elaboration of the mechanism of selection and (2) the lack of sufficiently detailed empirical evidence to support the theory.

Hayek offers the most influential theory of this kind, a general account of the spontaneous emergence of social order:

a state of affairs in which a multiplicity of elements of various kinds are so related to each other that we may learn from our acquaintance with some spatial or temporal part of the whole to form correct expectations concerning the rest, or at least expectations which have a good chance of proving correct. (1973: 36)[4]

---

4 There are several interesting questions related to Hayek's theory of spontaneous order that I cannot address here. Gray, 1984, offers a detailed analysis of the relationship of the theory to questions of liberal social and political philosophy. Kukathas, 1989, presents a sympathetic account of the importance of Hayek's epistemological ideas for an understanding of the practical implications of the theory of spontaneous order.

To explain the origin and development of this order, he invokes "the twin ideas of evolution and of the spontaneous formation of an order" (1978: 250). Note that the evolutionary process works at two levels in this analysis. A clarification of the effects of these two levels will show how a classical evolutionary account differs from other contemporary theories that acknowledge Hayek's theory as their precursor. As a related point, it is instructive to consider Hayek's ideas about spontaneous order because they reflect the conceptual tension of individual-versus-group selection.

To lay the groundwork for his analysis, Hayek separates rules of conduct and an overall social order: "the important distinction between the systems of rules of conduct which govern the behavior of the individual members of a group . . . on the one hand and, on the other hand, the order or pattern of actions which results from this for the group as a whole" (1967: 66). Here the social order has properties that cannot be reduced to the level of individual actors:

The overall order of actions in a group is in two respects more than the totality of regularities observable in the actions of the individuals and cannot be wholly reduced to them. It is so not only in the trivial sense in which a whole is more than the mere *sum* of its parts but presupposes also that these elements are related to each other in a particular manner. It is more also because the existence of those relations which are essential for the existence of the whole cannot be accounted for wholly by the interaction of the parts but only by their interaction with an outside world both of the individual parts and the whole. (1967: 70–1, emphasis in original)

Thus, this distinction, reminiscent of Durkheim's, between effects at the individual and group levels, entails differences in the required explanation.

At one level, the "spontaneous formation" of the rules of a given society's conduct is what Hayek labeled "the results of human action, but not of human design" (1967: 96). This is the Humean process in which social rules emerge as the unintended product of repeated social interactions. The unit of selection is the level of the individual; the criterion is the maximization of utility. Individuals learn about superior rules and then proceed to imitate them (1967: 78). This is the underlying idea of the contemporary theory of social conventions, whose validity I will discuss in the next section. At a more fundamental level, the evolutionary process of natural selection produces the overall social order for a society: "The natural *selection* of rules will operate on the basis of the greater or lesser efficiency of the resulting *order of the group*" (1967: 67, emphasis in original). Here the unit of selection is the group; the criterion is the "preservation of the group" (1967: 68). The elaboration of the mechanism that guarantees selection is unclear in Hayek's earlier accounts.

Although Hayek offers examples from economic theories of the market and from linguistic theory, this natural-selection account should be distinguished from other market-competition theories in that the selection is not one of the particular rules (e.g., property rights or language rules) but, rather, one of complete sets of rules (1967: 68). As a general theoretical claim, Hayek offers both a reference to theories of struggle among competing groups (1967: 67, n. 3) and a general statement of the logic of functionalist explanations (1967: 76–8). In later essays, Hayek places greater emphasis on classical models of Darwinian-like selection through competition for scarce resources and the resulting effects on the capacity for human reproduction (1988: 11–29).[5] Thus, the social orders are selected by a process of competition for productivity benefits for the group as a whole. The transmission of the selected rules is both genetic and cultural (1967: 67).

For this type of general evolutionary account to succeed, each of the following components must be satisfied: (1) the group as the unit of selection, (2) natural selection through the struggle for survival, and (3) a comparative metric of the fitness value of the overall social order. The conceptual problems of the group as the unit of selection have already been addressed. The requirement of a selection mechanism based on the struggle for survival is difficult to meet. We must show not only that a number of distinct groups in close proximity with one another are competing for scarce resources but also that there is discernible variation in the different social orders. Finally, we must be able to offer a measure of group fitness that can be related to the overall framework of a social order, a measure that allows us to identify the relative fitness qualities of the different social orders in the analysis.

It should be clear that the empirical requirements for satisfying such a general theory are unattainable. Hayek himself admits that we are unable to trace historically such an evolutionary process (1967: 74–8). Even advocates of somewhat less ambitious accounts of cultural evolution through natural selection such as Faia (1986: 87) and Boyd and Richerson (1985: 175) acknowledge that the empirical evidence supporting these theories is weak and inconclusive at best. What these theories

5 Note that Hayek explicitly rejects the Darwinian characterization. His substantive basis for the distinction is grounded in the issue of inheritance: Hayek relies on imitation, whereas social Darwinism invokes genetic inheritance. But the competition mechanism and the criterion of human reproduction are the same. (See Gray, 1984, for a similar interpretation of these later essays.) There are, however, two additional reasons that Hayek may want to insist on the distinction. The first is an exegetical one: He argues that Darwin in fact drew his basic theory from classical economics. The second is a practical one: Hayek is well aware of the intense opposition to social Darwinism.

leave us with is a choice: Either we can rest our arguments supporting general evolutionary theories of natural selection on functional explanations that lack a detailed mechanism of functional selection, or we can abandon general theories of group selection and look instead to more specific mechanisms of spontaneous emergence at the level of the individual. The first choice turns explanation into mere storytelling and protestations of faith, whereas theories of spontaneous emergence grounded in mechanisms of individual action attempt to achieve the second alternative.

The theory of social conventions

The logic of social conventions has been the source of numerous explanations of the development and existence of social institutions. It is the philosophical justification for the recent explosion of work in evolutionary game theory seeking to explain the general evolution of society.[6] It has long been the foundation for efforts to explain the emergence of specific social institutions – from language (Lewis, 1969) to norms (Ullman-Margalit, 1978) to property rights and morality (Sugden, 1986). Setting aside for a moment the more technical definitions of convention used in these theories, we can get a general sense of their implications by referring to the common definitions of the word *convention:* "general agreement or consent, deliberate or implicit, as constituting the origin and foundation of any custom, institution, opinion, etc. or as embodied in any accepted usage, standard of behavior, method of artistic treatment, or the like" or "a rule or practice based upon general consent, or accepted and upheld by society at large; an arbitrary rule or practice recognized in any particular art or practice" (OED, 1971). Thus, these self-enforcing rules are defined in terms of their customary character, which is based on the general acquiescence of a society's members. Note that even in its common usage the concept of convention refers not only to the existence of the rule or practice but also to the process of development and creation.

According to the theory of social conventions, a variety of existing feasible alternatives can serve as the informal rule. The selection mechanism is linked to repeated social interactions, and conventions are the unintended consequences of these interactions. Unintended consequences may be either positive or negative.[7] Evolutionary theories of institutional

---

6 For an introduction to the wide range of work in evolutionary game theory related to these issues, see the articles in the special 1991 issue of *Games and Economic Behavior.*
7 Boudon, 1982, provides a detailed account of the potential unintended effects of strategic interaction. Elster, 1978, takes up this question regarding the concept of social contradictions. And Van Parijs, 1982, offers an insightful critique of the strengths and weaknesses of these two accounts.

change are grounded in the positive consequences produced by social institutions. By basing explanations of institutional change on these unintended positive consequences, such theories must answer two questions. First, what is the mechanism that produces the unintended positive effects? Second, given the link to strategic action, what role do the strategic actors' goals play in the evolutionary process?

Let me highlight the general framework of the theory and then analyze the argument in detail. The key feature of a social convention is that adherence to its rules is beneficial for the actors in a particular interaction.[8] Each of the actors prefers to coordinate (either implicitly or by explicit agreement) on one of the beneficial conventions, as opposed to arriving at an outcome that involves a failure to coordinate. The rules of the convention provide the information about the future actions of others necessary to achieve that coordination. In formal terms, the convention constitutes an equilibrium outcome for the actors in the game: Compliance with the convention is their best reply to the strategic choices of the other actors. Hence, if they can coordinate on a particular rule, the rule will be self-enforcing. That is, as long as the individual actor can do better for himself or herself by acting in accordance with the institution than he or she can do by abandoning the institution, that actor will continue to respect its constraints, regardless of the absence of an external-enforcement mechanism.

The explanations of institutional development rest on different, but related, accounts of how the convention is recognized and coordination is achieved. The problem is one of expectation formation, and the main solution to it rests on Schelling's (1960) conception of salience. Because each of the actors prefers to coordinate at one of the cooperative outcomes, as opposed to the noncoordination alternatives, they readily use whatever salient information they have at their disposal as a way of achieving that coordination. Coordination on one of the beneficial outcomes is achieved as the actors come to recognize through repeated interactions similar salient characteristics of that outcome and formulate their expectations accordingly. The answer to the question of institutional development, therefore, emphasizes the following features: the jointly beneficial nature of certain outcomes, the problem of rationally

---

8 Throughout this discussion of the different theories of social conventions, I will continue to define and refer to a social institution as a set of rules. From this perspective, if a convention is an institution, a convention is also a set of rules. This is consistent with Sugden's definition of a convention. Lewis, on the other hand, defines a convention as a regularity in behavior. Given his exclusive reliance on information and expectation formation as the compliance mechanism for conventions, there is no problem with this definition. When the existence of informal sanctions (a characteristic of many self-enforcing institutions) is pertinent to the analysis, I will emphasize them and discuss their relevance to the theory.

coordinating on one of them, and the possibility that a particular solution to the coordination problem may evolve over time. We can best assess the implications of this theory by looking at those contemporary exponents who offer the most detailed formulations of the theory: Lewis, Sugden, and Schotter.

Consider first the case of conventions as solutions to pure-coordination problems. Lewis (1969) provides the original and most complete development of this argument. A pure-coordination situation is an interaction in which "a coincidence of interests predominates" (p. 14) among the actors. The task is coordinating on that universally preferred outcome. This outcome is defined as a coordination equilibrium "in which no one would have been better off had *any* agent alone acted otherwise, either himself or someone else" (p. 14, emphasis in original). The extent to which this outcome constitutes a real coincidence of interests among the actors is accentuated by the requirement that not only can I not do better by changing my own action but neither can I do better if any one else changes his or her action. If there were only one such coordination equilibrium, it would be easy for the parties to coordinate on it. The coordination problem is manifested in situations in which there are more than one such equilibrium available in the same situation. It is this latter case that is of interest to Lewis. Defining a proper equilibrium as an equilibrium in which "each agent likes it *better than* any other combination he could have reached, given the other choices" (p. 22, emphasis in original), he describes the type of coordination problem with which he is concerned as "situations of interdependent decision by two or more agents in which there are two or more proper coordination equilibria" (p. 24). This is the standard multiple-equilibria problem (see Table 3.3): There are no dominant strategies, and there is nothing in the incentive structure of the situation that would guide the actors in choosing among the equally acceptable alternatives.

It should be apparent that either of the two proper coordination equilibria would constitute a self-enforcing outcome if the actors could achieve the necessary coordination. Once the equilibrium is achieved, no individual actor can do better for himself or herself by choosing a unilateral strategy of abandoning that outcome. To the extent that an institution can provide the information necessary to achieve coordination, it is self-enforcing, and the question of institutional stability is resolved. More generally, for an institution to be self-enforcing, the conditions must be such that it is an equilibrium outcome for all of the actors in the situation. As long as the actors cannot do better by unilaterally abandoning the institution, that institution does not need an external agent to guarantee that individual actors will respect and maintain it. Note that the efficacy of the institutional rule depends on the quality of the information provided to the actors. The theory assumes that all of the members of the community have complete information about the rules.

The more interesting aspect of Lewis's theory is his explanation of how the convention comes to command the actors' attention. If the parties can enter into an explicit agreement, the problem will be resolved merely by the parties' agreeing to coordinate on a particular equilibrium. But the more interesting cases involve situations in which the actors are unable to enter into an explicit agreement. In such cases the actors' ability to coordinate tacitly on one of the proper equilibria depends on their ability to focus on something in their environment that will facilitate their coordination. If all the actors can focus on something that distinguishes one of the two equilibria, then over time they will be able to establish a regularity in behavior that, when confronted with similar interactions in the future, can serve as a guide to coordinated action. This is the question of expectation formation, whose key elements are an ability to develop a regularity in behavior in the direction of one of the mutually preferred outcomes, a set of mutual expectations that others will pick up on this regularity and follow it in the future, and the establishment of this regularity as common knowledge in the community. But all of this depends on the actors' initial ability to focus on a salient difference between the two coordination equilibria.

In his discussion of the importance of salience in the development of conventions, Lewis relies on Schelling's discussion (1960) of tacit coordination. Schelling offers several significant insights into the problem of coordination when the actors cannot explicitly agree on an outcome. In referring to solutions to tacit coordination problems, he stated that "[a] prime characteristic of most of these 'solutions' to the problems, that is, of the clues or coordinators or focal points, is some kind of prominence or conspicuousness" (p. 57). The key in such situations is to discover something in the environment that will catch the attention of enough actors so that they can establish a common action, a standard of behavior that will eventually be emulated by the other members of the community. Schelling asserts that these factors are often beyond the control of the actors in the situation:

If there are important conclusions to be drawn (from the analysis of tacit bargaining), they are probably these: (1) tacit agreements or agreements arrived at through partial or haphazard negotiation require terms that are qualitatively distinguishable from the alternatives and cannot simply be a matter of degree; (2) when agreement must be reached with incomplete communication, the participants must be ready to allow the situation itself to exercise substantial constraint over the outcomes. (p. 75)[9]

9 See Johnson, 1991, for an extended discussion of how cultural "focal points" can influence strategic decision making.

These are not factors that can be discerned from the incentive structure of the game but are, instead, factors that are specific to the particular environment in which the interaction takes place (p. 97). Without some kind of prominent signal directing the actors toward one of the desired outcomes, tacit coordination may be impossible.

Relying on the possibility of prominent signals in the environment, Lewis argues that regularities of behavior develop in accordance with these signals and that, given their expectations about their fellow actors, this leads rational actors to conform to these regularities. Because all of the actors prefer to coordinate on one of the proper equilibria, the existence of the prominent signals leads them to a common outcome. Therefore, the establishment of the self-enforcing solution to the coordination problem depends on the evolution of a regularity of coordinated behavior, with the aid of some prominent environmental differences among the alternative proper equilibria.

The key to the validity of Lewis's account is the assumption of a "coincidence of interest" among the actors. As long as there is close to a true coincidence of interests among the actors, which does exist in the pure-coordination case, Lewis's description of an arbitrary coordination over time with the aid of the prominent characteristics of one of the preferred outcomes is reasonable. But if we drop the "coincidence of interest" requirement and allow for the possibility that the actors differ in their preferences among the coordination equilibria – a real possibility if the alternative social conventions offer differential payoffs to the actors – then Lewis's theory seems open to serious question. Before dismissing the conventional explanation of self-enforcing institutions in such cases, however, we need to consider Sugden's (1986) proposed solution, which explicitly addresses the problem of the absence of coinciding interests.[10]

Sugden proposes a definition of a convention that is quite similar to Lewis's conception but that differs on the crucial issue of coincidence of interests: "For Lewis it is a part of the definition of a convention that each individual wants every other individual to follow it; my definition does not require this (1986: 33). Sugden means to distinguish his conception in two ways: (1) that the actors can rank the stable equilibria differently and (2) that actors need not have an interest in others following the convention. These differences are intended to allow the concept to cover cases in which the interests do not coincide.

---

10 Not only does Sugden propose the conventional explanation for pure-coordination problems ("conventions of coordination"), but he also extends the explanation to mixed-motive situations in which there is a conflict of interest over which equilibrium should be chosen ("conventions of property") and to situations that are structured as Prisoner's Dilemma problems ("conventions of reciprocity"). Because the main focus of my analysis is on the distributional effects of self-enforcing institutions, I will concentrate on his arguments supporting "conventions of property."

In developing his argument supporting conventions of property, Sugden uses several games of property distribution. To illustrate the main features of his argument, I will concentrate on the simplest of these games, the Division game, as it allows for the full range of cooperative and conflictual behavior. Two individuals are in conflict over a piece of divisible property. If they can coordinate on how to divide the property, there will be a mutually beneficial outcome. If the coordination fails, a fight will ensue that will be detrimental to both actors. The strategies consist of claims on a share of the property, claims that may range anywhere from nothing to the whole property. This strategy "may be either pure (i.e., a single claim) or mixed (i.e., two or more different claims, each with an associated probability)." A strategy consists of all claims that are assigned a nonzero probability, and "two claims are complementary if they sum to exactly one" (1986: 67). If the two claims are complementary, then the actors will peacefully receive their claimed share. But if the claims are not complementary, then a fight will ensue, and the actors will receive a negative payoff.

Two points about the logic of his analysis will facilitate our discussion. First, Sugden assumes that all of the actors have approximately equal power. This allows him to assume that both actors will be equally damaged by a failure to achieve a stable equilibrium: "If it comes to a fight, they are evenly matched" (1986: 59). Second, the game is played under two different informational conditions: symmetrical and asymmetrical. Under the condition of symmetry, the game looks exactly the same to both of the players and is described to them as a game between "you" and "your opponent." Under the condition of asymmetry, the presentation of the game is changed to distinguish the roles of the different players. The game is described as being between two players, A and B, and they are assigned one of the two roles. Although these differences in informational conditions may seem insignificant at first, they are, as I will show, crucial to Sugden's derivation of conventions of property.

Consider first the Division game as played in a symmetrical world. There are theoretically an infinite number of stable equilibria. Each equilibrium contains "a different pair of complementary claims c and $1 - c$ combined in a particular mix; there is an equilibrium for every value of c in the range $0 \leq c \leq 0.5$" (Sugden, 1986: 69). Conventions, as Sugden defines them, are possible in this formulation of the game. At one end of the range is the convention of equal division, achieved by adopting the pure strategy of $c = 0.5$. At the other end of the range is the convention of total conflict, achieved by adopting a mixed strategy of $c = 0$, in which the claims of 0 and 1 are made with equal probability. The problem with symmetric play is that a conventional resolution of games of property division is difficult to achieve. The possibilities for a conventional resolution of the Division game are theoretically numerous, but there is nothing in the game's analytical structure that suggests a particular resolution for the parties. In this symmetrical formulation, the actors do not have the necessary information to coordinate on a pattern of behavior that would stabilize their interaction on a satisfactory equilibrium. If the actors are going to coordinate on such an outcome, they must refer to features in their environment that are outside the structure of payoffs in the interaction.

By analyzing the asymmetrical form of the game Sugden seeks to discover whether the actors can exploit any additional information in their pursuit of a socially beneficial, stable equilibrium. In the asymmetrical play of the game, the actors have the opportunity to discover whether other actors play the game differently and whether the different forms of play open up possibilities for new stable equilibrium strategies. In the Division game, a strategy is now defined as a pair of probabilities $(c, 1 - c)$ representing the probabilities that a player plays one particular strategy when he is player A and another when he is player B: The set of stable equilibrium strategies are now the set of complementary claims of the form "if A, claim c; if B, claim $1 - c$." Any pair of such complementary claims would result in a stable equilibrium outcome.

Rather than seeking what amounts to a hypothetical symmetrical solution to the game, the task is now to select a strategy that is complementary to others with whom we are explicitly involved in conflicts over property division. The access to interactions with others expands the available information used in formulating our future strategies. For example, if as an A player, I begin to discern a pattern of behavior in B players – say to choose a fair division $(c = 0.5)$ – then in future interactions as an A player, I should adjust my strategy accordingly (also choosing $c = 0.5$). On the other hand, if B players consistently demand 75 percent of the property, the optimal strategy for me as an A player will be $c = 0.25$. According to Sugden's theory, over an extended series of plays, the actors come to focus on a particular asymmetry in the choices of A and B players, a specific pair of complementary choices, and given their preference for coordination over chaos, they develop a pattern of behavior that causes them to settle rationally on one of the stable equilibria.

But the question remains as to how the actors discover these asymmetries in behavior. Sugden devotes over a chapter to this question, but in the end his answer rests, as Lewis's does, on an elaboration of Schelling's notions of prominence and salience. Individual actors fix on those asymmetries most salient in their environment. This salience may be something in the relationship between a certain type of actor and the property in question (e.g., the property is already in the possession of one of the parties)[11] or something in the nature of the relationship between the actors. But note that given the assumption of equal power, the salient asymmetry cannot relate to asymmetries in power among the actors. Because all of the actors prefer to be at one of the stable equilibria, as opposed to being at one of the points of irresolvable conflict, some of them eventually focus on a particular asymmetry, and the others in time follow suit, establishing a convention as to how to divide the property:

> Provided that the players recognize *some* asymmetry, repeated playing of the division game can be expected to lead to the evolution of some convention assigning particular shares of the resource to each player. The convention that evolves might . . . assign the whole of the resource to one player; or it might prescribe an equal division; or it might prescribe a particular unequal division. Whatever the convention might be, it may be regarded as a *de facto* rule of property. (Sugden, 1986: 73, emphasis in original)

Respecting the convention becomes the rational thing for all the actors to do, even though it may produce unequal payoffs to the parties.

Interestingly, Sugden suggests that the actors generally establish conventions of property that produce unequal distributional effects. They do so because the equilibrium outcome of equal distribution is commonly less prominent than are other unequal alternatives. As Schelling (1960: 58) noted, the key to settling on a particular asymmetry is its uniqueness. Sugden argues that the equal distribution outcome may be open to problems of interpretation (e.g., exactly what constitutes an equal share) and may, therefore, lack the uniqueness necessary for tacit coordination. Although the equal distribution may seem preferable according to some criterion of fairness, it may not be as prominent as some arbitrary alternative producing unequal outcomes.

In the end Sugden offers an evolutionary theory for the development of conventions, more sophisticated than, but quite similar to, Lewis's account:

> A convention begins to develop when individuals begin to realize that it is in their interests to follow it. So we should ask what properties a convention must have in order for individuals to come to this conclusion quickly. It is both convenient and graphic to speak of conventions as being rivals, as in competition with one another; but of course it must be remembered that no element of purpose or intention is involved. There is only a process of natural selection in which some conventions are more successful than others; the most successful convention becomes established. (1986: 89)

---

11 But as Sugden readily notes, this underlying notion – "Possession is nine-tenths of the law" – is itself merely a social convention.

104

This summary interpretation has two significant aspects. The first is the conceptual confusion about the underlying mechanism of the evolutionary process. The force of Sugden's argument is based on the pursuit of utility by social actors. The social convention emerges as the unintended consequence of intentional choices, a consequence facilitated by salient features of the interaction external to the actors themselves. However, Sugden invokes natural selection as the force guaranteeing that the most successful rules will be established. Yet no case for a natural selection–like mechanism is made. This confusion exemplifies the tendency of these theories to slip back and forth among different mechanisms in order to justify the collectively beneficial emphasis of these evolutionary claims. But in order to understand the theory of social convention, the second feature of this summary interpretation is more important. Although Sugden does modify the pure "coincidence of interest" requirement central to Lewis's account, his argument retains the feature that the actors apparently gravitate toward a prominent asymmetry, regardless of its distributional effects.

Let us now consider the plausibility of Sugden's account, and the theory of social conventions more generally, by considering an example: According to the theory, how do conventions of time emerge? To make it even more concrete, we shall return to the evolution of the workweek. Weber (1952) attributes this evolution to the need to coordinate economic activity in the marketplace. All the economic actors prefer to coordinate on a particular market schedule, rather than to create a situation of chaotic interactions. Schotter (1981) treats this example as a pure-coordination problem. Given the historical evidence, it is more reasonable to assume that the actors differ in their preferences regarding the specific timing of the market, owing to distributional effects.[12] Sugden's argument suggests that the fundamental explanation should be the same for both assumptions.

The conventional explanation of the workweek has two crucial features. First, the rule evolves *arbitrarily*. The evolutionary process is unconsciously driven by whatever salient factor attracts the attention of the economic actors. The interests of any particular actor or group of actors do not determine the final institutional arrangement; that is, the distributional differences produced by different timing rules will not be used in the explanation. The information that leads to coordination on a particular time scheme may come from anywhere: environmental characteristics in the community, the nature of the economic activity, some visible

---

12 There are numerous available accounts of the evolution of rules governing the timing and location of economic activity. See Zerubavel, 1985, and Rifkin, 1987, for general discussions. For case studies, see, for example, Meillassaux, 1971, and Hodder and Ukwu, 1969.

characteristic of the actors involved (but not power asymmetries), or the like. The selection of information is arbitrary: Social actors use whatever information resources they can in order to coordinate their activity. Schotter's description reveals the underlying evolutionary process:

> The important point to be made, and the one that makes this approach unique, is that the social institution that is actually created . . . is a stochastic event, and that if history could be repeated, a totally different convention could be established for the identical situation. The point is that the set of institutions existing at any point in time is really an accident of history and that what exists today could have evolved in a very different manner. (1981: 79)

Second, the resultant time rule produces an outcome that is *Pareto superior* to uncoordinated exchange. Any evolutionary theory must detail the mechanism that guarantees Pareto superiority. These theories satisfy this part of their explanation by arguing that although the actors do not intentionally produce the time measure, they would not rationally adopt a rule that was not Pareto superior to uncoordinated exchange and, more important, that they would adopt any rule that was.

Many evolutionary theories acknowledge that this process will not necessarily lead to Pareto-*optimal* institutional arrangements. They offer various reasons for this failure. What is crucial to note here is that such theories do predict that changes in existing time rules will involve Pareto *improvements* over the status quo. This restriction is justified by the reasoning that rational actors do not respond to a movement toward a Pareto-inferior alternative, that they seek only Pareto-superior alternatives. To return to the simplified example shown in Table 3.6, any of the five equilibrium strategies may constitute an initial rule establishing the day for economic activity in the marketplace. Which one evolves depends on factors external to the structure of the known incentives. But we can say something about what the theory of social convention would predict in regard to institutional change: If the initial institutional rule directed the actors to choose day *A*, *B*, or *E*, no change from those institutional arrangements would be predicted, because no Pareto improvements would be possible. If, on the other hand, the initial rule dictated choosing either day *C* or day *D*, then movement toward a Pareto-superior institutional arrangement would be possible.

What does the primacy of distributional effects imply for this explanation? To the extent to which the theories rest on unintentional explanations of institutional development, the conclusion that the pursuit of collective benefits is inconsistent with narrow rationality is beside the point. All that is required of the theory is that it distinguish some mechanism that produces the collectively beneficial effects. The relevance of the distributive conception of social institutions is revealed when considering the elaboration of this mechanism. In this theory of the unintended

106

consequences of repeated social interactions, two factors – arbitrary and salient features in the environment that identify particular outcomes and repeated interactions characterized by the intentional pursuit of Pareto-superior outcomes – combine to ensure the development of collectively beneficial social institutions. Although the ultimate form of the institution is supposed to be arbitrary and unintended, the distributive effects of these institutions challenge the plausibility of the factors constituting this explanation.

The criticism of the Pareto superiority criterion was stated earlier. Given the path-dependence of institutional development, narrow rationality does not guarantee that strategic actors will respond to salient outcomes that are Pareto superior to present practices unless there is a direct benefit for them. This resistance can produce a countervailing force on the evolutionary development of more socially efficient rules of time measurement. Furthermore, this criterion fails to explain redistributive shifts in the development of self-enforcing institutions. Changes in the timing of economic activity that produce redistributive change cannot be explained by the Pareto-improvement criterion.

But even if we set aside for a moment this criticism of the Pareto-superiority criterion, we must question the persuasiveness of the first factor – the power of the arbitrary and salient features in the environment to influence strategic actors. To put the question simply: Would the desire for some institutional arrangement, however arbitrary, override the concern for distributional advantage in the establishment of institutions? Because the evolutionary theories focus on the individual interaction repeated throughout the community, we should look to that interaction for our answer. In the pure-coordination case, the arbitrariness of the evolutionary approach is acceptable, as there are no distributional effects with which to be concerned.

In mixed-motive cases, however, the distributional effects are relevant. Sugden argues against their relevance on the grounds that most social institutions evolving in these types of cases are "cross-cutting." Here, he separates the adverse effects of a single interaction from the cumulative effects of repeated interactions. If the relevant actors are not, in the long run, adversely affected by these rules of time measure, then they will have no reason to favor one asymmetry over another. Sugden emphasizes that even though actors may prefer one stable equilibrium to another in a particular game, they will have no similar preference in repeated plays of the game so long as the asymmetry on which the convention is based is cross-cutting. An asymmetry is cross-cutting if "each individual will sometimes find himself on one side of the asymmetry and sometimes on the other" (1986: 157–9). With such a convention, the disproportionate distributional effects even out over repeated interactions. Thus,

107

the persuasiveness of the social convention theory depends in part on the empirical question of whether social institutions are truly cross-cutting.

The problem with this argument is the dearth of cross-cutting social institutions. Instead, these institutions systematically favor particular groups in a given society. In the example of time measurements, this may be less evident now than it was when the rules were emerging. But for most informal social institutions, the ongoing distributional effects are more apparent. Consider the effects of rules governing the organization of the family, the organization of different groups in a society (race, class, age), or the structure of property relations. In these cases, the distributional effects are felt by the actors involved.[13]

Referring to the time-measurement example in Table 3.6, both players have important reasons for influencing the creation of the rule governing the timing of economic activity. In a single interaction not governed by an existing rule, the narrowly rational thing to do would be to try to force the issue. How this might be done and how it might lead to the development of social institutions are part of the strategic approach that I consider in Chapter 5. If the microfoundations for the emergence of social institutions are to rest on the strategic interactions repeated in everyday social life, then the motivations shaped by distributional effects must be taken into account, and the standard theory of social convention fails to do this.

Exchange and selection by competition

The conception of social institutions as contracts forms the basis for several theories of institutional development and change. From the contractarian analysis of political institutions and constitutions (Brennan and Buchanan, 1985; Heckathorn and Maser, 1987) through the transaction-costs analysis of economic organizations (Williamson, 1975, 1985) to the general transaction-costs theory of institutional change (Eggertsson, 1990; North, 1990), the contract serves as the model for explaining social institutions. There is some ambiguity in using these theories to explain spontaneous emergence and evolutionary change. On the one hand, they stress intentional efforts to design institutional rules, which introduces issues relevant to our understanding of formal social rules, especially the creation of political institutions. On the other hand, these theories incorporate, often implicitly, an evolutionary mechanism that selects out those contractual forms that do the best job of producing

13 An additional problem with the cross-cutting argument is that the cross-cutting will have no impact if social actors discount the future heavily. I thank Jon Elster for reminding me of this point.

some collective benefit. Thus, these theories offer a framework for explaining both spontaneous emergence and intentional design.

In this chapter I focus exclusively on explanations of evolutionary development and change, a process that synthesizes aspects of intentional decision making with a decentralized selection mechanism based on marketlike competition among contractual forms. The logic of this approach is described by Eggertsson:

> Central to Neoinstitutional Economics is the concept of *competition among contractual arrangements*. (1990: 52–3)

> Changes in contractual forms may often be a long process, particularly when there is a lack of experience with arrangements that would be best suited to a new situation. Once a successful experiment has been made, the forces of competition establish new *equilibrium contracts*. It is also reasonable to expect that a community that has a very long experience with stable technology and a stable range of relative prices has settled on contractual forms that minimize costs for each branch of production, given the state of knowledge about contractual arrangements and the basic structure of property rights. (p. 55, emphasis in original)

Although the *neoinstitutional economics* tradition, as Eggertsson labels it, is grounded in the assumption of rational self-interest, these explanations nonetheless invoke the collectively beneficial nature of social rules, in terms of either the minimization of costs or the maximization of wealth or other benefits.

It is important to remember that this does not mean that the theories do not account for certain failures to achieve a Pareto-optimal set of institutions but, rather, that they primarily emphasize the achievement of collective benefits in explaining institutional development and change. In order to justify this collective emphasis, these theories must locate mechanisms that either alleviate distributional conflict in the intentional creation of contracts or select rules on the basis of collective benefits. In analyzing these theories for such mechanisms, it is helpful to discuss separately the two main components of such an explanation: the individual exchange and the competition among alternatives. These components represent the forces of variation and selection in the evolutionary framework.

Individual exchange. Consider first the contracts produced by individual exchanges. The logic of the exchange relationship is one of mutual benefit: "Individuals must be convinced to join together to explore and ultimately to agree on the establishment of collective entities or arrangements that prove mutually beneficial" (Buchanan, 1985: 25). The motivation for drawing up a contract is quite simple: When any two social actors perceive that they can benefit from a mutual exchange, they

109

must agree on the terms of that exchange. Among these terms are rules governing the parties' actions during the exchange relationship. This is complicated by the fact that the underlying structure of the exchange relationship is that of the Prisoner's Dilemma (see Table 3.7).[14]

For a self-interested actor, the preferred outcome is to receive the benefits from the other party without having to give up anything in return. If the exchange does not require simultaneous performance, one actor will always be in the position of having to perform his half of the transaction without knowing with certainty that the other person will do likewise. Because this failure to complete one's half of the transaction – defection in the Prisoner's Dilemma framework – is the dominant strategy for both actors, the suboptimal outcome (2,2) is produced, a failure to achieve the mutually beneficial exchange. The purpose of a contract is to establish rules that either guarantee the compliance of both parties or establish penalties or sanctions for noncompliance. With the contract in place, the individual actors can be more confident that their compliance will not meet with a defection response. Thus, the contract facilitates the mutually beneficial outcome (3,3).

In the general theory, these contracts constitute the social institutions produced by social actors to facilitate the achievement of socially beneficial outcomes. The key point here is that the resulting institutions are the product of a *voluntary* agreement. Social actors create these institutional rules because they can gain benefits that they would not enjoy without them. The voluntary nature of these contracts, however, introduces a potential weakness in this form of explanation. The problem relates to the question of enforcing the promises embodied in the rules of the contract. In a one-shot Prisoner's Dilemma situation, the promises contained in the contract are not self-enforcing. That is, despite what one promises to do before one actually acts, it is still a dominant strategy to renege on that promise.

Without some external-enforcement mechanism to sanction noncompliance, the contractual rules will fail to induce the mutually beneficial outcome for which it is intended. Therefore, if the exchange relationships are conceived as one-shot interactions, it is hard to see how this contractual theory can explain the emergence of self-enforcing institutions. On the other hand, if the theory is based on the assumption that exchange relationships are characterized by ongoing and repeated interactions, the theory of collective action will demonstrate that there are many circumstances in which the contracts can be self-enforcing (Kreps, 1990: 505–15).

14 Hardin (1988) offers a more detailed critique of this approach than the one I offer here. I am merely emphasizing those aspects of the paradigm based on the notions of mutual gains from exchange and of agreement.

This raises a question about the intentions of those who employ a transaction-costs theory of institutional change. Are they trying to explain the initial emergence of property rights in a society, or are they merely trying to explain how social actors manipulate, through a voluntary agreement, existing property rights backed by the state's external-enforcement power? It seems clear that those who synthesize individual exchange with the selection mechanism of marketlike competition intend the former type of explanation. Therefore, in analyzing these theories, we can set aside the problem of noncompliance until a later discussion and assume that we are explaining repeated interactions that might produce self-enforcing contracts. This turns out to be a reasonable assumption when considering the spontaneous emergence of social institutions.

The contracts produced by voluntary agreement can take many forms. A second key element of this exchange approach can be found in the answer to the question of what kinds of contracts social actors will try to produce. The dominant answer builds on Coase's (1960) insights into the effects of transaction costs. That social actors would be concerned about transaction costs is understandable, because these are the costs incurred in establishing and enforcing institutional rules. The greater are the transaction costs of an exchange, the lower will be the level of aggregate benefits enjoyed by the social actors. Consider, for example, North's (1990) explanation of developing property rights in a society. Say that two actors share an interest in a common piece of property. Their task is to determine the best way to structure their use of that property. There are many possible choices, from some form of shared or common property rights to various divisions into private property shares. North (1990: 37–43) argues that these actors contract for rights that minimize the transaction costs of the ongoing exchange. They minimize the transaction costs in order to maximize the benefits they gain from the property. The contracting problem, therefore, is to structure the incentives in such a way that the person who has the greatest incentive to maximize the benefits from a piece of the property has the rights to that parcel.[15]

Once the actors have established the property rights according to the minimization standard, they will maintain them as long as the relevant external circumstances remain stable. But there is always the possibility that some factors external to the exchange relationship will change in such a way as to affect the enjoyment of the property's benefits. North (1990: 109) lists several changes in relative prices that can affect

---

15 Barzel (1989) emphasizes the complexity of the problem of structuring incentives in this way. He argues that one source of inefficiency in property rights schemes is the fact that it is impossible to account for and assign to the appropriate party every source of benefit from an asset.

111

benefits: in the ratio of factor prices, in the costs of information, and in technology. If any of these changes are substantial, they will affect the relative values of the different ways of institutionalizing property rights. If the result of these changes is that a new property rights scheme can produce greater aggregate benefits than the existing system does, the contracting parties will consider the following cost–benefit calculation: Do these additional benefits exceed the costs of changing the present contract? If the answer is yes, the actors will enter into a new contract institutionalizing new rights (North, 1990: 67). Here we see the third important element of the transaction-costs theory: Institutional change will occur only if the resulting outcome is Pareto superior to the previous institutional arrangement.

Note that at this point we are discussing only the motivations of the actors in the individual exchange. The fact that low-cost rules may be selected by marketlike competition has not yet entered the analysis. North's reliance on transaction-costs minimization reflects the approach of the new institutional economics. In analyzing the contractual arrangements of social organization, the theory proceeds from the "*working rule* that low-cost organizations tend to supersede high-cost ones" (Eggertsson, 1990: 213–14, emphasis in original). When exceptions to this rule are observed, three factors should be considered.

First, there may be hidden benefits that are not readily apparent. This reduces to a claim that the apparent exception to the working rule is in fact an instance of the more general rule of maximizing benefits. Here a higher-cost institutional rule in fact produces a more beneficial exchange than does a less costly one. Second, the efforts of social actors to create low-cost institutional forms may be constrained by the interests of the state. This latter issue is closely related to issues of intentional design and reform, but it is proposed as an explanation of why the voluntary arrangements being analyzed here can be restricted by some type of formal external constraint. The point relevant to this analysis is the implicit claim that if it were not for external constraints, rational social actors would voluntarily create the least costly forms of organization. This is consistent with the third exception to the minimization-of-costs rule: uncertainty. According to this account, actors may not create the least costly rules because they lack either the capacity or the knowledge to establish them.

This minimization-cost standard is a problematic one. As the arguments in Chapter 2 demonstrate, the claim that the minimization of aggregate transaction costs is the motivation for institutional development and change is inconsistent with individual rationality. The assumption of narrow rationality on which the transaction-costs approach is based implies that strategic actors will prefer more costly rules if these rules give them greater individual benefits than those from less costly ones. Remember that in this case the explanation is not inability or incapacity but, rather, self-interest. The transaction-costs approach does not predict costly rules produced by fully informed, self-interested behavior. Here we return to some of the same explanatory problems we encountered with the theory of social conventions. The standard transaction-costs approach fails to explain either the distributional features of informal social conventions or the redistributive changes in these rules.

I should clarify this criticism in the context of current attempts by Libecap and North, among others, to incorporate distributional considerations. The standard approach has traditionally avoided the question of power asymmetries and instead has focused on the problem of transaction-costs minimization among symmetrically endowed actors (North, 1981). North (1990) acknowledges the importance of asymmetries for explaining distributional differences; Libecap (1989) explicitly addresses the complications introduced by distributional concerns in the effort to contract for socially efficient property rights. These attempts are in the spirit of the sorts of arguments I am making. But what these authors seem to have in mind are efforts at intentionally creating formal property rights. The importance of power asymmetries for explaining the emergence of informal rules governing property rights and economic organization has not been pursued; and this is the basis of my criticism.[16] This failure can be explained by the reliance on competition as the selection mechanism for such decentralized emergence, competition thought to undercut the importance of power in individual exchange.

In regard to institutional change, the dubious relationship between a criterion of Pareto-superior change and strategic rationality has already been well exposed. Not only does the transaction-costs approach predict a Pareto-improving institutional change that might not be accepted by strategic actors (the path-dependent argument), but it also fails to explain either redistributive or Pareto-inferior change. This follows by implication from the combination of a reliance on voluntary agreement and a limitation to Pareto-superior change. If a change entails a loss to some

---

16 Eggertsson (1990: 256–62) reflects the confusion in the transaction-costs literature over the effect of distributional issues. In a discussion of the reasons that property rights must be established (as a mechanism for the governance and exclusion of property), he emphasizes the problem of free riding but abstracts out problems of distribution. What is striking about this formulation is that although distribution is not seen to be a major concern, free riding – which is a problem for the very reason that actors are interested in distributional advantage – is considered a serious problem! The only way that I can make sense of this formulation is to make the following distinction: Free riding is a problem in the creation of socially efficient institutions, whereas distribution is merely a problem in the division of such institutions' benefits. The arguments in this book assert that distributional concerns are a much greater problem than this distinction suggests.

individuals as a cost of establishing new property rights that produce greater aggregate benefits, narrowly rational actors will not voluntarily agree to the change.

The transaction-costs theory of exchange and competition has a way to resolve this weakness: a reconciliation of transaction-costs minimization (and the consequent maximization of aggregate benefits) with the pursuit of individual gain by means of compensation. We can see how the idea of compensation can be used in this way by examining Posner's (1980) interpretation of property rights and economic organization in primitive societies. He argues for an analogy between primitive economic institutions and insurance. That is, he explains the rules structuring economic activity in these primitive societies as a means of distributing risk in the community. The property rights scheme provides rules governing the enjoyment of community resources. Distributional advantages are granted to certain members of the community, and they are explained as the product of an exchange with the less advantaged, an exchange for protection in the future if the community is struck by hard times. Here Posner reconciles distributional differences with the long-term efficiency of the property rights scheme. This insurance analogy can be seen as a form of compensation: The less advantaged are compensated for the distributional bias in the economic rights scheme by the promise of future insurance protection.

It is easy to reduce this insurance explanation to a mere functionalist assertion without some fairly rigorous empirical evidence. To see this, consider the general logic of compensation. Say that two actors currently share the benefits of a parcel of land under a rights scheme distributing the annual benefits in the following manner: $60,000 to A and $40,000 to B. Now assume that circumstances change so that an alternative set of property rights allows the actors to produce an additional $25,000 per year but that this alternative scheme produces a new annual distribution: $50,000 to A and $75,000 to B. The logic of the new institutional economics predicts that as long as the aforementioned limitations on change are not applicable, the actors will adopt the new contract. But as long as the mechanism of change is one of voluntary agreement, my argument is that the new rules will not be adopted because they diminish A's benefits. If, however, B agreed to compensate A by giving her a side payment of at least $10,000 per year, then according to some accounts of individual rationality, it would be rational for A to agree to the changes.

Here the logic is plausible, and in the case of the intentional design of formal institutions, compensation is a possibility that must be considered. But the utility of this concept for explaining the spontaneous emergence of informal rights is highly questionable. The empirical requirements necessary to satisfy the theory are substantial, and there must be evidence of compensatory payments between the individuals in the institutional change, payments that are temporally related to these changes and are anticipated before the change. In the case of spontaneous emergence, an additional element must be shown: Either the form of compensation must be a common practice in similar exchanges in a society, or the compensation must be an element of the creation of those contractual rules that are subsequently selected out by the competitive process. Posner's insurance explanation exemplifies the weakness of most accounts of compensatory-like mechanisms: The evidence necessary to justify a compensation explanation is lacking.

Competition. But the transaction-costs approach invokes more than the actors' intentions in an individual exchange to explain the emergence of social institutions. Individual exchanges merely produce a variety of possible institutional forms, but the key selection mechanism is competition. Many explanations of institutional development and change situate the decision to establish social institutions in the context of a market or a marketlike environment. The main influence of the market on the choice of institutional form is in the competitive pressure it supposedly exerts on the institutionalization process. There are two related but conceptually distinct ways that competitive pressure can enter into this analysis. First, as a dynamic effect, competition can be a selection mechanism that determines the survival of various institutional forms on grounds of survival and reproductive fitness. This is the logic behind Alchian's (1950) model of evolutionary competition, used in most economic analyses of institutional emergence. The existence of a large number of firms seeking profits from a common pool of consumers produces pressure for survival. Over time those firms that employ less efficient techniques lose profits to those that are more efficient. Losing profits eventually translates into extinction. As the competitive process continues, only those firms that use efficient techniques survive. Second, as a static effect, competition can undermine the actors' bargaining power in a particular interaction:

The main curb on a person's bargaining power, and the main pacifying influence on trade in general, is competition. A person has competition if the party he wants to trade with has alternative opportunities of exchange. The people who offer these alternative opportunities to his opposite party are his competitors. Competition restricts a person's bargaining power by making the other less dependent and therefore less keen on striking a bargain with him. (Scitovsky, 1971: 14)

This latter effect enters into a theory of development and change only to the extent that it establishes the environment in which rational actors seek to produce institutions.

The existence of competition raises questions for theories of institutional emergence and change. The dynamic effect forms the basis of the theory of exchange and competition. The relevant question here is whether the competitive pressure is sufficient to select out less efficient institutional rules. The static effect relates mainly to arguments such as the one in the next chapter, that would invoke the asymmetries of power in a society in order to explain institutional emergence. The relevant question there is whether the existence of competition prevents social actors from using asymmetries in power to develop institutions that produce systematic distributional consequences. This static effect is also related to the theory of exchange and competition in that it justifies ignoring power asymmetries in its own analysis. It is important to remember that competition is not an either/or phenomenon; there are degrees of competition and therefore degrees of competitive effect. The best way to answer these questions is to establish the empirical conditions under which competition affects the emergence of social institutions. Because the issues are so closely related, the analysis is best presented by addressing both of these questions. I will clarify a few of the conclusions in my later discussion of bargaining theory.

What are the prerequisites for the existence of competition? Lists of the necessary conditions for marketlike competition are numerous. According to Scitovsky's analysis (1971) of competition, the following conditions are necessary for the existence of competition in social institutions: (1) a large number of competitors in pursuit of a common pool of resources, (2) a set of institutional alternatives differentiated only by their distributional consequences, (3) full information about the availability of alternatives, and (4) low transaction costs. If an explanation of institutional change is to invoke competition as a relevant factor, these conditions must be empirically satisfied.

Discussions of competition in the market are numerous. What I want to do is limit my analysis to those issues unique to the question of competition in regard to social institutions, as this will allow me to emphasize the difficulty of satisfying these conditions in the institutional case.[17] Central to my argument is the following distinction: *Institutions are not goods.* I am well aware that almost anything is considered a "good" in economic theory. But what I want to capture here is that institutions are not tangible, substantive goods, a fact that has three implications for any competition that might exist.

---

17 This also forces me to ignore certain general requirements of the competitive model that are seldom satisfied. One example is the problem of incomplete information. To the extent that the actors lack information about the different institutional alternatives, the effects of competition are diminished.

116

First, because institutions are rules structuring social interactions, they attach to people in ways that substantive goods do not. What do I mean by *attachment*? We create rules to govern classes of interactions in which we ourselves are involved. As long as we remain part of the interaction, we remain governed by the rule. Unlike a good that one can produce without any intention of consuming it, a rule cannot be alienated in the same way; generally when we produce a rule, we also figuratively consume it. Besides the enhanced concern for the continuing consequences of institutional rules that it produces in social actors, this attachment limits the number of actors in a community who might produce a particular institution. This in turn limits the number of potential competitors. An entrepreneur can, in principle, produce any kind of private good for which there is a demand in a community, but social actors generally produce only those institutions for which they have a personal demand.

Second, institutional rules are often related to interactions that are not interchangeable. Our level of benefits from social interactions may be contingent on a specific group of individuals; the interaction would not be the same if it involved other groups. This can be manifested in interactions as small as a marriage or other personal relationship, to an attachment to groups as large as an ethnic group or nationality. One of the requirements of competition is that the interaction be such that the actors can treat one another interchangeably. That is, an actor's choice of rules must be based on the distributional consequences and not on the identity of the other actors involved. If their identity is crucial to the interaction, those who make an institutional choice will be limited in their range of feasible alternatives.

Third and most important, rules are lumpy and coarse-grained. The set of possible rules from which most social institutions are developed is finite, suggesting that there are only a few ways of acting in most contexts, that is, only a few different rules to structure most social interactions. For example, in the family, there are a limited number of ways for men and women to divide their basic responsibilities; in social organizations, there are a limited number of ways to allocate decision-making responsibilities. From this it follows that the range of benefits produced by such rules is distributed discontinuously. Although the different possibilities can be characterized by their distributional consequences, the range is incomplete in the sense that there is not a rule for every possible distributional combination. The only exceptions to this discontinuity can be found in those institutions like certain property rights schemes that translate benefits into a continuous metric like money. This discontinuity affects both the range of institutional rules that can be established and the opportunities for some form of compensation in cases of redistributive change.[18]

With the requirements for competition and the distinctive character of institutional rules in mind, let us analyze the necessary empirical conditions for competition in the emergence of social institutions. Consider the dynamic effect of competition as a selection mechanism, remembering that it is important to clarify exactly what is selected in this theory. Competition exists among actors in common social interactions. These interactions are structured and facilitated by institutions. It is the institutional rule that is selected in the competitive process, the rule that does the best job of facilitating survival and reproduction. Thus, the relevant units of analysis for institutional selection are the sets of actors in a common interaction and not the isolated individuals. The relevant criterion for selection is the aggregate level of benefits produced in the interaction, not the level of benefits for any particular individual. For example, competition has been used to explain the emergence of rules of family organization and gender relations (Becker, 1973, 1974). This competition among different families depends on the reproductive fitness of the family and not on the benefits accruing to particular members. The question thus becomes under what conditions the most collectively beneficial (or socially efficient) social institution emerges from a process of competitive selection.

The various empirical issues here can be consolidated into two questions. The first is, How intense is the pressure for survival? It depends on the number of competitive groups, their capacity to consume resources, and the speed with which the competitive process takes place. For competition to create pressure for survival, there must be a demand for resources greater than the available supply. This translates into the following important condition:

$$[(\text{the number of competitors}) \times (\text{capacity to consume resources})] > (\text{available resources})$$

In the Alchian formulation, this condition is satisfied by two features of a market for goods: (1) There is, in principle, no limit on the profit consumption capacity of an individual firm, and (2) even if there were such a limit, the entry of new competitors would cause the demand for profits to exceed the availability.

---

18 Note that this problem is resolved in formal models by transforming the gaps in the distribution of alternatives into lotteries consisting of weighted probabilities of the existing alternatives. This establishes a continuous distribution of both strategies (pure and mixed) and benefits (Luce and Raiffa, 1957). Although this formulation resolves the computational problem for mathematical analysis, it fails to capture the actual experience of those who create real social institutions.

For many types of social institutions, neither of these conditions is easily satisfied. On the one hand, most social interactions are not structured so as to capture all of the available resources in a community; rather, they are structured to allow the actors to enjoy certain gains from collective activities. Consider the family again. It is an ongoing social interaction from which its individual members gain benefits that they would not enjoy in isolation. But unlike a profit-maximizing firm, an individual family does not seek to acquire all of the available resources in a community. In this case, the capacity for consuming resources by any particular "competitor" is, in this sense, limited. On the other hand, the number of competitors is limited in terms of the number of new entries. For many economic contexts, new entry remains a possibility, but in most other social situations the number of competitors is fixed by the nature of the social interaction. These limits are the result of both the attachment between actors and rules and the lack of interchangeability in many social interactions.

If, however, we conceptualize competition over several generations, the demand-exceeds-supply condition may be satisfied. That is, if we conceive of families and communities as increasing and expanding over generations, then extended families and communities may compete for available resources. But here the speed and nature of the competitive process are quite different from those of the Alchian logic. In principle a single firm can dominate a market in a single generation, but for most social institutions, this form of domination takes several generations. The intensity of the pressure as experienced by strategic actors is greatly diminished. The selection mechanism shifts from learning and imitation as a means of ensuring survival to some more general evolutionary process. Thus, as the time period for the analysis lengthens, this explanation is transformed from one – like the transaction-costs approach – based on the actors' rationality to one grounded in the classic evolutionary account criticized earlier for its unspecified functionalism and lack of empirical grounding.

The second empirical question is, How continuous is the distribution of institutional possibilities? This is a relevant question because selection occurs only among those rules that strategic actors find it in their self-interest to introduce. Nelson and Winter (1982: 218) emphasized this fact in the context of evolutionary theories of technical change to explain how incomplete information can produce technologies that are not Pareto optimal. They correctly point out that competition can select only the most efficient technology from among the available alternatives. If there are more efficient alternatives that firms unable to produce because of incomplete information about them, the competitive process will not be able to select them. Note that this argument applies equally to the emergence of social institutions. But the existence of discontinuities introduces a different effect on the range of feasible social institutions.

Discontinuity prevents the introduction and selection of more socially efficient alternatives when those alternatives are not the preferred rules of the more powerful members of a society. We can see this by returning to Table 3.6. Let us say that a rule exists at strategy combination 2,2 and that Buyers are the most powerful members of the community (and thus that they propose the rules). It is clear that more socially efficient alternatives – 3,3 and 4,4 – exist. But the feasible set is discontinuous. If we rule out the creation of some new rule based on mixed strategies, we will expect Buyers to maintain the 2,2 rule because it produces their best distributional outcome.[19] The discontinuity in benefits also rules out compensation plans that rearrange the distribution of new benefits so as to make the more socially efficient rule more attractive to Buyers. Therefore, the range of alternatives does not include the more socially efficient rules because it is not in the self-interest of those who can introduce them to do so. Once again, the explanation is not uncertainty or incapacity but, rather, self-interest.

At this point I should respond to a potential criticism of this argument. I can well imagine a transaction-costs proponent responding to this discussion by contending that regardless of the existing social institution, rational actors contract on their own to use a more socially efficient alternative and then compensate the losers with some other form of benefit. One possibility is a side payment of money. Such a response, I think, exemplifies the confusion between private arrangements and social institutions. I do not deny the possibility of such private arrangements, but I reject the idea that such arrangements become new social institutions.

My rejection is based on the difficulty of generalizing the private arrangement to the community as a whole. The discontinuity has been resolved in benefits, not in the set of feasible rules. For something to be a social institution, the rule must be generalized to and acknowledged by the community as a whole. For this private arrangement to become a social institution, the new rule must incorporate the practice of side-payment compensation in a systematic and generalized way. It is hard to conceive of how such complicated rules could emerge from a decentralized process.

---

19 The rejection of mixed strategies is a reasonable one. It is difficult to come up with examples of social institutions that embody true mixed strategies, and even if they were to exist as possibilities, they would be inherently unstable (Selten, 1980; Sugden, 1986). This instability indicates that such rules will eventually be replaced by pure-strategy alternatives.

Ultimately, the dynamic effect of competition as a selection mechanism depends on empirical conditions related to the number of competitors, the structure of the competitive process, and the nature of the rules to be selected. Given the distinctiveness of social institutions, there are many reasons that a marketlike competition mechanism does not select the most socially efficient institutional rules. Most important, we see that this includes cases in which distributional concerns preclude the selection of more socially efficient and available alternatives. Such a conclusion assumes the importance of asymmetries of power in a society, which shifts our attention to a possible static effect of competition on such asymmetries.

The competition affecting power asymmetries is competition among individual actors for the other individuals with whom they will interact. The different rules can be seen as the offers used in this competition. The relevant units of analysis are individual social actors, and the relevant criteria are the individual benefits that actors receive from different institutional forms. Competition reduces the importance of power asymmetries to the extent to which actors have other alternatives that are preferable to accepting the offer of any particular actor. The question here is under what conditions this form of competition diminishes the importance of asymmetries of power in resolving individual social interactions.

The important empirical issues are revealed in the following questions: First, how are the actors distributed for the different roles in a particular interaction? Competition requires that the actors who fill the various roles be approximately equal in distribution. For example, in the case of marriage and the informal rules structuring it, the pertinent question is whether there is an equal number of potential husbands and wives in the society. If there is a scarcity on one side of the relationship, it will weaken the effects of competition and strengthen the power of the actors in the scarce group.

Second, how continuous is the distribution of the alternatives? The principal implication of this condition is the same as that for the dynamic effect of competition, and so we need not restate the argument in detail. Given both the discontinuity of the feasible alternatives and the lack of compensation possibilities, the effects of power asymmetries are enhanced. An individual actor need not offer a rule with a better distributional division than the best offer made by any other actor in his subgroup. The discontinuity restricts the range of offers that are rational to propose. Note that this argument does not depend on oligopolistic-like behavior by the more powerful subgroup. However, if the members of the powerful subgroup are able to coordinate collusive offers in the community, the effects of competition will be weakened even more. For any decentralized process, such as the spontaneous emergence of social institutions, as the size of the group increases, the likelihood that oligopolistic strategies will be maintained decreases (Scitovsky, 1971: 424–31).

Third, how interchangeable are the different actors? If individual actors are not interchangeable, competition for social collaborators will be diminished. The fact that many social interactions are characterized by the lack of interchangeability suggests that the static effect of competition on asymmetries of power will not hold.

Each of these empirical features affects the conditions of competition and, therefore, the importance of asymmetries of power. Given the distinctiveness of institutional rules, it is unlikely that there will be many situations in which the conditions are satisfied sufficiently to neutralize power asymmetries completely. When such asymmetries do exist, we should expect them to play an important role in the emergence of social institutions.

CONCLUSIONS

In this analysis of evolutionary theories of institutional change, I focused on the mechanisms invoked by the different theories to justify a primary emphasis on the collective effects of social institutions. An assessment of the merits of the different theories rests on an analysis of the empirical conditions that must hold in order for the mechanisms to be effective. Rather than restating the theories, I will merely reemphasize the central empirical requirements vis-à-vis the issue of distribution. For the theory of social conventions, I argued that the necessary conditions relate to the institutional benefits: Either there must be no distributional differences among the institutional alternatives, or the distributional consequences must be cross-cutting. For the theory of exchange and competition, I contended that the necessary conditions relate to the mechanisms of compensation and competition. If the requisite conditions are present, the effects of distributional concerns will be offset by these mechanisms. Note that in the latter theory this does not mean that distributional differences will not exist but just that they will be a by-product of the main mechanism of institutional development. In such cases, distribution is not the main factor used in explaining the spontaneous emergence of social institutions.

But when these empirical conditions are not satisfied – and I have tried to show how restrictive these conditions are – distributional consequences and asymmetries of power are the logical places to look for an explanation of such an emergence.

5

The spontaneous emergence of social institutions: a bargaining theory of emergence and change

If institutions affect the distribution of benefits in social life, then we should expect strategic actors to seek those institutional rules that give them the greatest share of those benefits. Thus, the conflict over the substantive benefits of social life extends to the development of the institutional arrangements that structure it. Now on some accounts this logic of distributional conflict might be seen as consistent with the standard theories considered in the previous chapter. But there is an important difference in emphasis here. Although these standard theories often acknowledge the conflicts of interest existing in situations of institutional development, they concentrate on mechanisms that transform actions based on individual interests into institutions that are collectively beneficial.

We have already seen the necessary conditions for such mechanisms to be effective. Even in the situations in which the mechanisms obtain, much about the emergence of particular institutional forms remains to be explained. What I am arguing here is that in order to explain the substantive content of social institutions and, therefore, completely explain institutional development and change, our theories must focus primarily on the strategic conflict itself and on the mechanisms by which this conflict is resolved. Not only is such an emphasis dictated by the logic of assuming self-interested strategic behavior but also by our empirical understanding of social institutions.

The idea of invoking the conflict over distributional benefits as the major source of institutional development is straightforward in cases of intentional design: Preferences for particular institutional rules and the distributional outcomes that they produce can be incorporated into explanations of institutional design. Some efforts have taken account of distributional preferences in their explanations of the creation of formal social and political institutions (Bates, 1990; Libecap, 1989; North, 1990). But the importance of distributional conflict for explanations of a society's informal network of rules, norms, and conventions is more complex and has not been as readily pursued.

This lack of attention to the explanatory importance of distributional factors follows from the standard characterizations of the process of decentralized emergence discussed in the previous chapter. The general idea is that decentralized development insulates the process from the control of actors who want to fashion institutional rules for their own purposes. According to this characterization, the arbitrariness of the institutional outcome suggests that the asymmetries of power in a society are not important to explanations of these informal rules. And the voluntariness of the compliance inherent in self-enforcing rules is seen to imply that the outcomes are universally acceptable and that the disproportionate distributional benefits do not motivate conflict. For if they were not universally acceptable, rational actors would not voluntarily comply with them.

The problem here is that this characterization contradicts evidence from social life: Decentralized mechanisms produce informal networks that embody and reinforce the asymmetries characterizing a society. Examples are ubiquitous, but they differ in the degree to which the rules' content actually mirrors the asymmetries that foster them. In some contexts these asymmetries are obvious. Rules governing gender relations and family organizations have historically reflected asymmetric relationships between men and women: From classical antiquity (Starr, 1989) to developing communities (Papanek, 1990) to modern societies (Nash, 1989; Rhode, 1989), informal rules have structured relationships between men and women in such ways as to produce long-term distributional differences.[1] Similarly, informal rules governing the social organization of a community embody the underlying divisions in a society: from the stark discrimination of apartheid and slavery (Patterson, 1982; Thompson, 1990) to more subtle forms of hierarchy and authority (Nader, 1989).

In other contexts the distributional consequences are apparent, but the underlying asymmetries are less clear. Evolved systems of property rights are often characterized by this feature: from the shift from open-field to enclosed agricultural systems (Eggertsson, 1990) to the resolution of common-pool problems (Ostrom, 1990) to the evolution of various procedures for property division. In still other contexts the initial asymmetries appear to have lost their relevance. Measurements of time and space have historically been the subject of intense and sustained conflict, as the

---

1 For example, see the essays in Tinker, 1990, for a survey of recent findings on the long-term effects of rules of family organization on the economic development of women in developing societies.

criteria by which land, crops, and labor are measured produced significant distributional consequences (Kula, 1986). Today these measures usually appear to us as neutral metrics by which we structure everyday life (Whitrow, 1988).

In this chapter I offer a theory of decentralized emergence and change that captures the asymmetries characterizing these informal networks. In doing so I accomplish three important theoretical objectives. First, I propose microfoundations for the informal network of rules, conventions, and norms that capture some of the principal ideas of macro-level accounts in the Weberian and Marxian tradition.[2] Second, I show how the importance of distributional conflict and power asymmetries can be incorporated into a rational-choice theory of the spontaneous emergence of social institutions. One implication of this theory is that the long-standing debate between the Hume–Smith tradition on the one hand and the Weber–Marx tradition on the other comes down in part to a debate over the empirical conditions governing the process of decentralized emergence. Third, I offer a theory of spontaneous emergence that is more general than the other approaches because it is based on less restrictive empirical conditions. The theory starts with the logic of the basic strategic interaction from which social institutions are developed and then incorporates the effects of the context in which these interactions occur. In this approach the contemporary accounts of institutional emergence discussed in the previous chapter represent special cases of the more general conflict theory of spontaneous emergence.

In the next section I present this alternative theory. The theory is developed by drawing out the implications of a simple model of bargaining and demonstrating how these implications suggest a process of spontaneous emergence. Interspersed through this discussion are a range of examples of informal rules that can be explained in terms of distributional conflict. In the last section I present an extended discussion of the historical development of a set of rules of property division common to most societies in order to contrast my account with the theories of social convention and market competition.

2 A focus on the changing relationships among the interests of social actors can help us evaluate many macro-level theories of institutional creation and change. Such theories correlate macro-level conditions with particular institutional forms. Most fall back on a functionalist logic to explain institutional change. That is, institutional change is explained in terms of the social system's changing functional needs. If we looked instead at the effects of external changes on the interests of the relevant social actors, we could analyze the effects of these changes on the conflict over different institutional forms. See Taylor, 1989, for a telling and insightful analysis of the inadequate reasons given by macro-level theorists for their resistance to these micro-level explanations.

Institutions and social conflict

Let me begin by drawing on the arguments from previous chapters to sketch briefly the logic of institutional development based on distributional conflict. This is a logic applicable to all forms of institutional development, either decentralized or intentional processes. Social institutions are a by-product of strategic conflict over substantive social outcomes. By this I mean that social actors produce social institutions in the process of seeking distributional advantage in the conflict over substantive benefits. In some cases they create institutional rules consciously, and in other cases the rules emerge as unintended consequences of the pursuit of strategic advantage. In each case the main focus is on the substantive outcome; the development of institutional rules is merely a means to that substantive end. The importance of these institutional rules lies in the constraints that they place on strategic action.

Because social outcomes are the product of the interdependent strategies of all of those with whom we interact, in substantive conflicts we seek to constrain the strategies of others in such a way as to secure our own preferred alternatives. Given the interdependent nature of social life, strategic actors must anticipate the actions of others in order to choose what is best for them to do. Therefore, the way to influence the actions of others, to constrain their choices, is to affect their expectations about what we ourselves are going to do. Actors who are successful in individual interactions will try on future occasions to repeat the act of constraining.

Social institutions regularize these constraints. Institutional rules give us information about the expected actions of others and, in doing so, constrain our choices. Central to the process of institutional creation is the capacity to find a credible way to affect the expectations of others and to establish it as the recognized expected behavior for the community as a whole. In some cases this may be done merely through our own actions, producing self-enforcing institutions; in other cases, this may require the aid of third-party enforcers, producing externally enforced institutions. Although the tasks may differ in the various cases, the logic of institutionalization is the same: Social institutions are the product of efforts to constrain the actions of those with whom we interact.

The efficacy of social institutions as a resource for strategic conflict is found in the attraction of equilibrium outcomes. Strategic actors respect social institutions because they structure interactions to equilibrium conclusions. Institutional development is a contest among actors to establish rules that structure outcomes to those equilibria most favorable to them. This contest is determined by the parties' relative abilities *to force others*

126

to act in ways contrary to their unconstrained preferences. In this way, institutional development and change become an ongoing bargaining game among the members of a group.

To develop a bargaining theory of institutional change, we should allow for the possibility that some social actors are more powerful than others and investigate the effects of those differences. Those actors with a relative bargaining advantage can force others to comply with institutional rules because compliance is the best reply to the actions of the other members of the group. In the end, if strong actors can constrain others to choose a particular equilibrium strategy, the weak will comply whether or not they want to do so. From this it follows that social actors respect these institutional rules *not because they have agreed to them* and *not because they evolved as Pareto improvements* but simply *because they cannot do better than to do so.*

Once an institution is established, change comes slowly and often at considerable cost. Institutional change entails a change in the equilibrium outcome that social actors have come to recognize as the commonly anticipated solution to problems of social interaction. Strategic actors will continue to respect existing social institutions unless (1) assuming that they have the power to change them, external events change and alter the long-run benefits produced by them, or (2) assuming that other arrangements will produce a more favorable distributional division, they can resolve the formidable collective-action problems prerequisite to such institutional change. This is in large part a task of changing social expectations, with the difficulty of the task being directly related to the size of the relevant group: The larger the size of the group, the greater the costs of changing expectations will be, and therefore the greater the complexity of the problem of institutional change.

Interactions as bargaining problems

Having sketched the general logic of distributional conflict over institutions, I must now show how this logic forms the basis for a theory of the decentralized emergence of informal rules. Such a theory must answer two questions: (1) how the constraints are established in a single interaction and (2) how the constraints are generalized as a social institution governing the community as a whole. To answer these questions, we must begin with a conception of the basic strategic interaction that gives rise to informal social institutions.

This conception can be grounded in the features common to the various contexts in which informal rules exist. Whether it is the family, the neighborhood, the municipality, the workplace, other forms of social organization, opportunities for economic gain, the nation, or the international arena, each context shares common strategic features. In each situation, there are benefits to be gained from social actors working together, sharing resources, or coordinating their activities in some way. These actors need rules to structure their interdependent activities. More than one set of rules can satisfy this requirement, and the rules differ in their distributional properties. Because of this, people have conflicting preferences regarding the institutional alternatives. These features make up the standard bargaining problem: "a situation in which (i) individuals . . . have the possibility of concluding a mutually beneficial agreement, (ii) there is a conflict of interest about which agreement to conclude, and (iii) no agreement may be imposed on any individual without his approval" (Osborne and Rubinstein, 1990: 1).

Contemporary theories of institutional change usually conceive of the basic interaction giving rise to social institutions as either a coordination or a Prisoner's Dilemma game. Given the proper conditions, such games can easily be reformulated as a bargaining problem. For the coordination game, the only requirement is that the various coordination equilibria differ in their distribution of benefits. The mixed-motive game (see Table 3.4), which Sugden uses, represents a simple example of this structure. The requirements for the Prisoner's Dilemma game are more complex. For the bargaining solution to be self-enforcing (the implication of the third feature of Osborne's and Rubinstein's definition), cooperation must be a rational strategy.

The recent work on noncooperative game theory has demonstrated that there are many circumstances in which this might be the case (Kreps, 1990: 505–15). For my purpose here, the relevant conditions are that the interaction is repeated over time and that the actors are partners in ongoing relationships. As I suggested in my discussion of the transaction costs–market exchange theory, these also are the conditions necessary for the decentralized emergence of informal rules. So, for this part of the analysis, we can transform the Prisoner's Dilemma game into a bargaining problem and concentrate on the conflict among a range of cooperative solutions.[3] If these conditions break down, the appropriateness of treating the Prisoner's Dilemma game as a bargaining game will be called into question. But this raises more general questions about the stability of self-enforcing rules, an issue to which I shall return in the next chapter.

To facilitate the following discussion I propose a simple model of the bargaining problem (see Table 5.1). Although it abstracts from much of the complexity of many social interactions, it does allow us to identify the central elements of the process by which informal rules emerge. Many

3 See Snidal, 1985, for an analysis, in the context of international relations, of the implications of expanding the cooperation outcome of the Prisoner's Dilemma game into a range of possible cooperative solutions.

Table 5.1. *The basic bargaining game*

Player A	B	
	L	R
L	Δ_A, Δ_B	$x, x + \epsilon_B$
R	$x + \epsilon_A, x$	Δ_A, Δ_B

bargaining situations are characterized by a sequential series of offers and counteroffers, and the structure of this sequence has been found to affect the bargaining outcome. I choose here to simplify this process in order to present an analytical model that can cover the widest possible range of noncooperative bargaining situations. As I will show later, the conclusions drawn from this simple model capture the essential factors that affect more complex bargaining outcomes.

In this two-person model, if we set $\Delta_{A,B} < x$, there will be two equilibrium outcomes that can solve the bargaining problem, the R,L and L,R strategy combinations. The Δ values represent the payoffs that the actors will receive if they fail to achieve one of the equilibrium outcomes. Following Osborne and Rubinstein (1990: 70–1), I will refer to these as the *breakdown values*. If we require $\epsilon_{A,B} > 0$, the ϵ values will represent the distributional advantage accruing to one of the actors if a particular equilibrium outcome is chosen. The main goal for the actors in this game is to achieve ϵ.

With this basic framework I consider in turn the two questions that this theory must answer. In so doing, I will show how the major intuitions of macro-level accounts of institutional development and change can be incorporated into a micro-level explanation of the decentralized emergence of social institutions. The underlying mechanism by which distributive effects shape social institutions rests on the correlation between the resources that produce asymmetries in power in a society (the main focus of macro-level theories) and the factors that resolve the individual social interactions from which social institutions emerge. Bargaining theorists have found that bargaining success is a function of both the credibility of strategic commitments and the attitudes of bargainers toward risk and time. The key feature of my bargaining theory of institutional emergence is *the fundamental relationship between resource asymmetries, on the one hand, and credibility, risk aversion, and time preferences, on the other.*

First, how do social actors constrain the actions of others with whom they interact? The answer is that they do so by affecting the others' expectations of what they themselves are going to do in a given case. But here we arrive at a seemingly paradoxical result. In order to influence future expectations, they must constrain themselves. By constraining themselves to a future course of action, strategic actors alter the range of options open to those with whom they interact. The ability of a social actor to strategically constrain herself and, in doing so, establish her future course of action is the crucial first step in developing social institutions.

The strategic efficacy of any claim about a future course of action is contingent on how convincing it is to others; that is, the credibility of the commitment: Is it believable that they will do what they indicate they will do?[4] If it is convincing, then others must take that action into account when deciding their own best course of action. For example, in the basic bargaining model, the task for player A is to constrain the actions of player B so that he will choose to play L. To do so, player A must credibly commit to play R. More generally, if the rule that player A prefers is to be self-enforcing, she (and other A players) must find a way to commit to the R strategy in repeated plays of the game. If A players can make this commitment credible, the rational action for B players will be to follow the rule and play L. Although B players may prefer another alternative, the knowledge that A players will play R in any case constrains their choice to playing L. But what makes the commitments of the A players credible?

The first of two sources of credibility for social actors is the standard idea of precommitment: the capacity of actors to manipulate the benefits derived from their own strategies. In the preceding example, player A can enhance the credibility of her precommitment to strategy R by altering the benefits that she would receive if she chose strategy L. Let us say she found some way to diminish the benefits of choosing L (e.g., by some amount y) so that the new structure of payoffs has $x - y < \Delta_A$. Now choosing strategy R becomes the dominant strategy for player A, and so her precommitment to that strategy is quite credible. Much to his chagrin, player B now finds that his rational course of action is to choose strategy L.

What is necessary in order for player A to accomplish this strategic move is the availability of a technology of precommitment that enables the alteration of the benefits of choosing L. To see the value of such a technology, consider the following case, one of many fruitful examples that Schelling offers:

It was reported unofficially during the Korean War that when the Treasury Department blocked Communist Chinese financial assets, it also knowingly

---

4 This discussion of credibility is related to the general problem of equilibrium refinemenets in game theory: In a multiple-equilibria environment, what is the rational basis on which strategic actors choose some equilibria over others?

blocked some non-Communist assets as a means of immunizing the owners against extortionate threats against their relatives still in China. Quite likely, for owners located in the United States, the very penalties on transfer of funds to Communist China enhanced their capacity to resist extortion. Deliberately putting one's own assets in a form that made evasion of the law more difficult, or lobbying for more severe penalties on illegal transfer of one's own funds, or even getting one's self temporarily identified as a Communist sympathizer so that his funds would be blocked might have been an indicated tactic for potential victims, to discourage the extortionate threat in advance. (1960:159)

The constraints on the assets of the non-Communist Chinese put them in a better strategic position vis-à-vis those on the mainland who would seek their assets; the chance of retaining their funds was improved. This is an example of the general phenomenon of "burning one's bridges."

Although we can find many such examples in isolated bargaining situations, it is difficult to find similar, more systematic technologies in those interactions most likely to produce social institutions. Precommitment requires either a third party with whom a side agreement can be arranged or some other mechanism that can penalize the failure to follow through with one's commitment. As we see in Schelling's Korean War example, the external enforcement of the state can be an effective mechanism. We can also see how commitments to rank-and-file membership can precommit union officials to particular strategies when bargaining with management or leaders of revolutionary movements to particular strategies in actions against the state. But there are many situations in which the technology of precommitment is not available to social actors.[5]

The second, and more important, source of credibility is grounded directly in the relative bargaining power of the actors. As I suggested in Chapter 2, asymmetries in power can affect social outcomes in many ways. Generally, we can say that *A* has power over *B* if *A* can affect by some means the alternative actions available to *B*. This is the point of the commitment strategy here. Although there are many sources of the asymmetry in power that characterize bargaining interactions, we need to isolate those most likely to govern the spontaneous emergence of informal institutions. Such institutions emerge from repeated social interactions.

---

5 In his extended discussion of the importance of precommitment in bargaining situations, Schelling stresses the counterintuitive notion that precommitment allows the weak to take the strategic advantage away from the strong. Although this insight is unquestionably borne out in various isolated situations, this result is less likely in the repeated social interactions that are the groundwork for creating social institutions. Consider the method of "burning one's bridges," Schelling's favorite example. Although the weak may use such tactics in isolated situations, we would not expect such technology to be available in an ongoing and systematic way. Furthermore, if such technology were available, we would expect the more powerful members of the community eventually to find a way to destroy it. This suggests that if precommitment is a source of institutional development, it will tend, contra Schelling, to be a strategy available to the more powerful members of a group.

In any single bargaining interaction, various factors can determine relative bargaining power: the resources available to the actors, their intelligence, their previous experiences – all intangibles that, for want of a better term, we might call *bargaining savvy* (Bachrach and Lawler, 1981; Raiffa, 1982). Although any of these may determine a particular outcome, only those factors common to a wide range of bargainers can resolve repeated interactions and lead to the emergence of informal rules. These factors are unlikely to be related to the characteristics of particular individuals. Rather, they are more likely to be related to the possession of substantive resources, what Maynard-Smith referred to as "resource-holding power" (1982:35–6).

In bargaining interactions, the most important resources are those available to the actors in the event that bargaining is either lengthy and costly or ultimately unsuccessful. For any particular bargaining interaction, many factors may determine the availability of these resources. We can think of these as the existing resources that an actor might retain after the effort to achieve a bargain breaks down. Or we might think of them as the other options available to the actors if they are left to conclude a bargain with some other party. Here we see how the existence of competition can affect relative bargaining power: It affects the other options available to the actors. In the bargaining model in Table 5.1, these resources determine the breakdown values, $\Delta_{A,B}$, a measure of the costs of noncoordination on an equilibrium outcome. If $\Delta_A = \Delta_B$, the breakdown values are equal, and we can conclude that there are no key asymmetries of power in the game. But if either $\Delta_A > \Delta_B$ or $\Delta_A < \Delta_B$, we have an example of asymmetric bargaining power.

The standard view in bargaining theory is that if A has greater bargaining power than B does, A will usually get a greater share of the benefits of the bargaining outcome (Maynard-Smith, 1982: 105; Osborne and Rubinstein, 1990: 88–9).[6] We can see the underlying idea of this view through the effects of differences in the breakdown values. Here the mechanism by which relative bargaining power influences social outcomes is in its effect on the credibility of the commitments in the bargaining interaction. To see this, consider a game with asymmetric breakdown values, $\Delta_A > \Delta_B$. Now the costs of breakdown are greater for player B than for player A. If player A is now able to communicate to player B that she will choose R regardless of what B does, what will B do?[7] That is,

6 This view has been formalized in several bargaining solutions: in the asymmetric Nash and the Kalai–Smorodinsky solutions in cooperative theory and in some variants of the Rubinstein noncooperative solution (see Elster, 1989a: 50–96, for a nontechnical introduction to these solutions).

7 I use the word *communicate* loosely at this point. Later, when we consider the generalization of commitments throughout a society, I will discuss the nature of this communication.

what will this information do to B's choice? The answer depends on how credible B finds A's commitment to be. There are important reasons to believe that B will accept the credibility of the commitment in this case and respond by choosing L.

The principal idea here pertains to the relationship between available resources and attitudes toward risk. Resource ownership influences one's attitude toward risky situations. There is a positive relationship between ownership of resources and risk acceptance, and a negative relationship between ownership and risk aversion. Considered from the perspective of player B, this relationship suggests two related reasons that he would find A's commitment credible and choose L. First, because A will suffer fewer costs of breakdown, A is more likely to accept the risk and attempt the commitment to R. As Maynard-Smith puts it in his highly relevant analysis of asymmetric evolutionary games, "A player who has less to lose from a breakdown is more likely to risk one" (1982: 153). If B is aware of the asymmetry, he has good reason to believe that A is sincere in his commitment. Second, because B will suffer greater costs of the breakdown, he is more likely to be risk averse and is, therefore, less likely to challenge A's commitment. This risk aversion leads to a willingness to accept the commitment and to choose L. The greater the differences are in resources between the actors, the stronger the relationship will be between breakdown values and risk attitudes. That is, the greater the differential is between Δ_A and Δ_B, the higher the probability will be that B will choose L.

Up to this point I have assumed that both parties completely understand the nature of the interaction, including the asymmetry in breakdown values. The certainty of the resource asymmetry leads B to accept the credibility of A's commitment. But even if B is not certain about the differential in breakdown values between A and himself, there is reason to believe that if he knows that he is weak, he is more likely to respond to A's commitment. We can see why by working through the way in which B assesses the likelihood that he is bargaining with a strong person. Let us say that B knows that strong players commit to R and that weak players choose L. If B does not know which type he is playing against, he must base his decision on his subjective probability, p, that he is playing against a strong person. What we need to know is the threshold probability above which it will be rational for him to act as if he is playing against a strong person and choose L. We can obtain this threshold by calculating the mixed-strategy equilibrium in the game.

The question of interpreting mixed strategies in game theory is rather problematic.[8] One acceptable way of interpreting them in the context of

---

8 See Rubinstein, 1988, for an excellent discussion of the general issue of interpretation of game-theoretic models, including the problem of mixed strategies.

repeated games is as the probability distribution of players in a society. For example, in this bargaining context we can interpret the probability assigned to R as the likelihood that one will meet a strong person. The equilibrium mixed-strategy combination for player A in this game is play R with probability

$$(x + \epsilon_B - \Delta_B) / (2x + \epsilon_B - 2\Delta_B)$$

and L with probability

$$(x - \Delta_B) / (2x + \epsilon_B - 2\Delta_B)$$

The mixed-strategy probabilities for A give us the threshold values for B. If

$$p = (x + \epsilon_B - \Delta_B) / (2x + \epsilon_B - 2\Delta_B)$$

then B is indifferent between the choice of L and R.[9] But if

$$p > (x + \epsilon_B - \Delta_B) / (2x + \epsilon_B - 2\Delta_B)$$

he will prefer to choose L and accept his lesser payoff x.

Note now the relationship between p and Δ_B. Does the value of p differ for strong and weak actors? If we take $\partial p / \partial \Delta_B$, we can determine how p changes for different values of Δ_B. In this case,

$$\partial p / \partial \Delta_B = \epsilon_B / (2x + \epsilon_B - 2\Delta_B)^2$$

Because by definition $\epsilon_B > 0$ and because the denominator also must be positive, we can conclude that as breakdown values increase, the threshold p increases. This implies that as an actor's breakdown value decreases, the proportion of the population that needs to be strong for him to prefer L goes down as well. Thus, if he is weak, it will take a lower probability that he is meeting a strong person for him to accept the commitment of A than it would if he were a strong person. Therefore, even if B is uncertain about A, if he knows that he is weak, he is more likely than a strong person is to accept the commitment. Of course, his willingness still depends on his subjective probability of the likelihood that A is a strong person. The weaker that he is, the lower that the probability needs to be for the commitment to be efficacious.

There are two additional implications of asymmetries in power that might influence B's choice of L. The first involves the costliness of extended bargaining. Attempts at commitment (such as the one by A) can extend the bargaining process and delay its resolution. Like attitudes toward risk, time preferences can affect the outcomes of a bargaining prob-

---

9 Note here that as long as $\epsilon_B > 0$ (i.e., as long as B prefers the L,R outcome to the R,L one), the probability of meeting a strong person must always be greater than the probability of meeting a weak one, in order for B to avoid choosing R.

lem. Attitudes toward risk relate to failures to achieve a successful resolution; time preferences relate to the timing of achieving that resolution. Although they are distinct, both are affected by the ownership of resources. If an individual has more resources, thereby making him less dependent on the bargaining outcome, he will generally be more patient in the bargaining process. Extensive bargaining is time-consuming, but a patient bargainer is less concerned about the timing of the outcome. This patience translates into a bargaining advantage.

Time preferences are measured in terms of the parameters with which we discount the future. Rubinstein (1982) showed that differentials in discount parameters among the bargainers affect the distribution of the solution: The bargainer with the higher discount parameter receives a greater share of the benefits. The idea is as follows: If A and B have different time preferences, the value of future bargains will be greater for A than for B. Because bargaining is costly, B will be more willing to accept a smaller share now than a possibly larger share later if that share will be diminished by a serious discount factor. In the bargaining model (Table 5.1) there is some parameter d for which B will be indifferent between $d(x + \epsilon_B)$ and x. If A's commitment delays a resolution of the bargain, the costs of delay may influence B's strategy. If B's d is greater than $x/(x + \epsilon_B)$, she will accept A's commitment to R and select L.

A final implication of asymmetries in power involves possible threats of retaliatory action. Here threats mean the actors' capacity to affect the benefits derived by others from their own choice of action. For example, A may threaten retaliation against B if he fails to choose L. The effect of the threat can be to increase the pressure on B to adopt his less-preferred alternative. The reason is that the threatened retaliation (if carried out) would increase the costs of adopting R. In Table 5.1, if A can inflict a punishment, c, on B that will alter the benefits of the L,R equilibrium outcome so that

$$\Delta_B > x + \epsilon_B - c$$

then L will be a dominant strategy for B. For B, because retaliation is costly, the question is whether the threat is credible: If B ignores the threat and chooses R, will A retaliate? This introduces the issue of the rationality of informal sanctioning. As I shall show in the next chapter, in an isolated interaction, the threat is not rational, but in an ongoing relationship of repeated interactions, incurring the threat can be a rational strategy. Thus, in ongoing relationships, the asymmetry of power between the actors can introduce the possibility of threats, threats that further reinforce A's efforts to commit to R and constrain B's actions.

In sum, this last discussion of threats should not confuse the underlying issue of power asymmetries and commitments. Although there may be instances in which social actors can achieve their preferred outcomes by threatening punishment, the commitment to which I am referring here need not be, and is usually not, so explicit. What I want to demonstrate here is a more general phenomenon: Social actors suffer significant costs for failing to coordinate on equilibrium outcomes, yet these costs need not be suffered uniformly. When social actors are aware of these differentials, they can influence the credibility of certain strategies. Those who have either fewer alternatives or less beneficial ones are more inclined to respect the commitments of those in the opposite situation. In this way, the commitment of the powerful can significantly influence the choice of equilibrium alternatives.

A few examples will show how asymmetries of power can resolve distributional conflict in common social interactions. They are offered merely to illustrate both the wide variety of contexts to which the bargaining theory applies and the different effects of power asymmetries. Each can be characterized as an ongoing relationship with a mixed-motive incentive structure: Each individual benefits from the joint activity, but he or she differs in preference regarding how the activity ought to be conducted.

Marriage, family, and gender relations.[10] The family is a complex social organization involving a large number of activities for which some rule determines responsibility and authority. The activities can be described according to their division of authority between the sexes and among the generations. Starr (1989) offers an account of family and gender relations in ancient Rome that represents a fairly common distribution of authority and benefits. Roman society, as documented in such texts as the Twelve Tables (451 B.C.) and Gaius's *Institutes* (second century A.D.), had a fully developed network of informal rules governing such activities. It is instructive here to examine two related categories of activities: authority over property and over marriage.

There are many ways that such activities can be structured; they differ mainly in the authority granted to the different sexes. Not surprisingly, Roman families followed rules strongly favorable to men. In the area of family property, men were granted authority over not only the common property of the family but also the property that wives brought to the marriage. Women had no authority to alienate or transfer property. Even after their husband's death, the rules restricted women's authority to

10 See Manser and Brown, 1980, and McElroy and Horney, 1981, for two formal attempts (using the Nash cooperative solution) to treat the distribution of resources and time responsibility in a marriage as a bargaining problem. Sen, 1990, offers a sympathetic critique of this approach in which he argues that the bargaining model of the family should be extended to include other-regarding motivations.

control the family's assets. Indeed, the rules created incentives for widows to remarry so as to place the property under the control of another male who could then use it for productive purposes. Here women's choices were also limited by the rules governing marriage. There were three forms of marriage in Roman society: *usus, confarreatio,* and *coemptio.* Each of these restricted, to varying degrees, women's freedom to choose their own mates. The first two were arranged by the woman's father; the third, which grew in importance in the second century A.D., allowed a woman whose father was dead some choice of a husband. Regardless of form, marriage entailed guardianship and placed women under the control of their husbands.

These rules can be explained by the relative bargaining power of the different sexes. Because the family has historically been the social organization through which individuals meet their basic needs for nourishment and protection, we should look to the resources that they use for these purposes. In Roman society these resources were strongly skewed in favor of men. Not only did men control wealth, but they also dominated access to economic productivity and development. A related factor demonstrates how different rules interact to reinforce one another. The other family options available to women – a basic source of bargaining power – were limited by the constraints on marriage: Because women had limited freedom to choose marriage partners, the value of the option to marry someone else also was diminished. Because of these substantial differences in bargaining power, Roman men were able to commit to strategies for family activities that granted them considerable distributional advantages in both property and authority. Given their lack of feasible alternatives, Roman women rationally accepted their subordinate position.

Weights and measures: structuring social activity. Social interaction requires some underlying criterion of time and space, which is contained in part in a society's system of weights and measures. Although these systems often seem today to be made up of neutral criteria, they have historically been the source of considerable distributional conflict. The choice of a particular metric often produced significant changes in the distribution of benefits of a particular activity. There are many examples, but consider a particularly clear one: procedures for measuring land and produce in feudal Europe. Kula (1986) provides an excellent historical account from which we can draw the relevant facts. Agricultural and commercial activities can be conceptualized as joint economic interactions requiring some standard system of measure. In agricultural matters the distribution of benefits between the lord and the peasants depended in large part on the criterion of land measurement.

The alternative criteria differed in whether the basic unit of land was to be established by (1) the labor time necessary for a certain amount of production, (2) the amount of seed required for a certain production level, or (3) the amount of land necessary for the survival and reproduction of a peasant family.

Feudal society was marked by persistent conflict between lords and peasants over this criterion. The established measures reflect the relative bargaining-power advantage of the lords. The relevant resources, land and other options for wages, strongly favored the lords. An additional important feature of these feudal relationships – given the lords' more general control over social life – was the threat of punishment against the peasants for not complying. As we would expect, units of land measure were established in different contexts in ways to favor lords in distribution. For example, because the overall distributional share going to lords increased as the unit of measure decreased, the unit of measure for the more productive areas was smaller than that for less fertile land. Given the lords' advantages in land and other alternatives, the peasants had to accept these measures.

The value of using power asymmetries to explain these criteria is further demonstrated by the conflicts over measures of grain. Consider merely the question of whether or not the unit of grain measure was to be "heaped." A heap measure was, as its name implies, one in which the measuring container was filled to capacity; a nonheaped measure was one in which the grain was leveled at the container's rim. Lords used different measures in different contexts. When they dealt with peasants, the heaped unit was generally the standard; with other commercial actors in the marketplace, the nonheaped unit was the standard. Different communities in Europe reflected variations on these basic forms. The lords' ability to establish these measures can be explained by their relative bargaining advantage vis-à-vis peasants and merchants. Deviations from these standards that worked against the lord's interests can be attributed to the increased power, due in large part to other options, of merchants in urban areas.

Economic firms: the organization and distribution of revenues. The economic firm has evolved into the basic form of economic organization in industrialized societies. Here joint activity requires rules and procedures governing both production and distribution. Consider as one such example the conflict over the distribution of profits in the workplace. The informal rules structuring labor–management relations in the firm take many different forms. One possible rule entails individual negotiations between the firm and unorganized workers. An alternative rule establishes collective bargaining between representatives of the firm and

138

the workers. Advanced industrial societies can be distinguished by which set of rules emerged as the informal structure of labor–management relations. In western Europe informal rules establishing collective bargaining were the standard. In other areas, such as the United States and Japan, the dominant informal rule was wage negotiation with unorganized workers (Clegg, 1976; Sturmthal, 1943, 1972). These national differences can be explained by the relative bargaining power of the workers in the different countries.

It is easy to conceptualize firm activity as a bargaining problem. Here we shall focus on the rules that emerge as bargaining over profits takes place. Such rules are important because they affect the ultimate distribution of the firm's resources. An organized work force can commit to a strategy of collective bargaining. Either the firm can accept this strategy and bargain a wage rate accordingly, or it can reject collective bargaining and face the possibility of a strike. If the work force is sufficiently organized and disciplined, its commitment can be credible, and in anticipation of a strike, the firm will accept the collective bargaining alternative. If, on the other hand, the work force is poorly organized, the firm will find the collective-bargaining strategy lacking in credibility and might attempt instead to commit itself to a strategy of individual negotiations. The efficacy of the alternative strategies depends crucially here on the level of the workers' organization.

The organization of workers affects their relative bargaining power in two ways. First, organized workers can pool their resources and in doing so decrease the importance of the wealth advantage enjoyed by the firm's owners. In the case of an extended work stoppage, these pooled resources can sustain workers in the face of lost wages. Second, organized workers can decrease the availability of the firm's outside options. If the firm cannot turn to other workers in the event of a work stoppage, the value of its resources will fall when a bargaining solution is not reached. Given the much higher level of organization of European workers, the fact that they, unlike their U.S. or Japanese counterparts, were able to establish informal collective-bargaining procedures is understandable because of the basic differences in their relative bargaining power. In the face of an organized work force, firms in Europe were compelled to adopt such procedures, whereas in the United States and Japan, firms could ignore worker representatives until the workers sought the outside intervention of the state.

The recognition of commitments

When strategic actors achieve successful commitments, they face the second half of the task of institutionalization: generalizing these constraints as rules governing the community as a whole. Generalization occurs when social actors recognize that the committed strategies have become the socially anticipated action and realize that compliance with them is their best response to the actions of others. Institutionalization thus becomes a process of social recognition of strategic rules of action. This recognition is quite simple for externally enforced institutions: The use of standard procedures by state officials to establish such rules serves to ensure their recognition (Hart, 1961). The interesting problem relates to the generalization of self-enforcing rules through a decentralized emergence process: how commitments established in individual interactions come to be recognized and respected as the accepted rule of action for the society as a whole. An answer can be found in the ability of strategic actors to recognize those asymmetries in power that support those commitments.

Decentralized emergence means that recognition is a dynamic process. Recognition requires a capacity for learning and an ability to adapt and adjust to the actions of others with whom we interact. The structure of the process is quite simple. Over time people come to identify certain recurrent strategies that they face in common social situations. From their experience they gain information about the behavior of others that they use to plan their future actions. If the common interactions are frequent enough, these persons will converge through a process of adjustment on a stable combination of actions, combinations which come to be recognized as the informal rules of behavior governing future interactions. My task now is to show how this decentralized recognition process is generated by commitments supported by asymmetries in power.

Decentralized emergence can be modeled as a configuration of repeated games (Calvert, 1991; Schotter, 1981). The specific structure of the configuration depends on the underlying social situation. Although ongoing social interactions can take many forms, it is helpful to identify two extremes on a continuum of relationship types.[11] One type is best characterized by the family. In the family an individual is in an ongoing relationship with a small set of actors. The learning process is one of communication and adjustment in repeated interactions with the same persons. The family thus can be viewed as an iterated bargaining game involving a relatively stable set of actors. The recognition problem requires learning and adjusting to the strategies of the same actors in the

---

11 Note that communication in social interactions can take many forms, from unspoken implicit acknowledgment to extensive explicit negotiations. In analyzing cases of decentralized institutional emergence, the focus should be on those factors communicating important information in the least explicit way so as to capture the effects of communication in the largest number of cases.

repeated plays of the game. To the extent that others outside the family are relevant to the recognition process, they serve as models of new strategies for family interactions that might be tested or imitated in the context of the basic relationship.[12]

A second type of relationship is best characterized by certain forms of economic activity. In such activities a person is part of a set of repeated interactions, but the particular individuals with whom he is involved may change from interaction to interaction. The learning process is one of communication and adjustment with an array of social actors in different interactions that share the same basic bargaining structure. Economic activity can be viewed as a repeated bargaining game in which the actors change. The recognition problem entails learning and adjusting to the different types of strategies confronted in the repeated plays of the game. To the extent that ongoing relationships with the same actors play a role in the recognition process, it can be seen as a way of stabilizing expectations about different types of strategies.

Many social relationships are characterized by a mix of these two extreme forms,[13] as in the context of the economic firm. In the firm, workers and management develop an ongoing relationship that places them in repeated interactions with roughly the same individuals, but each of these persons may also be part of related interactions with actors in other firms and those outside the firm's environment. For them the learning process is more complex, requiring adjustment to a range of social strategies. A similar configuration can be found in gender relationships. Although the family serves as a major source of learning, family members also gain information about gender relations from their interactions with others outside the family.

My main purpose in highlighting the more extreme cases is to illustrate how the structure of the ongoing relationship dictates the types of information most likely to influence the learning process. Learning in re-

12 Of course, the modern proliferation of variations on the traditional family organization has expanded the possible configurations of this most basic social organization. These changes have increased both the number and the duration of an individual's experiences. Given the commensurate increase in the range of potentially relevant actors necessary for successful learning, this could significantly alter the social recognition process.

13 In this analysis I do not use *n*-person conceptualizations of social situations. The general problem of social cooperation as an *n*-person game has been thoroughly treated by others (see Taylor, 1987). My main reason for treating decentralized emergence as a set of small-*n* interactions is a conviction that this is the most appropriate way of capturing the process of learning as it is experienced by social actors. This is not to say that size is not a relevant variable for issues related to social institutions. When it is, I address it as such. However, on the question of emergence, the recognition of social institutions is best viewed as the result of small-*n* interactions. See Schotter, 1981, for an alternative that does treat emergence as an *n*-person problem.

peated games has been modeled in various ways. Milgrom and Roberts (1991) provide a review of the literature. The different approaches can be distinguished by their assumptions regarding the types of information employed by the actors as they establish their expectations.

One set of models emphasizes past play. These models are purely adaptative, assuming that actors rely exclusively on information about the past behavior of their opponents. The "best reply" logic bases expectations on the last play of the game: "At each round each firm selects the quantity that would maximize its payoff if its competitors continued to produce the same quantities as at the preceding round" (Milgrom and Roberts, 1991: 83). The assumption is that a player's action in game t is a perfect predictor of his play in game $t + 1$. The "fictitious play" logic bases expectations on the full set of past plays of the game: The players "choose the strategies that maximize their payoffs given the prediction that the probability distribution of competitor's play at the next round is the same as the empirical frequency distribution of past play" (p. 83). The assumption is that a player's action in game t can be predicted by the distribution of his choice in the $t - 1$ previous games.

A second set of models, including "rationalizability" (Bernheim, 1984) and "correlated" equilibrium (Aumann, 1987), ignores the past behavior of particular actors and focuses exclusively on information about the payoffs in the game. In these models strategic actors use their understanding of existing payoffs and their knowledge of the rationality and the information possessed by their opponents to establish expectations about these opponents' strategy.

These different models reveal the problems confronting social actors in their attempt to establish shared expectations. In relationships like the family, repeated play with the same players dictates a primary focus on past play, that is, the history of the behavior of the members of the group. In relationships like those in many economic activities, repeated play with a changing set of players dictates a primary focus on the structure of the payoffs. Milgrom and Roberts point out the weaknesses of both approaches. In past-play approaches, "best reply" reasoning places too much emphasis on the recent past, ignoring the information from any previous plays; "fictitious play" reasoning places too much emphasis on the distant past, weighting the first play equally with the last and ignoring the possibility that others also learn in the process of repeated play. Payoff-oriented approaches ignore whatever information can be deduced from the relationship between payoffs and the types of players who tend to seek them. For social actors seeking to stabilize their expectations in common social situations, excessive reliance on any single type of information can produce either a delay in convergence or convergence on an outcome inferior to the one that they might otherwise prefer. Milgrom

A bargaining theory of emergence and change

and Roberts conclude that a "sophisticated" learning model would allow strategic actors to incorporate each of these types of information.

Because most of the relationships from which social institutions emerge do in fact involve some mixture of these different types of learning, we should concentrate on the kinds of information that will be most effective in such a sophisticated reasoning process. Doing so will allow me to show why we would expect asymmetries in power, if they exist, to generate decentralized emergence. If institutions are to arise out of bargaining interactions, then we should anticipate the following emergence process. Individual bargaining is resolved by the commitments of those who enjoy a relative advantage in substantive resources. Through a series of interactions with various members of the group, actors with similar resources establish a pattern of successful action in a particular type of interaction. As others recognize that they are interacting with one of the actors who possess these resources, they adjust their strategies to achieve their best outcome given the anticipated commitments of others. Over time rational actors continue to adjust their strategies until an equilibrium is reached. As this becomes recognized as the socially expected combination of equilibrium strategies, a self-enforcing social institution is established.

To support this scenario, I suggest three reasons that information related to power asymmetries is more likely than other kinds of information are to resolve the recognition problem. First, the substantive resources that determine power asymmetries can, on average, be more easily observed than can other kinds of information. In a single interaction, resource-holding information can be observed more easily than can information about the motivations of the actors, including information about their understanding of the payoffs' logic. Because of this, Maynard-Smith concludes that the very observability of resource-holding power reinforces the credibility of the commitments on which it is based (1982: 147–8).

Second, the kind of resource-holding power most likely to resolve repeated bargaining interactions is power possessed similarly by a substantial segment of the population; that is, power based on resources that are systematically distributed in a society. Note that this is an argument about frequency. In a wide-ranging set of interactions, convergence on a particular way of solving a bargaining problem ought to result from the factor that most often resolves individual problems. If resource-holding power is distributed systematically in a society, that form of power should be the factor most frequently resolving such problems. Such resources identify characteristic divisions within a population and correlate power asymmetries with those divisions. In a dynamic process of multiple-bargaining interactions, this relationship between power

143

asymmetries and recognizable differences among the actors simplifies the adjustment process.

Third, because resource-holding power determines the breakdown values in the bargaining problem, commitments based on power asymmetries produce information that correlate player types, strategies, and payoffs. If we accept the Milgrom and Roberts conception of the sophisticated learning problem, the information generated by asymmetries in power should be most likely to converge expectations toward stable combinations, because the kinds of information affecting strategic expectations which are transmitted in different learning environments reinforce one another. Commitments, breakdown values, and the characteristics of the actors with whom we are involved each reinforce expectations about future strategies. The main implication of this correlation is that strategy combinations generated by asymmetries in power are the most salient feature of the bargaining process. Together, these three reasons suggest that the asymmetries of power characterizing fundamental cleavages in a society form the basis of the recognition process.

Although the learning and adjustment process is akin to that found in the standard evolutionary theories, there is a crucial difference among the approaches: The underlying mechanism that produces the institution is fundamentally different. This strategic-conflict approach is grounded in the ability of social actors to constrain the actions of others through a commitment to a future course of action. The standard evolutionary approach is based on the arbitrary development of social institutions through tacit coordination on salient features in the interaction's structure. Although the learning process may be similar – such as Schotter's model (1981) of a Bayesian learning procedure – the motivation for the adjustment in strategies is different. One approach explains the final form of the institution in terms of the interests of those capable of future commitment; the other approach explains it in terms of the unconscious movement toward an arbitrarily prominent outcome. One depends crucially on the asymmetries of power in a society; the other does not.

The various examples of self-enforcing institutions examined earlier can be explained using this recognition process: family and gender relations, through the asymmetries between men and women; weights and measures, through the asymmetries among lords, merchants, and peasants; and collective bargaining, through the asymmetries between workers and management. Consider one example in more detail: the origin of the informal labor–management bargaining rules in many western European nations. The development of centralized collective bargaining between labor and firm associations can be seen as an emerging pattern of strategies originating at the individual firm level (Sturmthal, 1972). As workers began to organize at the plant level and to commit to a collective-bargaining strategy for individual contract negotiations, firms increasingly recognized this as a set pattern of worker behavior. Because the workers' power derived from their significant level of organization, the firm's response to this strategy was to accept union negotiations but to strengthen its own collective associations. This spiral of collectivization was advanced by a centralization of local union organizations. Over time both workers and capitalists recognized a set of bargaining institutions that were respected without reference to external sanctions.

In summary, this bargaining theory of institutional development explains the spontaneous emergence of informal networks of rules that form the basis of society. In doing so, it also explains how these rules can come to embody and reinforce the underlying asymmetries characterizing a society: between sexes, races, classes, age groups, and so forth. It demonstrates that although rules emerge from a decentralized process, this does not mean that they are arbitrary and that they do not reflect the interests of the actors involved. This is an explanation of decentralized emergence that invokes the reality of distributional conflict: Institutions emerge as the by-product of substantive conflicts. The key empirical conditions necessary for the theory to work are systematic distributional consequences of informal rules, systematic asymmetries of power in a society, and a network of common and repeated social interactions.

Spontaneous change

The distributional effects of this informal network of rules produce an ongoing tension that threatens its stability and creates incentives for continuous institutional change. Yet contrary to the conclusions of many who study the rationality of social institutions (McKelvey and Ordeshook, 1984; Riker, 1980), institutional change is not easily accomplished. Such change entails changing expectations throughout a group or society; it requires those actors who can commit to a future course of action to shift the equilibrium outcome on which social actors expect others to focus. My analysis here suggests the following conditions for institutional change: *A change in the informal rules of a society can be generated by changes in either the distributional consequences of those rules or the relative bargaining power of the actors.*

Changes in distributional consequences affect actors' preferences for social institutions, which affect the actors' incentives to undertake institutional change. There is always, of course, an incentive for those disadvantaged by the status quo to change institutions. But there are two important changes in distributional consequences that increase the incentives for change. First, the external conditions and circumstances producing the benefits of social outcomes can change. Here I have in mind

145

any factor influencing the production of social outcomes other than the actors' strategy choices. For example, either external economic conditions or technologies may change, affecting a firm's level of profits and producing new ways of structuring its activities (North, 1990). Second, the existing institutional arrangement may produce distributional effects that were not anticipated by the actors involved. Dominant actors may pursue a substantive strategy that produces differences between short-term and long-term effects. The long-term effects may be unintended, but they affect the benefits produced by social institutions. For example, marriage rules were changed in Canton Province in China in the late nineteenth century (from delayed-transfer marriage to compensation marriage) when the existing practices were found to produce a demand for jobs that conflicted with economic productivity in the dominant sericulture industry (Stockard, 1989). Both of these forms of change can affect the ways in which different institutional alternatives produce distributional benefits, creating the possibility that a new institutional rule will be preferred to the status quo. If the changes work to the detriment of those actors who have the resources to shift the group to a new equilibrium outcome, then a change in the social institution is possible.

Changes in the actors' relative bargaining power can also precipitate institutional change. Such change can come about because of a change in resource-holding power external to the specific social institution. But remember that such a change must be systematic throughout the society. Honore (1981) provides evidence of efforts by Roman women to avoid the effects of the restrictive marriage and property rules. Those women who had private resource-holding power went to court to plead their own cases and establish private arrangements outside the restrictive rules. Some were quite successful, although these new arrangements did not precipitate a change in the basic institutions. We can explain this by the fact that there were no systematic changes in the relative bargaining position of women in Roman society.

Or a shift in relative bargaining power can occur because those members of society with less resource-holding power affect the other options available to more powerful actors. From the perspective of an individual social actor, this implies the following calculus of interests. An actor's best individual strategy is to comply with the social institutions, even though she would prefer other alternative arrangements: She cannot do better for herself by unilaterally changing her strategy. But she can achieve a more favorable institutional arrangement if she can coordinate her strategy with others who share her institutional preferences. To make this strategy individually rational, she must be confident that a sufficient number of those who are similarly situated will also select it. If such coordination is possible, then both the relationship of interests and the

146

asymmetries of power change, and a change in social institutions is possible. This latter effect means some kind of oligopolic behavior on the part of resource-poor actors, an extremely difficult collective-action problem.

More generally, this last discussion emphasizes the principal obstacle to decentralized institutional change: resolving problems of collective action. It is a problem inherent in any attempt to alter existing institutional arrangements, and it explains why neither a preference for new institutions nor shifts in power may lead to immediate change through a decentralized process. For institutions such as these, for which recognition emerges slowly from repeated substantive conflicts, the process of changing expectations is considerable. It requires repeating the emergence process developed in this chapter: (1) recognition of the changes in either consequences or power, (2) efforts at change at the level of the individual interaction, and (3) a gradual shift in strategy to the new equilibrium combination, leading to convergence on a newly recognized rule. This process is made even more difficult by the fact that unlike the case of initial emergence when expectations are not fixed on a particular rule, change requires persuading social actors to alter an expectation that is now fixed.[14]

A closer analysis of the risk involved in efforts to change expectations and thus change an informal social institution suggests what kinds of decentralized change are more likely. Consider the logic of strategic decision making in this situation by referring to Table 5.1. For example, the status quo may be an informal rule dictating that *A* players choose *R* and *B* players choose *L*. Remember that an actor's strategic choice is determined by the expected utility of the various choices available to her, and the expected utility of any particular choice depends in part on the probabilities she places on the actions of those with whom she interacts. When an informal institution exists, it stabilizes expectations and establishes an actor's probabilities.

In this example, the status-quo rule informs player *B* that *A* players will choose *R* with a probability approaching 1. This probability makes the expected utility of choosing *L* the rational choice for *B*. Now, if a *B* player wants to change the status quo to a new institutional rule (say one in which *A* players choose *L* and *B* players *R*), she will be confronted with the fact that a change in her strategy will not be in her self-interest unless the probability of an *A* player's choosing *L* exceeds some threshold, say p_c, that will make her expected utility of choosing *R* greater than that of choosing *L*. If we interpret these probabilities as I suggested earlier, as percentages of the population of *A* players choosing a particular

---

14 For a related discussion of the relationship between social expectations and changes in cultural symbols, see Johnson, 1991.

strategy, the problem of institutional change for B players can be formulated as follows: At a minimum, get the threshold percentage, p_c, of A players to switch to the L strategy. Unless such a shift can be achieved, the pursuit of a new institutional rule will not be to the benefit of B players.

By focusing on the effects of different changes in conditions (either in bargaining power or in distributional consequences) on the threshold values for change, we can develop some measure of the risk involved in attempts at decentralized change and, through that, measure some sense of the more likely types of change. In doing so we can follow the same procedure used in the previous analysis of power asymmetries and establish these threshold values by calculating the mixed-strategies of the various actors. In the example in Table 5.1, the relevant threshold probability for B players is the probability,

$$p_c = (x - \Delta_B) / (2x + \epsilon_B - 2\Delta_B)$$

that A players will choose L.

First, consider the effects of changes in bargaining power. If, for example, we take

$$\partial p_c / \partial \Delta_B = -\epsilon_B / (2x + \epsilon_B - 2\Delta_B)^2$$

we will find a negative relationship between an actor's bargaining power and the threshold value for change. That is, as a B player's power increases, the percentage of A players playing L necessary for B's R strategy to give her the higher expected utility will decrease.[15] The implications of this effect of changes in bargaining power differ depending on whether the social actors are advantaged or disadvantaged by the status-quo rule. On the one hand, if the bargaining power of the more powerful members of society increases, it will have the effect of increasing the stability of the status quo. Unless the more powerful groups in a society also recognize the existence of a new institutional form that will give them additional benefits, the increase in their power will reinforce their preferred institutional arrangement, the status quo.

On the other hand, if the bargaining power of the less powerful group in a society increases, it will have the effect of diminishing the threshold necessary for the less powerful actors to change the status quo. If we abstract out for the moment the effects of changes in an institution's distributional consequences, the relative effects of changes in bargaining power will do one of two things: reinforce the status quo or shift the relative bargaining asymmetries in the direction of those institutional forms more favorable to the less powerful groups under the status quo.

15 Note that a similar relationship exists for A players.

Table 5.2(a). *Institutional change favoring*
the more powerful

Player A	Player B	
	L	L'
R'	Δ_A, Δ_B	$x + \epsilon'_A, x$
R	$x + \epsilon_A, x$	Δ_A, Δ_B

Thus, in seeking to explain decentralized change, the more likely effects of changes in bargaining power are in the direction of changes to the advantage of the less powerful members of the society, in the direction, that is, of redistributive change.

Second, consider the effects of changes in the distributional consequences of feasible institutional rules. If, for example, we take

$$\partial p_c / \partial \epsilon_B = (\Delta_B - x) / (2x + \epsilon_B - 2\Delta_B)^2$$

we will find that because $x > \Delta_B$, there is a negative relationship between an increase in the favorable distributional consequences of a new rule and the threshold value for change. That is, as the favorable distributional consequences of a new rule increases, the percentage of A players playing L necessary for B's R strategy to give her the higher expected utility will decrease.[16]

To assess the general implications of this relationship, we need to consider two different situations. The first is a change in circumstances that introduces a new institutional rule producing greater benefits for those advantaged by the status quo. The structure of such an interaction is illustrated in Table 5.2(a): The status quo is a rule having the strategy combination R,L, and the new institutional rule, which will produce additional benefits for the A players, has the strategy combination R',L'. The second situation is the existence of an institutional rule that produces greater benefits for those disadvantaged by the status quo. The structure of such an interaction is illustrated in Table 5.2(b): The status quo is a rule having the strategy combination R,L, and the new institutional rule, which will produce additional benefits for the B players, has the strategy combination L',R'. In both situations, the greater the increase is in benefits available from an institutional change, the lower the threshold will be for change necessary to accomplish that change.

In determining what types of decentralized change are more likely, the relevant question is whether the effects of improved distributional

16 Note again that a similar relationship exists for A players.

Table 5.2(b). *Institutional change favoring
the less powerful*

Player A	B	
	L	*R'*
L'	Δ_A, Δ_B	$x, x + \epsilon'_B$
R	$x + \epsilon_A, x$	Δ_A, Δ_B

consequences are greater in one of these two cases. The answer rests in a comparison of the two thresholds for change:

$$p_c = (x + \epsilon_A - \Delta_A) / (2x + \epsilon'_A + \epsilon_A - 2\Delta_A)$$

for those favored by the status quo, that is, Table 5.2(a), and

$$p_c = (x - \Delta_B) / (2x + \epsilon'_B - 2\Delta_B)$$

for those disfavored by the status quo, that is, Table 5.2(b). When these thresholds are equal, the effects of improved distributional consequences are the same. It turns out that the thresholds are equal when the relative gains from institutional change are equal. That is, if

$$[(x + \epsilon_A) - \Delta_A] / [(x + \epsilon'_A) - \Delta_A] = [x - \Delta_B] / [(x + \epsilon'_B) - \Delta_B]$$

the effects of the increased distributional consequences will be the same for both of the cases.

When they are not equal, the actor who achieves the greater proportional increase in benefits from a change in institutional form has the lower threshold for change. This suggests that those who are advantaged by the status quo must face a greater absolute increase in benefits from the new institutional form than do those disadvantaged by the status quo, in order for the thresholds of change to be the same. If we abstract out for the moment the effects of changes in bargaining power, the relative effects of changes in the distributional consequences of feasible institutional rules will depend on the relative magnitude of the potential increases in benefits. It will take a smaller absolute increase in the potential benefits of those disadvantaged by the status quo to enable a comparable decrease in the threshold values for change. Thus, given the somewhat greater risk facing those advantaged by the status quo, this analysis suggests that distributional changes are more likely to produce institutional changes that benefit the less advantaged groups under the status quo.

To summarize, under any circumstances the process of decentralized institutional change is difficult. In the best of circumstances the difficulty in changing expectations indicates that institutional change lags behind the changes in the interests of the social actors. Now I acknowledge that the complexity of this problem prevents us from making definitive assertions about the direction of decentralized institutional change. But this brief analysis of the effects of external conditions on the logic of strategic decision making implies that the changes in both bargaining power and distributional consequences more readily and more positively affect the task of those who are disadvantaged by the status quo. When we combine the effects of both sets of conditions, we can reasonably expect that *in those instances in which we see spontaneous institutional change, it is redistributive.*[17]

A COMPARATIVE ANALYSIS: THE EMERGENCE OF RULES OF PROPERTY DIVISION

Conflicts over property exist in all societies. The resolution of disputed claims is fundamental to maintaining ongoing social relationships. As groups repeatedly confront interactions that generate disputes, they institutionalize criteria for resolving them. The failure to develop such criteria can lead to serious breakdowns in social interaction.

Such rules are found in primitive as well as in more developed societies. In primitive societies, elaborate social rules have been devised to facilitate social and economic interactions. In more developed societies, such social rules were originally established to resolve problems not adequately covered by the emerging legal system. Initially, these rules were enacted informally through a decentralized process, and they became self-enforcing procedures. Over time, many of these rules were translated into legal prescriptions, especially in more advanced societies. Once these rules became law, they were reinforced by an external agent who sanctioned deviations.

Consider the following problems:

1. A ship on the high seas encounters a threatening storm. In order to save the ship, the captain orders that the cargo belonging to A be thrown overboard. The cargoes of B and C are saved.

2. A, B, and C are creditors of T, whose assets are insufficient to satisfy all three of their claims.

3. T dies without a will. A, B, and C are T's surviving children. D is T's wife. Each of them claims to be the true and rightful beneficiary of T's estate.

Each of these examples shares a similar problem related to the division of property: How do we resolve claims to a piece of property when the sum

17 I continue this discussion of the stability of informal rules in Chapter 6.

of the valid claims exceeds the available property from which they are to be satisfied? If the sum of the claims is greater than the available property, what should the rule of division be?

Societies have established social rules for resolving each of these types of problems. In this section I consider the emergence and the path of change of these informal rules. Each problem is characterized by a set of possible rules which would resolve the property dispute; the different alternatives are characterized by disproportionate distributional effects. This gives us an opportunity to contrast the important elements of the different theories of institutional change. For the theory of social conventions, we focus on the possibility of cross-cutting effects. For the theory of exchange and competition, we focus on the existence of competition, as either a selection mechanism or a constraint on relative bargaining power. For the bargaining theory we focus on the existence of systematic features in a society, both asymmetries of power and the distributional consequences of institutional rules, which are reflected in the rules.

Basic property rights are particularly good examples for comparing the different theories of spontaneous emergence and change, because they are the types of rules that the standard theories are best equipped to explain. Here we can best see the strengths and weaknesses of the standard approaches and determine in what ways their explanations are enhanced by invoking distributional concerns. If the introduction of distribution and power is relevant to the property rights case, there should be little doubt of their importance in explaining the wide range of social institutions whose emergence more clearly lacks the necessary empirical conditions in order for the standard theories to apply.

These extended histories allow us to concentrate on explanations of both emergence and change (and the particular problem of redistributive change). Through this analysis I can demonstrate how the bargaining theory is based on less restrictive conditions and is, therefore, a more general theory. The standard approaches are special cases of this theory: the theory of social conventions as a case when there are no systematic distributional effects and the theory of exchange and competition as a case when there are no systematic asymmetries of power.

Problem 1: The "general average" problem

For over two thousand years the question of jettisoned cargo has been a source of conflict over property rights. The circumstances that originally led to the conflict are quite simple. Merchants presented their cargo to a ship's captain whose responsibility it was to transport it to the destination of purchase. But ships were often confronted with catastrophic

152

events that could cause the loss of the ship, cargo, and crew. In these moments of emergency the captain and the crew were forced to make decisions concerning the safety of the ship. One of the standard procedures was to jettison some or all of the cargo in an effort to lighten the ship. If the ship was saved, when it reached its destination, representatives of the merchants were left with only a percentage of their anticipated cargo (or nothing at all).

The basic question was who should bear the loss that all agreed was necessary to save the ship? If A's cargo were jettisoned in the emergency, could he look to merchants B and C for indemnification? What about the shipowner or the captain and crew? Furthermore, what about other extraordinary damages that the ship might have suffered in the process of saving the remaining cargo and the voyage itself? These additional damages – which came to be considered part of the more general problem of losses for the "common benefit" (Gilmore and Black, 1957; Lowndes and Rudolf, 1975) – could be subject to indemnification from the remaining cargo. Considered in general terms, the problem of property division involved the merchants and the ship's personnel (including owner, captain, and crew), each of whom wanted to end the voyage with his share of the property. Yet there was not enough property between cargo and ship to satisfy the claims.

Original discussions of the problem can be found as far back as the Old Testament and the Babylonian Talmud.[18] It was a problem acknowledged by all ancient societies involved in maritime commerce. The contributory issue was addressed in the Rhodian Sea Laws, in which it was enlarged to take account of losses due to causal damages as well as those of voluntary jettison. Although there was no specific mention of the nature of the contributions, the problem was described generally as one of mutual insurance (Felde, 1953: 411). The Rules of Oleron suggested that such losses be resolved through some ratable contribution of the parties, but the specific shares were not mentioned (Gilmore and Black, 1957: 220). In the sixth century, the Digest of Justinian reports that losses due to jettisoned cargo were to be resolved by the "contribution of all" (Gilmore and Black, 1957: 220), but it is not clear what the ship's responsibilities were to this contribution (Selmer, 1958: 21–3).

It is apparent from these texts that the underlying premise was that the loss of jettisoned cargo was a problem shared by all of the merchants. Some type of contribution was required, but the extent to which the shipowner would contribute was open to question. Selmer states that from antiquity to the medieval period it was standard procedure for the

---

18 Two short but illuminating accounts of the historical development of solutions to this problem are those by Barclay (1891) and Felde (1953).

shipowner not to contribute (1958: 45), but others are less certain about the ship's responsibility (Felde, 1953). Although the specific rate of contribution differed in various locations, the basic rule for dividing the surviving property became known as the rule of *general average*, a method of calculating loss according to the relative value of the parties' initial contribution to the overall enterprise.

This general average solution reflected a sense of common interest among those involved in maritime commerce in its infancy. Selmer points out that this sense of shared interest began to decline in the Middle Ages, owing to both an increase in specialization in maritime commerce and the introduction of marine insurance (1958: 40–5). Yet despite the decline of this shared interest, the issue of jettisoned cargo continued to be treated as a general average problem.

In the modern period the rules of most maritime nations have continued to treat jettisoned cargo as a joint catastrophe but differ on the rate of contribution of the relevant actors. All countries usually expand the problem to include damages to the ship suffered in the process of saving the vessel and the cargo. In the nineteenth century, some maritime legal scholars tried to change the rule to bring it in line with the general method of treating loss at sea (each bears his own loss unless fault can be established), but their efforts failed. More recently, representatives from most of those nations active in maritime commerce have met in a series of conferences (1890, 1924, 1949) in an effort to standardize national variations. The resulting guidelines, known as the York–Antwerp Rules, establish a general average solution with ratable contributions from both cargo owners and shipowners. Although most of the countries whose rules deviate from this criterion have refrained from adopting the York–Antwerp Rules, these provisions are regularly incorporated into shipping contracts among merchants and carriers (Gilmore and Black, 1958; Lowndes and Rudolf, 1975).

In analyzing the effects of this property rule on maritime affairs, three alternative formulations must be considered: (1) each bears his own loss, (2) pure general average, and (3) variations on pure general average. The first alternative, known as the *particular average* rule, is the general solution for problems of maritime loss in nonvoluntary cases (Paulsen, 1983; Yasgoor, 1977). That is, unless fault can be attributed to another actor, losers of property are forced to suffer without indemnification. This rule distributes the remaining property strictly in terms of prior right: Each party retains whatever percentage of his or her original property survives. Although this could be a stable rule if established (and it has been in most other areas of maritime affairs), it is not currently used in any modern society.

The second alternative, the general average, divides the remaining property in such a way as to "insure that all shall have suffered equally": "The value of each of the contributing interests is multiplied by a fraction which has as its numerator the sum of the general average expense and has as its denominator the sum of the contributing values" (Gilmore and Black, 1958: 222). In its pure form, general average exacts contributions from each cargo owner, the shipowner, and the owner of the freight, which is the compensation that the shipowner receives for transporting the goods. To understand the effects of general average, consider the following simplified example taken from Gilmore and Black. To avoid a catastrophe during a voyage, a ship voluntarily incurs general average expenses (all expenses for the common benefit) totaling $115,000 ($100,000 in jettisoned cargo, $10,000 in lost freight, and $5,000 in damages to the ship). The losses must be distributed among the cargo, the ship, and the freight, which had prevoyage values of $1 million, $1 million, and $100,000, respectively. Each interest must bear a loss in an amount equal to (115,000/2.1 million) times its original value, which amounts to a loss of $54,761.90 each for the cargo and the ship and $5,476.20 for the freight. The general average distribution is completed by requiring the shipowner to indemnify the cargo owners for their excessive loss. Here, the equality in the definition of general average refers not to the same amount of loss but, rather, to the same proportion of loss relative to the value of the initial contribution. This pure general average approach has been adopted in the United States, Great Britain, and the Netherlands, among other nations, as well as in the York–Antwerp Rules.

The third alternative consists of variations on the general average approach. The variations affect the share of the contributions required of the three main interests. The general average apportionment rule is used, but the initial interests are weighted according to their relative contributions. The result is an unequal distribution of the proportional losses borne by the parties. For example, the French commercial codes have always recognized a smaller contribution from shipowners than from cargo owners who have suffered losses (Felde, 1953: 417). Similar rules tend to favor the ship or freight contributions in several countries influenced by either the French or German traditions: one-half from the ship (France, Italy), one-half from the freight (Belgium, Scandinavia), and two-thirds from the freight (Germany, Brazil, Turkey).[19]

19 More detailed descriptions of the developments of differences among the rules of maritime nations can be found in Felde, 1953, and Lowndes and Rudolf, 1975. Great Britain has an interesting variation that is limited to cases in which fault can somehow be attributed to one of the parties. If it can be determined that the negligence of one of the parties was responsible for the catastrophe that led to the "general average" sacrifice, that party will be precluded from receiving indemnification.

Some rule for dividing losses for the "common benefit" was necessary for maritime commerce. If a rule had not been agreed on, the continuing conflict among the relevant actors would have caused serious harm to this commerce (especially before the introduction of marine insurance). Yet although all of the parties have an interest in some rule of division, the distributional effects of the different alternatives suggest that the parties might prefer different formulations. This shows that the general average problem can be characterized as a bargaining problem among the different actors on any one voyage.

In explaining the emergence of the maritime rules that came to apply throughout a society, we should note that no rule was cross-cutting for all of the actors and that the one rule that was cross-cutting for the cargo owners did not evolve. The different alternatives produced systematic distributional effects in maritime affairs, indicating that the bargaining model might also explain the emergence of a general rule. We can see this by looking at the preferences of the different actors. The general average approach seems at first to be an equitable solution to the problem. Everyone who benefits from the joint enterprise of the voyage suffers a ratable share of the loss. But the historical evidence suggests that general average has hurt the shipowners and benefited the merchants (Gilmore and Black, 1958; Selmer, 1958). The major cause of this harm has been the difficulty of incorporating many of the ship's losses into the general average expense. Therefore, although the shipowner is responsible for indemnifying a share of the merchant's full loss, he is not in fact fully indemnified for his total expenses. This discrepancy suggests why the shipowners would prefer one of the variations on the general average rule, which, in principle, seems to favor the shipowner at the expense of the cargo owners. The third alternative, the particular average rule with its emphasis on each party's bearing its own loss, would probably be the least preferred by the merchants but might be the most preferred by the shipowners.

In regard to the cargo owners, any of the rules would be acceptable, as the particular average rule would be cross-cutting. In any particular instance of loss, the particular average might treat the cargo owners more or less favorably (this is contingent on the extent of their own losses), but over time the probability that any merchant would end up on either side of the loss ledger is fairly equal. For the shipowners, however, the rules are not cross-cutting, as the distributional effects would always be the same in each instance of loss under a given rule. The extent to which they would attempt to affect the establishment of a particular rule depends in the end on the extent to which they are adversely affected by the general average approach.

The emergence of rules to resolve what has come to be known as the *general average problem* can be explained by the existence of asymmetries of power in the maritime world. But here we also see the effects of competition on relative bargaining power. The earliest rules appear to have favored the shipowners. This is consistent with the relative power advantage enjoyed by early shipowners: They owned the ships; they were willing to accept the personal risks; and they were few in number. Shipowners could announce in advance that they would accept cargo only from those cargo owners who would accept responsibility for any losses that might ensue. Because the cargo owners had no other alternatives, they would be better off accepting these terms than they would be if they failed to ship their cargo. In fact, this bargaining scenario resulted in either a particular average or a general average minus the shipowner-contribution rule. As the cargo owners came to be able to choose from a number of shipowners, the relative bargaining advantage of the shipowners was reduced. Cargo owners now could force a shipowner to accept terms that would divide responsibility for loss among the cargo owners and the shipowner. And this changed the rules along the lines of general average, which includes a contribution from the shipowner.

Competition is relevant in this case because the actors are interchangeable and the range of strategies is closer to a continuous distribution. The interchangeability worked to the benefit of the cargo owners, increasing their breakdown values by enlarging their outside options in the event that bargaining with a particular shipowner failed. The fact that the indemnification for losses could in principle be distributed along a continuous range strengthened the effects of competition on bargaining power.

The existence of competition, however, has not ruled out the importance of such power. Why has the rule for jettisoned cargo not changed to the particular average rule that resolves most issues in maritime affairs? Describing the general average rule as a continuous range fails to capture the importance of the decision as to what losses are to be covered by indemnification. As we see in the jettisoned case, this decision has historically worked to the detriment of shipowners. The existence of general average rules that disfavor shipowners can be explained by the relative power of the cargo owners. They prefer these rules to a change to a particular average alternative that they can offset with marine insurance, because the general average rule tends to extract a greater contribution from shipowners than they get back in indemnification.

Problem 2: Bankruptcy

What appears to be a simple case of too many debts and too few assets produces several problems for ongoing economic interactions. Not only must some provision be made for the continuing economic activities of the debtor, but several issues affecting the relationship of the creditors to the insufficient assets also must be considered.[20] A debtor who has an incentive to enter into preferential agreements with individual creditors may complicate this problem of property division. Because the debtor is concerned about his own future economic status, such preferential agreements may give him an opportunity to acquire additional resources or, at the very least, improve his postinsolvency prospects. These concerns motivate the debtor to offer additional security to a creditor in exchange for a break on the creditor's outstanding claim, a security that may give the individual creditor an advantage over other claimants. Indeed, this problem of collusion has led some to argue that one reason for establishing rules to govern this problem is to protect the creditors from one another (Gessner et al., 1978; Levinthal, 1919). Let me set aside for now the problem of fraudulent preferences (I shall consider the stability of self-enforcing rules in the next chapter) and address the more general problem: How do we divide the insolvent's remaining assets among the creditors' valid claims?

Throughout history the problem of unpaid debts has been the subject of various rules governing creditors' rights. The earliest discussions of a solution to the problem can be found in such ancient documents as the Code of Hammurabi and the Twelve Tables of Rome (Dalhuisen, 1968: 6–7; Levinthal, 1919: 230–1). Creditors were allowed to take action directly against debtors, either enslaving them or killing them. Obviously this approach was a difficult way for multiple creditors to satisfy their claims! A more acceptable solution developed as an extension of execution of the person – execution of the person's available assets. Early attempts at devising criteria governing such executions are discussed in the Babylonian Talmud and in various documents describing Roman debt procedures (Aumann and Meschler, 1985; Levinthal, 1919: 232).

Two general approaches were devised, each of which has had a lasting influence on modern rules and procedures. The first approach was execution by individual creditors. Each creditor would seek satisfaction for his or her own claim. If the debtor became insolvent, the remaining assets would be used to satisfy all outstanding claims according to some designated criterion for ranking the individual creditors (Levinthal, 1919: 233–4). One criterion for ranking was "first come – first served"; that is, the claims were satisfied in the order in which the debts were incurred. For example, such procedures were found in ancient Jewish and Indian communities. Another criterion was to satisfy the claims in

20 For intelligent and concise accounts of the underlying logic of the problem of creditors' rights and bankruptcy, see Levinthal, 1919, Radin, 1940, and Gessner, Rhode, Strate, and Ziegert, 1978.

the order in which individual creditors sought payment as the debtor's insolvency became apparent, a procedure found in early Germanic systems. Eventually, various societies began to rank creditors according to specific features of their claims.

The second approach, originating in Rome, was a general execution in which all of the creditors joined in seeking satisfaction of their claims. The general execution took one of two forms. There is evidence from as early as 118 B.C. that creditors satisfied their claims by accepting a percentage of the proceeds from the sale of the debtor's assets (Countryman, 1976: 226). Although the records are unclear as to the exact distribution of percentages among the creditors, Jones (1979:12) observes that these general sales and distributions were one of the first attempts to achieve equality among the claims. These early insolvency sales were the first recorded instances of what eventually became the modern process of bankruptcy. In the first century A.D. a second method of general execution was established. During this period creditors came together and negotiated their own distribution of the debtor's assets (Levinthal, 1919: 235–6). Any division of property was possible under this bargaining procedure, which was the precursor of the modern procedure of composition.[21]

From these early procedures a variety of rules developed, but they were basically variations on two features of the original procedures: the ranking of creditors by common characteristics and the joint division of assets according to a percentage of their original claims. There is little available evidence of the further development of these rules from this early period until after the Middle Ages.[22] After this period, however, there is evidence of these rules being significantly expanded throughout the

21 Although the institutionalization of the composition has offered modern creditors a strategic alternative to bankruptcy in many countries, they did not initiate the original procedures. These negotiated arrangements were initially proposed by debtors as a way of avoiding the embarrassment and humiliation of public insolvency and as a way of possibly salvaging something from their remaining assets. Dalhuisen (1968) offers an excellent account of the history of the institution of composition and an exhaustive comparative analysis of modern composition procedures in western Europe and the United States. Under most modern procedures, either the debtor or a group of creditors can propose a composition as an alternative to bankruptcy. If a majority of the creditors (in both number and size of the shares of their claims) approve the proposed distribution, the composition will be binding on the creditors as a whole. The procedures of the various nations differ on the percentage of shares of the total debt required for approval of the composition and on the effect of the composition vote on the validity of the claims of secured creditors.

22 In fact, this lack of further development leads Dalhuisen (1968) to assert that modern bankruptcy and composition rules are more closely related to Renaissance insolvency laws than to those of the Roman period. Other writers maintain the close relationship between the ancient rules and modern procedures (Countryman, 1976; Jones, 1979; Levinthal, 1919). The substantial evidence of numerous similarities suggests that the standard interpretation of a close relationship is more accurate.

developing commercial nations. Although some nations put greater emphasis on the ranking of priority creditors (e.g., France until the late sixteenth century, Germany until the late seventeenth century) and others focused more on the equality of claims (e.g., Italy and Britain), all established rules for cooperatively resolving the problem of the insolvent debtor.[23] Although the nations differed on the circumstances under which these rules became applicable (e.g., which types of debtors would be covered by the bankruptcy procedures and what the effect of these procedures was on the debtor's remaining liability), the rules governing the division of assets settled into a basic pattern. Subsequent developments have emphasized the establishment of different priorities among the categories of creditors.

The bankruptcy problem can be characterized as an instance of bargaining among creditors. If the creditors are involved in ongoing financial interactions in a community, they will be better off establishing a rule of division than relying on a destructive fight for assets that might be devalued in the process. The alternative division rules affect distributional outcomes, but the extent to which the effects are systematic or cross-cutting depends on the likelihood that the different categories of creditors will be systematically distributed. To compare the alternative rules of division, we can consider rules that vary within the two main criteria of priority ranking and proportional distribution. There are three alternatives: (1) rules ranking creditors according to some criterion, (2) rules first ranking creditors by class and then satisfying claims within a class by some proportional distribution, and (3) rules satisfying claims simply by some proportional distribution. That these procedures produce different patterns of claim satisfaction should be obvious. These differences can be clarified by comparing the two extreme cases, simple priority ranking and simple proportional division.

The simple priority ranking favors some creditors over others based on an established criterion. I mentioned earlier the historical examples of a "first-come–first-served" criterion for priority ranking. The most prevalent modern criterion for ranking is based on the secured–unsecured feature of most claims.[24] The rule generally provides for first satisfying the claims of secured creditors and only then satisfying unsecured claims (Fama and Miller, 1972; White, 1980). If the assets are exhausted by se-

---

23 There are detailed accounts of the history of bankruptcy rules for many countries. Short accounts of these histories can be found in Dalhuisen, 1968; for more extended discussions, see, for example, Gessner et al., 1978, or Peltzer, 1975, for Germany; Livadas, 1983, for France; Jones, 1979, Weisberg, 1986, or Boshkoff, 1982, for Great Britain; and Countryman, 1976, Boshkoff, 1982, and Weisberg, 1986, for the United States.

24 Note here that the reference is to valid secured claims and not to the fraudulent security granted by a debtor in anticipation of insolvency.

cured claims, the unsecured creditors will not be satisfied. Because the basic problem is insufficient funds to meet all of the claims, such a rule produces a distribution that disproportionately favors some creditors over others.

In considering the simple proportional division rules, several alternatives have been proposed. Aumann and Meschler (1982), in a fascinating game-theoretic study of the bankruptcy procedures in the Babylonian Talmud, look at three different rules for proportional division. The first is a pure-proportional criterion, a pro rata satisfaction based on the dollar value of the claims. The share of a creditor's reimbursement is equal to the product of the ratio of the dollar value of his own claim to the dollar value of all claims times the total available assets. The second alternative is an equal division among all creditors. Aumann and Meschler define it as a rule by which "all claimants get the same award q, except that those who claim less than q get their claims" (1982: 202). The rule "divides each additional dollar equally between those claimants who still have an outstanding claim" (p. 203). A creditor gets an equal percentage of each dollar of available assets until either his claim is satisfied or the assets are exhausted.

The third alternative is a formulation proposed by Aumann and Meschler as the bankruptcy rule contemplated by the Babylonian Talmud:

A famous Mishna (Baba Metea 2a) states: "Two hold a garment; one claims it, the other claims half. Then the one is awarded ¾, the other ¼."

The principle is clear. The lesser claimant concedes half the garment to the greater one. It is only the remaining half that is at issue; this remaining half is therefore divided equally. (1982: 198)

This procedure, the *contested garment* rule, can be stated formally in the two-person bankruptcy case. First, the creditors announce their claims, d_1 and d_2. Second, we calculate the amount of the debtor's assets, E, that each concedes to the other: Creditor 1 gets $(E - d_2)$, creditor 2 $(E - d_1)$. If the value of the concession is positive $- (E - d_i) > 0 -$ the creditor will automatically receive that amount in partial satisfaction of his claim. Third, the remainder of the assets still at issue,

$$\{E - (E - d_1)_+ - (E - d_2)_+\}$$

are divided equally among the creditors.[25] Thus, the total award for each of the creditors is equal to that conceded to him plus an equal share of the remaining contested assets:

$$x_1 = \{[E - (E - d_1)_+ - (E - d_2)_+] / 2\} + (E - d_2)_+$$

25 Note that the + subscript signifies that only positive concessions enter into the calculation of the remainder.

Aumann and Meschler extend the rule to the n-person case, adding additional criteria when necessary to produce an order-preserving outcome that ensures that those with larger claims will not receive smaller awards than do those with smaller claims.

These alternative rules of division can produce significantly different distributional outcomes. The simple priority rule favors some groups of creditors over others. Some creditors have their claims satisfied (or receive a high percentage of their claims), whereas others receive only partial satisfaction (or nothing at all). The proportional rules, on the other hand, make a greater effort to equalize the effects of insolvency. The pro rata division rule allows each creditor to suffer a loss of equal magnitude. The other two proportional division rules tend to favor certain categories of creditors. The equal division rule favors the smaller creditors by allowing them a higher proportional share of their outstanding claims than that recovered by the larger creditors. The contested garment rule favors smaller creditors when

$$E \leq (nd_1/2)$$

and favors larger creditors when

$$E \geq (D - nd_1/2)$$

where D is the sum of all outstanding claims.

The remaining alternative that I have not yet discussed is the mixed rule of ranking by class and then proportional division within each class. This is the rule adopted with some variation in virtually all modern commercial societies.[26] Creditors are ranked by class, with secured creditors receiving top priority, followed by certain categories of creditors who are given preferential status by law (e.g., tax officials, bankruptcy officials, etc.). Within each class the creditors are satisfied according to the pro rata rule of distribution. The distributional effect of this rule is similar to the simple priority rule, in which some creditors receive a greater satisfaction of their claims.

The only rule that guarantees the absence of disproportionate distributional effects is the pure pro rata division rule. Each of the other rules tends to favor a particular group of creditors. Different classes of creditors prefer different alternatives to resolve the disputes. A rule based exclusively on the equal division or the contested garment procedure would, however, be cross-cutting if we could reasonably assume that creditors sometimes find themselves with small claims and that on other

---

26 In addition to the country-specific studies of bankruptcy to which I have previously referred, detailed information on the variations within particular societies can be found in Anton, 1985, on Spain and MacNeil, 1967, on Africa.

occasions they are the larger creditors. It is more difficult to make this claim for the mixed rule or the simple priority-ranking procedure. Alan Schwartz (1981) points out that secured and unsecured creditors usually come from different segments of society. Secured creditors are more "sophisticated and relatively affluent," and unsecured creditors often are "relatively poor and unsophisticated." Creditors can require security for loans because they have the economic leverage to do so. Others, such as wage-earning employees and less significant creditors, lack the leverage to demand security as a prerequisite for providing loans or services on credit. Here we should anticipate the absence of the cross-cutting feature necessary for a theory of conventions to explain the development of property rules for dividing the assets of an insolvent debtor. The circumstances suggest that there would be conflict among the competing economic interests over establishing a particular rule of division.

The history of the emergence of bankruptcy rules is a complicated one, with a variety of rules still in force, but there is considerable evidence that this history has been marked by distributional conflict resolved by relative bargaining power. The long history of preferential treatment for some classes of creditors suggests as much. Given the disproportionate distributional consequences, efforts to commit to a particular form of division would be expected from some of the creditors. If the creditors were relatively equal in bargaining power, we would expect either a first-come–first-served or an equal-division rule. If some of the creditors were more powerful than the others, we would expect them to try to establish a procedure that would give them preference in the case of bankruptcy. That is, they would refuse to offer credit without guaranteed security. If some of the creditors have the resources to demand security and others do not, an unequal division of property would be anticipated. And this is exactly what the history of bankruptcy rules demonstrates: Over time, a dominant standard – the preference of secured creditors – emerged that favored those creditors who had the economic leverage to demand guaranteed security in individual transactions (Dalhuisen, 1968; Schwartz, 1981).

Here the relative bargaining power that affects the creditor relationship pertains to the debtor. Does a creditor have the power to demand a preference ahead of other creditors seeking the same protection? Clearly this depends on the types of resource-holding power that determine relative bargaining power. Competition can play a role in this process, but it is not as strong as in the general average case. First, the actors' interchangeability is limited. Not all creditors offer the same form of credit to borrowers: Some offer capital, whereas others offer only labor and services. To the extent that some forms of credit are more difficult to secure, they have more leverage to demand preferential treatment. Second, the rules of bankruptcy are not continuously distributed. If the only alternatives were some form of proportional distribution, they would be, but the existence of preferential treatment for some types of creditors establishes a multitiered rule that violates continuity. Such a rule is analogous to the idea of lexicographic preferences in an individual: The claims of the top tier of creditors must be satisfied before anything will be distributed to the lower levels. These factors diminish the power-diluting effects of competition and open up ways for that power to influence rules of bargaining.

Problem 3: The intergenerational transfer of property

The problem of dividing property at death is fundamental to all societies. The future security and well-being of the survivors are often contingent on the distribution. In many societies it is not only the distribution of an individual's estate to his or her heirs but also the transference of the deceased's status. This is most clearly seen in primitive societies, in which it is common for the possessor of the estate to assume the deceased's leadership positions in the community (Comaroff and Roberts, 1981; Geertz, 1982; Hoebel, 1954; Nader, 1969).

The problem of distribution typically focuses on the spouse and the children of the deceased: What is the appropriate way to distribute the deceased's estate among the closest surviving relatives? Rules governing this type of property distribution, generally known as *intestate succession,* were originally established because the option of individual testamentary distribution was either restricted or not available.[27] Later, when the general right to distribute estates by means of testamentary will was firmly established, the rules retained their importance in those situations such as Problem 3 in which a will either was not found or did not exist.

---

27 In primitive societies, the ability to transfer property by means of a will did not generally exist, although many people circumvented the community standards by distributing much of their property during their lifetime. In ancient Rome there is evidence of the widespread use of wills among the elites as a way of avoiding some of the harsher features of the succession laws (Maine, 1986; Watson, 1971). As the use of wills began to be accepted in modern Europe, they were limited to the transfer of certain parts of a person's estate. When the testamentary will developed in Britain in the fourteenth century, it was limited to the transfer of personal property (Miller, 1977). As its use became established in those Western societies emulating the Roman rules as collected in the Code of Justinian, the will was limited to those parts of the estate that were not part of the *legitime,* the assets from the estate set aside for the protection of the immediate family (Lloyd, 1877). After the use of the will was extended to real property, there was a persistent trend to exclude a certain portion of the estate for the benefit of the immediate family. These efforts to prevent the testator from disinheriting the immediate family remain today in the laws of most countries. Examples include the homestead rights in the United States, the *réserve héréditaire* in France, and the *Pflichtfeil* in Germany (Miller, 1977).

A bargaining theory of emergence and change

A simple and concise description of the historical development of intestate succession rules is hard to provide. There have been discernible
patterns of change during the social development of modern societies,
but there remain today primitive societies maintaining rules that do not
follow these modern patterns.[28] Therefore, it seems appropriate to discuss the variety of rules in primitive communities before describing the
patterns of change in modern societies. Although the rules are basically
the same, the variety still existing in the primitive societies has given way
to a greater consensus among modern nations.

The problem of property succession remains at the center of social life
in primitive societies. The source of greatest conflict in many of these
communities is the conflict over whether or not relatives qualify under
the succession rules of their society (Comaroff and Roberts, 1981; Marcus, 1981; Starr, 1978). Two general categories of rules have been established to govern the division of estates. In the first category are those
rules singling out one of the sons to receive the bulk of the estate. Most
societies that adopt such rules practice *primogeniture*, distribution to the
eldest son.[29] The extent to which the eldest son is responsible for the continued well-being of the other family members varies among these societies, but some provision for their ongoing security is generally required.
A few societies, such as a number of communities in Thailand (Hooker,
1982), practice some form of *ultimogeniture*, distribution to the young-
est son.

The second category of primitive rules of succession consists of rules
that attempt a more equitable distribution of the estate. Some, such as
the tribes in Kenya (Saltzman, 1981) and in many traditional Islamic societies (Makdisi, 1984), extend the distribution to provide for an equal
division among all of the sons. Others, from such diverse areas as the
isolated, rural communities of Turkey (Starr, 1978), tribes in Indonesia
and Batu (Hooker, 1982), and the villages of the Yoruba (Coker, 1958),
extend the distribution even further, setting aside an explicit percentage
of the estate for the daughters or the spouse.

The persistent diversity of criteria for distributing estates in primitive
societies reflects a similar variety found in the historical development of
such rules in modern Western societies. The earliest reports of intestate
succession in Rome describe rules in which the spouse and the children of
the deceased all were treated equally. The Twelve Tables explain that the

---

28 Hooker (1975) presents an interesting account of the effects of British colonialism on
    the inheritance laws of many less-developed societies. He describes in detail British ef-
    forts to change indigenous succession patterns and the considerable resistance that they
    encountered.
29 Anthropological studies of the practice of primogeniture include those by Marcus
    (1981) on the Friendly Islands, Hooker (1975) on New Guinea and Papua, and Co-
    maroff and Roberts (1981) on Tswana.

estate of a Roman citizen was divided equally among all of his children (sons and daughters) and his spouse (Watson, 1971). Maine (1986) points out that the actual application of the rules often excluded emancipated children, a possibility also indicated in legal documents discovered from the first century B.C. (Watson, 1971).

The earliest records of rules of succession after the Middle Ages portray standards of favoritism and equality established in close proximity to one another. Before the nineteenth century, the criterion for dividing estates varied widely on the continent of Europe. Intestate succession was governed by either the principle of primogeniture or a standard of equality among children. Rules of each type could be found in the different regions of individual nations (Goody, 1983; Thirsk, 1976).[30] Even in those areas in which one rule was established, members of the community often recognized other acceptable alternatives. For example, in the sixteenth and seventeenth centuries, in various parts of France and Germany where equality had become the established practice, favoritism toward the eldest son was still practiced (Berkner, 1976; Cooper, 1976; Lloyd, 1877).

In Britain, primogeniture was the dominant criterion. The rule of inheritance by the eldest son was well established as early as the thirteenth century (Miller, 1977). As the rules of succession were codified in a series of parliamentary acts in the sixteenth and seventeenth centuries, the rule of primogeniture was retained for both real and personal property. In the eighteenth century the rules were changed to require a more equitable division of a decedent's personalty (Lloyd, 1877). However, this dominance of primogeniture did not extend to the pre-Revolution American colonies. In the eighteenth century the southern colonies maintained rules of favoritism toward the eldest child, but the northern colonies commonly adopted a relatively equal division among all of the children (Alston and Schapiro, 1984). Katz (1977) states that some of the northern colonies deviated from a straight equal division by allowing a double share to the male children.

The nineteenth century was a period of change in the rules of succession in continental Europe and the United States. Primogeniture was replaced in those areas in which it had been the dominant principle by more equitable rules of property division. For example, in 1849 the Code of Napoleon explicitly prohibited primogeniture throughout France (Cooper, 1976). The new criterion usually divided the estate equally among the children and provided lifetime security for any living spouses.

---

30 For interesting accounts of the diversity of succession practices during this period, see, for example, LeRoy Ladurie, 1976, on France and Berkner, 1976, on Germany.

Similar rules of division were established throughout the United States in the early decades of the nineteenth century.[31]

Britain was the last modern nation to change its rules of intestate succession. In the 1920s the British government undertook a study of the prevailing patterns of testamentary distribution of estates (Miller, 1977), which revealed that an equal distribution of property was the overwhelmingly dominant criterion of division. This evidence of testamentary patterns of equality set the standard for the 1924 reforms in the British laws. With these changes the rule of primogeniture was no longer dominant in any modern Western society.[32]

This review of the development of rules of intestate succession reveals three alternatives for dividing property in instances such as Problem 3: (1) all of the estate to one child, (2) an unequal division with shares to some or all of the children, and (3) equality in distribution. The distributional effects of each of these rules are straightforward: The first alternative produces the starkest effects. All of the property is distributed to one child (usually the oldest living son), and the other children receive no direct ownership rights in any of the estate. The actual practice of primogeniture generally alleviated the harshness of this distribution by making the eldest son responsible for the continued maintenance of the other living children (Goody, 1983; Thirsk, 1976). But the rule itself dictates an indivisible transfer to one favored child. The second alternative, *preferential partibility* (Berkner and Mendels, 1978), produces unequal distributions but expands the number of possible heirs to at least two of the children. Examples include the rules in several American colonies giving double shares to the sons and rules distributing half of the estate to the eldest son and dividing the remaining half equally among the remaining children (Alston and Schapiro, 1984). The third alternative is the only rule that does not produce substantial distributional effects: The estate is divided equally among all of the decedent's children.[33]

---

31 Lloyd (1877) presents an exhaustive study of the rules of succession throughout "the Christian world" as of the late nineteenth century. Anyone interested in regional variations in such rules need go no further.

32 Favoritism toward male children remains the dominant rule in other societies. Although provisions are now made for partial fixed shares for daughters, Islamic rules of succession maintain a standard of preferential treatment for sons (Hooker, 1975; Makdisi, 1984).

33 Given the potential importance of the distribution of property among generations for the distribution of income and wealth in a society, the distributional effects of these rules across generations is of some interest. Several studies have used intergenerational growth models to analyze these long-term effects (see, e.g., Blinder, 1973; Menchik, 1980; Pryor, 1973; Stiglitz, 1969). Not surprisingly, these studies have demonstrated that the first rule of unigeniture tends to exacerbate income and wealth inequalities

Again we can characterize this problem of intergenerational transfer as a bargaining problem. The rules govern the distribution of assets at the death of a parent, but one of the rule's main effects is to determine the ongoing social and economic relations among parents and children. The greatest concern of all is future economic well-being: for the parents, economic security and protection through the remainder of their lives; for the children, their long-term economic prospects. One important resource for achieving these goals is the family estate. The efforts to achieve these goals can create conflicts between parent and child and among the children themselves. An explanation of the development of intestate succession rules can be found in (1) the effects of the rule on these conflicting goals and (2) the alternative sources of economic well-being for the actors.

Competition can indirectly affect the emergence of rules of intestate succession through its effects on the relative bargaining power of the children vis-à-vis the parents. If the children have sources of income other than the family estate, their bargaining power will be enhanced, and the parents must respond accordingly. But the features of interchangeability and continuity are also an issue here. For most children, not all economic alternatives are interchangeable, and so we would expect them to have some preference to stay with their parents. But this in fact works against the parents and the eldest child, because the set of feasible alternative rules is discontinuous. Unless a private arrangement is worked out (a will), the set of alternatives will be limited to one child, equal division, or some discontinuous division of shares.

With the distributive theory we would expect the following scenarios: In communities characterized by a subsistence agriculture economy and little real access to other sources of land, the asymmetries of power rest with the parent who controls the family estate. The parent can introduce unigeniture rules that maintain the estate and tie the children to its continuing economic productivity. Because the abilities of the eldest son are the most immediately valuable to the parent, it is in the parent's interest to favor him with the unigeniture rule. In communities characterized by a developing commercial economy and other sources of available land, the asymmetries rest with those children who have other sources of economic income. The parent who depends on the continuing support of his children is forced to introduce rules of equal division that give the children a greater economic interest in the continuing productivity of that estate. Given the alternative sources of income available to the children, the promise of a more equitable division of resources is

over time. On the other hand, the studies also show that given a few simplifying assumptions about mating patterns and the size of families, both of the two multigeniture rules tend to produce more equitable distributions over time.

necessary to ensure their continued support. The favored status of the eldest child is thus modified to reflect the increased leverage of his younger siblings.

These are the basic relationships between asymmetries in resources and institutional criteria that we find in the history of rules of intestate succession. The relationship between alternative economic resources and the degree of equality embodied in succession rules existed throughout Europe and the United States. The earliest records of rules of succession after the Middle Ages portray standards of favoritism and equality established in close proximity to one another. Into the nineteenth century, patterns of primogeniture and equality could be found in areas distinguished by the alternative sources of income available to the children (Berkner, 1976; Cooper, 1976; LeRoy Ladurie, 1976; Lloyd, 1877). The establishment of rules in the United States reflects a similar pattern. The standard historical account of the late eighteenth and early nineteenth century shows that whereas the South (a land-based agriculture economy) maintained rules of favoritism toward the eldest son, the North (a developing commercial and industrial economy) commonly adopted a relatively equal division among the children (Alston and Schapiro, 1984; Shammas, Salmon, and Dahlin, 1987).[34]

Although this standard understanding supports the distributive theory, a few more recent accounts – which suggest that the relationship between U.S. succession patterns and economic conditions was more complex – provide even more compelling evidence. In a more detailed analysis of succession patterns in Connecticut, Ditz (1986) found that unigeniture patterns were maintained in communities that had subsistence economies, whereas patterns of greater equality were established in developing commercial areas.[35] As the number of commercial alternatives expanded in Connecticut, the prevalence of equal division rules spread. This is the direction of change that we would anticipate with the distributive theory. More generally, the history of change in Europe and the United States reflects the basic scenario: As alternative sources of income became available to the children, the rules began to reflect a greater equality in distribution.

34 As I suggested in the previous section, the question of widows' property rights to the family estate can also be formulated as a bargaining problem between husbands and wives. Carr and Walsh (1977), Shammas (1987), and Salmon (1986) offer empirical evidence to support this: During the eighteenth century in the United States, women who moved to colonies in the Chesapeake Bay area, in which there was a shortage of women (thus enhancing their bargaining power), received much greater bequests at the death of their husbands than did women in the more populated colonies (New England).

35 Other analyses of inheritance in the United States that found a similar correlation between partible inheritance and the employment alternatives available to children include those by Censer (1984) and Crowley (1984).

Institutions and social conflict

Summary

This comparative analysis of the emergence of rules of property division emphasizes the importance of distributional concerns in explaining institutional development and change. The invocation of asymmetries of power is central to understanding the development of each of these approaches. On the issue of emergence, the initial rules of property division in each case produce systematic distributional effects, ruling out the cross-cutting property necessary for the standard formulation of the social convention theory. Although competition plays a varying role in the three accounts, it is clear that it is not as a selection mechanism of a particular rule (as in the theory of exchange and competition) but as an effect on relative bargaining power. This means that even when competition is introduced into the analysis, the emergence of the initial rules can be best explained by referring to systematic distributions of bargaining power in a society.

When we turn to the issue of changes in the initial rules, the explanatory importance of distributional conflict becomes even clearer. These changes are redistributive: The main benefactors of the initial rules lose their distributive advantage in the change. Thus, the changes cannot be explained by referring to social efficiency, Pareto superiority, or even compensation. Rather, these changes can be explained by a shift in the relevant asymmetries of resources in a society, shifts that reflect systematic changes in the distribution of bargaining power.

170

6

Stability and change: conflicts over formal institutions

This process of spontaneous emergence produces the informal institutions constituting the foundation of society. By providing information about the anticipated behavior of social actors, these conventions and norms stabilize social expectations and structure social life. Because they are self-enforcing, the efficacy of these rules depends on the extent to which social actors find it in their self-interest to comply with them. There are many circumstances in which self-interest dictates either simple noncompliance or an effort to change the rule. If these circumstances become too pervasive, the stability of the informal institution will be threatened.

Formal institutions are designed and created on this foundation of informal conventions and norms. In some cases, the formal rules are established as a way of stabilizing or changing existing informal rules. In other cases, the rules are created to structure those social interactions that lack an informal institutional framework. The most important of these are the rules created to structure collective decision making. Compliance with formal rules is reinforced by the sanctions of an external-enforcement mechanism. Thus, the creation of formal institutions introduces both law and the state into the structure of social life.

The introduction of the state helps distinguish theories of institutional development and change. Such explanations can be characterized by a primary, if not an exclusive, focus on either formal or informal institutions.[1] This sharp distinction might be explained by differences in the underlying mechanism of institutional creation: an intentional one for formal institutions and an unintentional one for informal rules. Implicit in this distinction, I think, is the idea that factors like distributional conflict and asymmetries of power, though appropriate to explanations

1 See Shepsle, 1989, and Langlois, 1985, for discussions of the existence of this distinction in political science and economics, respectively.

171

of intentional creation by the state, are less relevant to explanations of unintentional emergence. The main argument of the last two chapters was that even though the process of spontaneous emergence is decentralized and the resulting product is unintentional, they do not prevent this framework from reflecting the main cleavages of interest and power in a society.

In this chapter I investigate the conflict over the intentional creation of formal institutions. My previous arguments imply that although the logic of the mechanism of intentional creation may differ from that of spontaneous emergence, the underlying factors, which are central to both mechanisms, are the same. In order to assess the implications of this similarity, my analysis will focus on the relationship between the existing network of conventions and norms and the conflict over formal rules.

Usually when the relationship between formal and informal rules is considered, the main focus is from the top down: the effects of the state's formal institutions on informal rules and conventions. Ostrom offers an instructive example in her three-level typology of institutional rules: operational (rules affecting daily activities), collective-choice (rules governing the process by which policy decisions, including the creation of operational rules, are made), and constitutional-choice (rules "affect-[ing] operational activities and results through their effects in determining who is eligible and determining the specific rules to be used in crafting the set of collective-choice rules that in turn affect the set of operational rules") (1990:50–5). The analysis starts with constitutional-choice rules and works down to operational rules. Because of their effects on lower-level rules, upper-level rules are given priority in the analysis.[2]

My analysis is structured from the bottom up, emphasizing the conditions under which informal rules lead to the development of formal social institutions. There are many reasons for assigning analytical priority to informal social institutions. Let me merely list some of them now and then develop them later throughout the chapter. Informal rules are the foundation on which formal rules are built. Informal rules can limit the number of feasible alternatives from which formal institutions are developed. Informal rules persist when efforts at formal change are attempted. Most important, informal rules influence the distribution of resources, which in turn affect the power asymmetries in the conflict over the establishment of formal institutions.

---

2 Note that in this formulation of the Ostrom typology, the operational rules appear to be limited to those formal rules (laws) governing everyday activities. But Ostrom goes on to acknowledge the importance of informal conventions, norms, and rules in her analysis. The general point about the top-down focus of the relationship among the different types of rules holds.

Note that the process of spontaneous emergence is continuous. The "spontaneous order" problem is often posed as a pre-state process: How does social cooperation emerge without external enforcement? Although this is a significant question, it underestimates the importance of the decentralized emergence of informal rules. Informal rules continue to emerge and change within and around the state's formal institutions as the unintended consequences of everyday social interactions. And these emerging rules can affect the social consequences produced by formal institutions.

In the next section I concentrate on the stability of self-enforcing social institutions. Under what conditions are informal rules sufficient to structure social interactions? When do actors seek to establish an external enforcement mechanism to ensure compliance? The tension created by the distributional consequences of these informal rules complicates this analysis. We must consider stability from the perspective of both those favored and those disfavored by existing informal rules. This requires an analysis of cases of (1) maintaining existing rules and (2) intentionally reforming those rules. In both cases my emphasis will be on intentional change.

Then, in the following section, I focus on a set of issues related to the actual conflict over intentional institutional design. What are the implications of introducing an additional actor, the external enforcer, into the bargaining process? The point of the analysis is to highlight what is distinctive about the introduction of the state into the distributional conflict over social institutions. At the end of the chapter I offer a historical analysis of institutional change in rules governing labor–management relations in order to consider the relative effects of formal and informal rules as strategic resources in conflicts over distributional benefits. In so doing, I return to the basic question, When will social actors rely on informal rules, and when will they turn to the state for reinforcement of their interests?

THE STABILITY OF INFORMAL INSTITUTIONS

In order to analyze the stability of these informal rules, it is helpful to return to a simple example of how such rules structure social interactions. Consider the informal conventions and norms that structure gender relations in a society. There are many ways of dividing responsibilities and benefits among men and women in a community. Such a division is necessary for many social interactions, from the organization and management of the nuclear family to general standards of behavior between the sexes in casual contact. It is important that social rules establish the ways in which the responsibilities and benefits are to be

173

divided in these contexts, and, in doing so, they define expectations about the future actions of men and women in a community.

According to the analytical model of bargaining (Table 5.1), the institutional rules governing gender relations tell men and women which actions (equilibrium strategies) represent the socially shared expectations for a particular community. In an expected-utility calculus, these rules establish a probability approximating one that the person with whom one is interacting will adopt the anticipated equilibrium strategy. Given this probability estimate, men and women can determine their own best course of action, which will, if the information is reliable, be the corresponding equilibrium strategy. Therefore, compliance is ensured – if it is at all – by the information that the rules provide. As long as men and women share the same expectations and comply with the rules, they both will gain from the interaction.

Remember that this does not mean all of the men and women in a community will be satisfied with the existing set of gender rules. It merely means that because of the rule's existence, the knowledge of which is shared by the members of the community, they cannot do better for themselves in this interaction by choosing another action. Some people may prefer other rules, on distributional grounds. If so, then there will always be an incentive for those actors to change the status quo.

The tension created by distributional consequences raises questions about the long-term stability of informal institutions. If institutional development pertains mainly to efforts to constrain other social actors for the sake of distributional advantage, we should concentrate on the conditions under which informal social institutions do satisfy those efforts. When they fail to do so, we should look for those conditions under which some members of the society have an incentive to resort to the state to reinforce their particular interests. This allows us to address the question, When will informal institutions be replaced by formal ones? Here we need to separate those questions related to the maintenance of existing institutions from those related to the intentional change of the status quo.

Maintenance of the status quo

The stability of self-enforcing institutions is usually discussed in regard to the general issue of social cooperation in a stateless world. This approach introduces the Prisoner's Dilemma analogy and raises the standard challenges of free riding and defection. The various analyses differ in the manner in which they model the basic interaction from which self-enforcing cooperation emerges. For example, Axelrod (1984) conceptualizes the question of stability as the product of bilateral interactions among the various members of a society; Taylor (1987) models it as an *n*-person game in which cooperation is the product of the interdependent choices of all of the society's members. It seems to me that the choice of a particular model depends on the structure of the specific case. What is important to my analysis is highlighting the common features of both models that are fundamental to the question of stability. These are the characteristics affecting the long-term benefits of compliance with informal social institutions.

The distributional tension inherent in these rules suggests that the issues raised by this approach should be analyzed by distinguishing the interests of those favored and those disfavored by the status quo. We can do this by considering two threats to maintaining the status quo: information and incentives.

Information. The challenge of information to the stability of informal institutions rests on the question of the rules' "socially shared" character. Do social actors have the requisite knowledge of the rules' substance to justify relying on them as a source of social expectations? If men and women lack knowledge of the existing rules governing gender relations, they often will not act in the way that the rules prescribe. From the perspective of a woman seeking to interact with a man in her community, if knowledge of the informal rules is not socially shared, she will often be confronted by behavior that she does not expect. When this is the case, the process of expectation formation breaks down, and the efficacy of the informal gender rules declines.

The lack of shared information can depend on many factors, but two are of special importance. First, the rule may be ambiguous and open to multiple interpretations. For example, Comaroff and Roberts (1981) offer numerous accounts of the ambiguity of informal rules of marriage and kinship relations among the Tsawana in southern Africa. The rules govern the responsibilities of men and women within the extended family and the distribution of benefits and status in both the family and the general community. One of the problems faced by the members of a Tswana community is the difficulty in determining which of the various rules apply to a particular relationship between a man and a woman. The problem arises because a valid marriage is not a function of a particular ritual or practice. Rather, valid marriage, for purposes of the applicability of the Tsawana marriage and kinship rules, is a function of several factors, the combination of which may vary among cases.

The consequences of this ambiguity for social relations in a Tsawana village are numerous. The marriage and kinship rules affect both the responsibilities and the benefits of the man and woman in the relationship. This in turn affects the rights and status of the man and woman in the

175

community and therefore the ways in which others in the village interact with the couple. Although everyone in the village may know that rules exist governing marriage relationships, they may differ in their interpretation of the actions that the rules prescribe. The result of the ambiguity is that social expectations are less stable; social interactions are more conflictual; and the number of ex post disputes over interpretations of the rules is quite high. To resolve these conflicts, the Tsawana resort to various dispute-settlement procedures, some of which involve third-party enforcement mechanisms.

A second factor that can affect the extent to which information is socially shared is the size of the group. Problems with the quality and comprehensiveness of information provision vary with the size of the relevant community. Here I have in mind a problem with the multiplicity of possible rules and not the ambiguity of a particular rule. Questions concerning which rules are in force in a particular community can affect the stability of informal rules. In smaller communities this is less likely to be a problem. The ongoing nature of relationships in these communities increases the probability that social actors are aware of self-enforcing rules and the information that they provide. In the Tsawana example, in a particular village the problem with its informal marriage and kinship rules is not uncertainty about the existence of a particular set of rules. If the villagers can agree on the applicability of the rule, they understand its consequences for the division of responsibilities and benefits. In a small village, therefore, the villagers know which rules apply to marriage relationships.

As the size of the community increases, the problem of uncertainty also increases. In larger groups, uncertainty as to whether social actors share the same understanding of the rules governing their interactions affects social expectations. As we move from a small village to larger Tsawana communities, the possibility that two actors may differ as to which marriage practices they think should apply increases. This greater uncertainty is a function of size. Socially shared knowledge is mainly a product of shared experience: As the number of actors increases, the likelihood that a person will have ongoing interactions with the same actors declines. The effect here is to decrease reliance on informal rules to establish expectations.

The Tsawana example reinforces the earlier discussion in Chapter 3 concerning the effects of ambiguity and uncertainty on the reliability of the information derived from institutional rules. The more complex the informal rules are, the more serious the problem of interpreting these rules will become. As the ambiguity of the rules increases, our confidence in the expectations that we derive from social institutions should decline. According to the logic of strategic decision making, the practical effect of ambiguity and uncertainty is to complicate a social actor's expected-utility calculation; that is, convergence on a particular equilibrium outcome is less assured. In this way the force of informal institutions on the strategic choices of social actors is diminished.

These information problems affect the efficacy of the informal rules. Those who are favored by the rules have a strong incentive to force those who deviate to learn the proper rules and act accordingly. Those who are disfavored by the rules have an incentive to exploit any strategic maneuvering made available by deviations. As in the Tsawana example, problems with the reliability of the information provided by social institutions increase the incentive for those favored actors to seek external enforcement of the rules.

Incentives. A major challenge to the stability of informal rules comes from the apparent incentives provided by noncompliance. Social institutions are self-enforcing if they constitute an equilibrium outcome for the individual actors. As long as an individual actor cannot do better by pursuing a different strategy – given the strategies of the other actors – he or she will continue to act in accordance with that institution. And the individual actor will continue to respect the institution's constraints, even though he reaps fewer benefits from the institution than do other actors with whom he is involved. He does so because without the ability to coordinate the strategies of others toward a different equilibrium, he has no other rational choice. This logic suggests that even those rules producing significant distributional consequences can be self-enforcing.

What if the circumstances are such that the actors do have better alternatives than complying with the informal rules? For example, consider a potential problem with the self-enforcing nature of bankruptcy rules. The existence of rules of priority in bankruptcy can alter the incentives governing interactions with those who seek credit. The priority rules for secured creditors enhance the possibility that borrowers who are a higher loan risk will be granted loans. Lenders treat the security as a hedge against the chance of failure of repayment. Without this security, it is unlikely that these high-risk borrowers would obtain their desired loans.[3] Sometimes even this security is not enough to encourage high-risk loans, thereby putting pressure on debtors to make special arrangements with creditors as a way of giving them an unfair advantage in the event of bankruptcy. The potential for these arrangements to develop un-

---

3 Although this is the common understanding of the effects of rules of priority, there still is a debate over the overall efficiency effects of these rules. The dominant view is that priority rules produce more efficient lending (Buckley, 1986), but others have argued that the evidence is inconclusive and, therefore, that the claim that priority rules produce the incentive for efficient lending is unfounded (Schwartz, 1981; White, 1980).

derlies the argument of those who think that the bankruptcy problem is really one of protecting the creditors from one another.

Perhaps the problem of the insolvent debtor should be structured as a Prisoner's Dilemma game among creditors. Individual creditors can earn a greater return by acting unilaterally than they can by acting cooperatively, but because each creditor has the same dominant strategy, they will end up with a Pareto-suboptimal outcome. This suboptimal outcome is based on the assumption that mutual conflict over the debtor's assets will destroy some of those assets and adversely affect the productive capacity of the remaining property.[4] If the problem is structured in this way, the stability of informal bankruptcy rules will be threatened by the incentive to agree to fraudulent conveyances.

The extensive analysis of cooperation in Prisoner's Dilemma–like social interactions offers an answer to the question of stability. The results are well known. In a single interaction, noncompliance with the rule is a dominant strategy. The only circumstances in which the rule can be self-enforcing and stable are those in which compliance solves an iterated Prisoner's Dilemma game. Thus the relevant question is, What are the conditions under which the *long-term* benefits of compliance with informal rules exceed those of noncompliance?

The long-term benefits of compliance are a function of (1) the extent to which an actor discounts the future, (2) the benefits of compliance and noncompliance in a single interaction, and (3) the effect of noncompliance on the future behavior of other actors. They are a weighted sum of the discounted benefits from each individual interaction. Here I should say something about the benefits provided by the informal rules. The standard formulation of the Prisoner's Dilemma game treats the payoffs from cooperation as equal for each of the players. But there is no reason to treat them as equal; the distributional consequences of social institutions indicate that the benefits from compliance should differ for those favored and disfavored by the informal rules. If they do, the incentive for noncompliance will differ for those favored and disfavored by the status-quo rule. It will take a lower value of the outside alternative for those disfavored by the rule to choose noncompliance.

The key to the value of compliance as a long-term strategy is the discount rate: The more that one values the future, the greater will be the likelihood that compliance will be the long-term rational strategy (Taylor, 1987). An actor's discount rate is in large part a function of the likelihood that she will continue to engage in social interactions with the

---

4 This is a common assumption in arguments offered in support of bankruptcy rules and procedures. One of the justifying arguments for these rules is that in the absence of such cooperative procedures, the assets would be devalued or destroyed by the conflict among the creditors (Gessner et al., 1978; Jackson and Kronman, 1976).

same basic group of actors. This likelihood is affected by her time horizon (how long she thinks that she will be in a particular community) and by the number and distribution of actors in the community (Hardin, 1982).

We can see the importance of these factors by returning to the fraudulent conveyance example. If a creditor thinks that she is involved in a relatively anonymous and isolated exchange with people with whom she will not interact in the future, she will be motivated by the short-term gain provided by noncompliance with the bankruptcy rules. If, on the other hand, she is involved in an exchange with actors with whom she will repeatedly have occasion to interact, she will be motivated by the long-term effects of her actions. In the long term, any additional benefits gained from an isolated act of noncompliance can be offset by the retaliatory response it engenders in the other actors. The subsequent sanctions inflicted by the other actors against a fraudulent conveyance in violation of the bankruptcy rules can take many forms, from an isolated penalty to a decision to discontinue future transactions. The most significant effect of these sanctions can be to reduce the expected benefits of noncompliance and make compliance the more beneficial long-term strategy.

Thus, the conditions under which informal rules are stable are those conditions under which the threat of informal sanctions can make compliance a rational long-term strategy. This returns us to the issue of the size of the group with whom an individual interacts. Note that the relevant group may not be the community as a whole. If the distribution of actors in a community is divided into distinct subgroups whose members interact predominantly with those within that subgroup, it will be the size of the subgroup that is relevant to the long-term calculation of benefits. If there is no such systematic distribution, it will be the size of the community as a whole that must be considered. In either case, as the size of the relevant group increases, the likelihood that an individual will be confronted by someone who will sanction noncompliance decreases. There are two reasons for this.

First, there is a relationship between the number of actors with whom you are involved and the frequency with which you will interact with the same actors: the greater the number of actors is, the lower the probability will be that you will interact with the same actors in the future. If you are a lender, you will assess the long-term benefit of a fraudulent conveyance in terms of the probability that this conveyance will result in future sanctions against you. If there is a low probability that you will have future interactions with those in the initial exchange, then probability of a sanction will be low, and the value of the fraudulent conveyance will increase.

It is possible that the future costs of noncompliance will be less direct. For example, a defecting creditor may acquire a reputation as someone who fails to comply with the informal rules. If she acquires such a reputation, others in the community who have not previously had any transactions with her may refuse to interact with her in the future. This indirect effect of reputation can diminish the long-term benefits of noncompliance. But here, too, the effects of reputation depend on the size of the group with whom the creditor interacts. Reputation will affect future choices only when the information about the defecting creditor can be effectively transmitted throughout the community. As the size of the group increases, widespread transmission of reputation should become more difficult.

The second reason for the relationship between group size and the effects of informal sanctions involves the rationality of carrying out the threats of those sanctions: As the size of the group increases, the incentive to sanction others declines. We can see this by asking who has the incentive to carry out the informal sanction. Because sanctions are costly, following through with a threat to sanction noncompliance is not a rational strategy unless those costs can be recouped in the future. Such costs are offset by the future benefits from cooperative behavior that the threat of sanctions induces in other actors.

The incentives once again differ for those favored and disfavored by the status quo. Let us distinguish between a general sanction against the noncompliance with social rules and a specific sanction against the violation of a particular rule. The standard analysis of the rationality of informal sanctions applies to general sanctions and treats the incentives as equal for all of the actors (Kreps, 1990). If we focus instead on the incentives for specific sanctions of particular rules, we will see that the incentives for sanctioning are greater for some actors because the long-term benefits for compliance are higher for those favored by the rule. Because of this difference, it is more likely that informal sanctions will be a rational strategy for those favored by the status quo. The greater is the distributional advantage produced by the status quo, the greater will be the incentive for informal sanctions.

But an informal sanctioner cannot offset costs with long-term benefits unless she will continue to interact in the future with those whom she sanctions. Here again we see the connection with group size. In small groups, ongoing relationships among the actors may provide the additional incentives for maintaining these sanctions. If I sanction a noncomplying creditor in one transaction in order to ensure his compliance in future interactions with me, the additional benefits to me may be sufficient to justify the sanction. However, in larger communities with fewer ongoing relationships, though it may be in the collective interest of a community (or a segment of that community) to reinforce informal bankruptcy rules with informal sanctions, it is not in the individual interest of any of the actors to enforce such sanctions. In such communities the threat of informal sanctions does not induce compliance with informal rules.

To summarize, the factors which determine whether the long-term benefits of compliance exceed noncompliance are the size and distribution of the group with whom social actors interact and the magnitude of the distributional advantage accruing to those favored by the status quo. As the size of a community increases, the stability of informal rules is threatened by the incentives for noncompliance. As we see in the case of fraudulent conveyances, this threat can lead those favored by the rules to seek external enforcement of the status quo. In an effort to avoid the problem of noncompliance with the rules of priority, laws were established to penalize preferential arrangements between individual creditors and debtors. These rules against preferences void any such transaction that takes place for the main purpose of favoring one creditor in anticipation of the debtor's becoming insolvent. Originally intended to address the problem of fraud for creditors, such rules evolved into statutory requirements that void any such transactions taking place within a set period of time before the declaration of insolvency.[5] Such rules vitiate the advantages of the creditors' acting unilaterally.

Discussion. When we combine information problems with the lack of effective informal sanctions in large communities, the viability of informal institutions that produce unequal distributional outcomes is open to question. On the one hand, the efficacy of the institution for those favored by the rules is diminished by noncompliance. On the other hand, the effort to enact a law that reinforces the status quo with an external-enforcement mechanism is costly. This is where transaction costs enter the analysis. The two main forms of transaction costs here are (1) the costs of organizing the favored group into a political interest group and (2) the costs of incorporating state actors and their interests into the sanctioning process.

5 The history of the development of rules against preferences is complex and beyond the scope of this analysis. The decision as to what constitutes a valid secured debt is a difficult one. Jackson and Kronman (1976) point out that the establishment of a rule against preferences requires a difficult balancing of "the competing interests of secured and unsecured creditors" (pp. 976–7). The resulting rule must address the conflicting goals of (1) "the protection of the secured party's pre-bankruptcy contractual expectations" and (2) the "minimization of the social costs of bankruptcy itself" (p. 980). For an account of the debates over the development of such rules, see, for example, McCoid, 1981, and Weisberg, 1986.

These costs point to one reason that informal institutions may persist in the face of noncompliance by those who are disfavored by the rules. The costs of establishing an external-enforcement mechanism to reinforce the status quo may be prohibitive. The relevant question is how much noncompliance will be acceptable to those favored by the rule before they seek a formalization of the status quo. To answer this, we must compare two expected values: long-term benefits under the informal rule and those under a formal law. These expected values are calculated as follows.

Let us say that someone favored by the rule discounts the future by some factor, d. The expected value of the status quo is the discounted sum of the benefits of the individual interactions. In order to take account of the possibility of noncompliance, the benefit of the status quo in a single interaction must be treated as the sum of the benefits of compliance and noncompliance weighted by the probabilities of the two events

$$p_c(x + \epsilon_A) + (1 - p_c)(\Delta_A)$$

with p_c representing the probability of compliance with the status quo. If we assume for purposes of analysis an infinite time horizon, the long-term benefits of the status quo will be[6]

$$E \text{ (status quo)} = [p_c(x + \epsilon_A) + (1 - p_c)(\Delta_A)] / (1 - d)$$

Similarly, the long-term benefits of a new formal rule must be discounted and offset by the costs of formalization. Note that the costs of formalization are a function of time, because the costs of maintaining an external-enforcement mechanism are continuous. Because these long-term costs enter into the present value of formalization, these costs must also be discounted. If we ignore for the sake of analysis the possibility that someone may ignore the formal sanctions, the long-term benefits of the new rule will be

$$E \text{ (new law)} = (x + \epsilon_A) / (1 - d) - C / (1 - d)$$

If we compare the two expected values, we can see that those favored by the status quo will go to the state to reinforce their distributional

6 Two points here. First, there has been some debate over the appropriateness of assuming an infinite time horizon. I follow Rubinstein (1988) here, who argues that an infinite time horizon is an appropriate way of modeling (and interpreting) a decision in which the actor does not in fact know the end point of the process. Second, to calculate the present discounted stream of future benefits, I treat the future as a set of discrete interactions. Thus, the sum of $[p_c(x + \epsilon_A) + (1 - p_c)(\Delta_A)] + [p_c(x + \epsilon_A) + (1 - p_c)(\Delta_A)]d + [p_c(x + \epsilon_A) + (1 - p_c)(\Delta_A)]d^2 + \ldots + [p_c(x + \epsilon_A) + (1 - p_c)(\Delta_A)]d^t = [p_c(x + \epsilon_A) + (1 - p_c)(\Delta_A)] / (1 - d)$ as $t \to \infty$. See Taylor, 1987, for an explanation of this calculation.

advantage when the expected losses from noncompliance exceed the various costs of obtaining and maintaining an external-enforcement mechanism. These losses are a function of both the magnitude of the distributional advantage produced by the status quo and the percentage of interactions resulting in noncompliance. As either of these values increases, the expected losses from noncompliance increase as well. When they exceed the political costs of state enforcement, we would expect the status quo to be formalized. When they do not exceed these costs, we would expect to see the informal rules persist in the face of some degree of noncompliance.

Intentional change

The stability of informal institutions is also affected by circumstances concerning the attractiveness of the status quo. In Chapter 5 I introduced the two main conditions that produce incentives for change from the status quo: (1) changes in the asymmetries of power among the actors and (2) changes in the distributional consequences of the institutions. There I discussed the effects of changes in these conditions on the possibility of spontaneous change in the informal rules. Here I want to focus on the effects of these conditions on efforts at intentional reform through formalization of a new rule. Some of my conclusions from the earlier analysis are relevant to this discussion.

The effects of changes in bargaining power on the possibility of intentional change depends in which direction the change occurs. If the change merely enhances the power of those favored by the status quo, they will have no incentive to seek the state's enforcement power unless the maintenance of the status quo is threatened by the information and incentive problems previously considered. If the change alters the relative bargaining power in favor of those disfavored by the status quo, they will be faced with a choice. They could use this bargaining power to pursue an advantage in their own interactions, possibly producing over time a spontaneous change in the informal rule that structures the relevant social interaction. Or they could organize and intentionally try to change the status quo to a new formal rule that produces for them a better distributional outcome.

Changes in the distributional consequences of informal rules can produce incentives for intentional change for all of the actors. Whether they are favored or disfavored by the status quo, the existence of an alternative institutional arrangement that increases their own benefits creates an incentive for change. If they reject the individualistic strategy of seeking the advantage in their own interactions, they will have an incentive to seek change through the formalization of the new rule.

The decision to change the status quo intentionally is based in each of these cases on a comparison of the expected long-term benefits of the different institutional rules. Because the logic of the decision is the same for those favored and disfavored by the status quo, we can examine the factors that influence the decision by looking at one case. Consider the decision of those favored by the existing rule, by returning to the game shown in Table 5.2(a). The comparison is between the expected value of the old rule (R,L) and the new one (R', L').

The expected values are calculated in the manner just described. Under the status quo, someone favored by the rule can expect a payoff of $x + \epsilon_A$ for a single interaction. Assuming for the sake of analysis that there is compliance with the status quo, the long-term benefits of the old rule will be

$$E\ (R,\ L) = (x + \epsilon_A) / (1 - d)$$

Calculating the expected value of the new rule is more complicated. We must take account of two factors: the costs of formalization and the losses incurred in those cases in which the other actors do not comply with the new rule. In the next subsection I discuss various reasons that the new rule might not be followed. To take account of the interactions in which the new rule is not followed, we must treat the expected benefits of the new rule in a single interaction as a sum of the payoff of the new rule and the payoff of lack of coordination weighted by the probabilities that each will occur:

$$p_n\ (x + \epsilon'_A) + (1 - p_n)\ (\Delta_A)$$

with p_n as the probability of compliance with the new rule. Note that the probability of compliance can be a function of time. It is reasonable to assume that as the new rule becomes better established over time, more people will come to understand and correctly apply it and that p_n will increase. Thus, we should treat p_n as a function of time, $p_n\ (t)$.[7]

With these definitions we can calculate the present discounted expected value of the new rule:

$$E\ (R',\ L') = [p_{n(t)}\ (x + \epsilon'_A) + (1 - p_{n(t)})\ (\Delta_A)] / (1 - d) - C / (1 - d)$$

From this, a number of interesting and important relationships follow. First, the more that an actor values the future (i.e., the higher the d), the greater will be the expected value of the new rule. Second, the higher the probability of compliance is, the greater the expected value will be. Thus,

7 For my purposes, there is no reason to define a particular functional form for $p_n\ (t)$, as there are many forms that could be used to define how p_n is a function of time. The particular form would determine how quickly p_n converges to 1. The choice depends on a number of empirical factors affecting the speed of this convergence.

the more quickly the actors in the community converge on the new rule, the greater its expected value will be. Third, the greater the costs of formalization are, the lower the expected value will be.

In the end, the decision to change an existing institution intentionally rests on whether

$$E\ (R',\ L') > E\ (R,\ L)$$

This relationship will hold when, in the long term, the additional benefits produced by the new rule exceed the sum of three forms of cost (the losses due to interactions in which the new rule was not followed, the political costs of change, and the costs of submitting to an external enforcer). If they do, we should expect a formal change in the social institution. If they do not, we should expect the existing rule to be maintained.

Stability and the difficulty of changing expectations

This analysis of intentional change offers an additional explanation for the stability of informal institutions: the difficulty of changing established social expectations. Formal institutional change (1) alters the information about the equilibrium that the rule seeks to produce and (2) establishes sanctions against the strategies dictated by the old rule. The efficacy of intentional change depends on the ability of this new information and the sanctions to change existing expectations.

To see the difficulty of this task, reconsider the logic of strategic decision making. The expected utility of a strategy is based on an actor's expectations about the behavior of two sets of actors: those involved in interactions and third-party enforcers. The status quo stabilizes the actor's expectations regarding a particular equilibrium outcome. It establishes a probability approximating 1 that the others with whom he interacts will conform to the equilibrium strategy. If it is a formal rule, it also will inform him about the sanctions for noncompliance. Sanctions have the dual effect of diminishing the value of noncompliance and of reinforcing expectations about the actions of others. Those actors who introduce a new formal rule seek to change the equilibrium outcome by reorienting the expectations to that new equilibrium.

To be successful, the new rule must cause social actors to shift their probability estimates to the strategies associated with that equilibrium. But unless an actor is confident that the new rule will be recognized and applied by those with whom he interacts, there is no reason for him to change his probability estimates. If he fails to do so, the expected utility of the strategy dictated by the old rule will still be greater than that of the new one. In such cases the informal rule can persist despite efforts to change them.

This raises the question of why an actor might lack confidence that the new rule will be recognized and followed. The answer can be found in the earlier discussion of the reliability of social expectations. Consider three reasons. The first involves the strength of enduring expectations. Kuran argues that individuals develop ties to long-standing institutions in the face of pressure for change. One aspect of these ties can be a "personal conservatism, a personal attachment to some aspect of the past" (1988:144). This attachment is not grounded in self-interest, in that the status quo is valued because it gives someone a distributional advantage. It is, rather, an unwillingness to change long-standing expectations.

Although Kuran offers little explanation of how and why this personal conservatism has such an effect, it seems to be related to the effect on change often attributed to ideology. Social actors become so accustomed to complying with particular rules that they come to accept those rules as the natural way of doing something. Adam Smith (1969: 261–82) extended this idea even further to contend that enduring rules that have the initial effect of stabilizing expectations come to have a normative effect: a shift from influencing how we perceive the way the world is to how we think the world ought to be. Although I cannot explain why this transformation occurs, it does seem to reveal a possible effect of enduring informal rules. For my purposes here, it is enough to acknowledge that if someone thinks that a rule dictates the way that we ought to act, an attempt to change these expectations grounded in self-interest and incentives will face some resistance.

A second reason that a strategic actor may question other actors' compliance with a new rule relates to the ambiguity of rules. If an informal rule has been in place for a long time, any ambiguity in it should, over time, be diminished. If the new rule is subject to multiple interpretations, there will be some doubt as to which of those interpretations should guide expectations. If the ambiguity is significant enough to prevent swift convergence on one interpretation, a strategic actor may decide that the expectations produced by the old rule will better predict future behavior.

A third reason pertains to uncertainty in the probability that the sanctions under the new rule will actually be invoked. A number of factors can influence the likelihood of punishment: the difficulty of monitoring compliance, the complexity of the interaction subject to the rule, and the interests of the third-party enforcers in actually carrying out the sanctions. If an actor doubts that he will be sanctioned for noncompliance, he will prefer to comply with the old rule if it would otherwise give him a higher expected utility. Similarly, if I doubt that he will be sanctioned for noncompliance, this will affect my expectations about the likelihood of his compliance with the new rule.

Any of these factors can create doubts as to whether the rule will be recognized by those with whom we interact. These doubts threaten the efficacy of formalization by diminishing the probability that the new rule will be recognized and applied. This can explain many of the difficulties that arise when attempting to establish new social institutions. These difficulties are especially relevant to efforts to make revolutionary changes.

Some attempts at intentional change result in the outright rejection of the rule. In November 1793 the revolutionary government in France introduced a new calendar as part of a general effort to transform social life in the country.[8] This change, which replaced the Gregorian calendar with a new Republican one, was instituted as a way of reducing the influence of the Catholic church in French society (Rifkin, 1987: 76–8). It restructured all of the existing temporal rules, removing all of the Christian rest days and holidays and establishing twelve new months with the equivalent of three ten-day weeks. Opposition to the reform and efforts to circumvent its effects were widespread among the French people. The revolutionary calendar lasted for thirteen years before Napoleon reestablished the old calendar in 1806.

The opposition can be explained in two ways. The new calendar was not in the self-interest of the working class, in that it reduced the number of rest days from 180 to 36. So the resistance was in part a matter of distributional conflict. But the new time rules also violated both enduring ideological beliefs and ingrained expectations about the way social life was to be conducted. Given the additional fact that the ability of the French state to monitor and sanction noncompliance was stretched beyond capacity, the new rules never succeeded in completely reorienting social expectations.

Other efforts at intentional change result not in outright rejection but in the establishment of a dual or pluralist system of formal and informal rules. Such systems were common in colonial societies. Hooker's account of the Dutch East Indies (1975: 250–300) is representative of the colonial experience. In the nineteenth century, Dutch authorities established a legal system to govern the Indonesian colonies. Although it was more comprehensive in administrative and criminal matters, it sought also to reform many aspects of the indigenous domestic and commercial conventions. These reforms conflicted with the existing *adat* system that structured village life and produced considerable resistance to the new

---

8 This is an example of a more general problem faced by revolutionary movements: the destruction of the informal network of conventions and norms defining the prerevolutionary society. The efforts by Stalin in the Soviet Union in the 1930s and 1940s to change the length of the workweek suffered a fate similar to the French reform effort (Zerubavel, 1981: 73).

rules. Over time a pluralist system developed in which the *adat* rules were used in most domestic and commercial interactions among the villagers, and the Dutch rules were applied when the interaction involved a Dutch citizen. This legal pluralism, to adopt Hooker's term, made for a complicated system of social expectations. The native resistance to the colonial reforms can also be explained by the effects of ideology, ambiguity, and uncertainty on the traditional social expectations.

These examples reinforce the idea that the difficulty in changing stable expectations can enhance the stability of informal social institutions. Much of the resistance to intentional change can be explained by distributional factors, but some of the persistence of informal social rules in the face of intentional change and external enforcement can be traced to ideological and cognitive factors. When these factors are prevalent, there are good reasons for a strategic actor to doubt that a new rule will provide reliable information about the future behavior of others in the community. When such doubts are well founded, informal conventions and norms can be maintained in the presence of contrary formal laws.

THE STATE AND CONFLICTS OVER FORMAL INSTITUTIONS

The analysis of the stability of informal institutions underscores the conditions under which the state enters into the process of institutional development and change. When the efficacy of informal institutions is threatened, social actors try to invoke the external-enforcement mechanism of the state to establish institutional constraints that give them a distributional advantage. But the introduction of the state changes the underlying conflict over social institutions. The logic of informal institutionalization is to constrain the actions of others through our own commitments. The logic of formal institutionalization is to constrain the actions of others through the actions of a third party.

To investigate the formalization of institutional constraints is to investigate the basic politics of state decision making. The many details of such politics are beyond the scope of this analysis. But it is important to show how the formulation of intentional design as a contract among social actors fails to reveal the complexity of the state's involvement in this process. In this section I address issues essential to understanding the structure of political bargaining over formal institutions. To do so I shall point out the distinctive features of the distributional conflict over social institutions when the state participates in the bargaining process: the new mechanisms for institutional creation, the interests of the state, the effects on the bargaining power of the actors, and the additional sources of institutional conflict.

New mechanisms for institutional creation

When social actors, acting under the authority of the state, can create an institution by means of decree or enactment, the process of institutional development and change is transformed. The existence of the state expands the number of ways in which the two aspects of the institutionalization process, the creation and the social recognition of a new rule, can be accomplished.

The creation of a new law is the product of a formal decision-making process that requires intentional bargaining over institutional constraints. The structure of the bargaining depends on the decision-making process in a particular state. Consider the difference between a nondemocratic and a democratic state. Levi's (1988) accounts of revenue production and taxation policy in medieval France and Britain and in modern Australia provide relevant insights into the different ways that state decision making can be influenced by nonstate actors. Her main argument is that state actors are subject to economic (the need for continuing revenue) and political (the desire to maintain political power and social stability) constraints. Because these constraints depend in part on the strategies of the other actors in the society, state actors who seek to maximize tax revenue must attend to the interests of those who can affect these constraints in creating new legal institutions.

In a nondemocratic state such as medieval France and Britain, those actors who hold the power and authority over state decision making try to impose new institutions by decree. The opportunity for other social actors to influence these decrees is indirect. The structure of institutional bargaining is mainly between the state and powerful interest groups, and formal institutions are the product of private contracts between the state and those groups and not the product of a general contract among the various social actors.

In a democratic society such as modern Australia, on the other hand, formal institutions are in large part a product of competition for control of the state's decision-making process. The effect of nonstate actors on state decision making is more direct in this system, but state actors do have an independent effect on the long-term consequences of formal institutions. This effect is related mainly to the state's administrative function (interpreting, monitoring, and enforcing laws). The bargaining is primarily among the different interest groups, with state actors serving as an additional and often important bargainer. Formal institutions are the product of the bargaining among these various groups.

The recognition process for a new law is itself institutionalized, unlike the decentralized recognition process for institutions that emerge spontaneously. The mechanism for recognizing externally enforced rules is in principle quite simple: The state officials' use of standard procedures to establish such rules ensures their recognition (Hart, 1961). But the formal process is restricted by the difficulty of changing enduring expectations. These constraints suggest another way in which institutional change is path dependent: Existing informal rules can limit the extent of formal institutional change through the effects of enduring expectations on the formal recognition process.

The overall effect of these new mechanisms should be to increase the rate of institutional change. As opposed to the slow pace of change that occurs through commitment and learning in the process of decentralized emergence, the institutionalization process is itself the product of social institutions. These established procedures for institutional change appear to enhance the social actors' capacity to respond to changes in asymmetries of power and in distributional consequences. Though this is often the case, the implications of state involvement are more pronounced than mere procedural changes.

The interests of the state

State actors, either administrative officials or political representatives, have their own interests. Whether they are a preference for political power or material gain, these interests must be considered in the bargaining over formal institutions. These interests enter the bargaining in two forms: the direct interest in the benefits accruing to those actors who serve as external enforcers and the indirect interest in the effects of the distributional consequences of formal institutions on the long-term interests of the state.

The direct interest is straightforward. The administrative task of sanctioning noncompliance is costly, with problems of interpretation, monitoring, and sanctioning that must be resolved. The logic of externally enforced institutions is that these costs are not borne by the actors in a decentralized way, and so someone has to be paid to perform these tasks. Thus, the administrative costs of external enforcement to some actors are the direct benefits to the external enforcers.

The indirect interest is more important to explanations of the creation of formal institutions. Return to North's analysis (1981) of the conflict between the state and owners of economic resources. Both have an interest in the structure of property rights in the society. Economic actors want to establish rights that give them the distributional advantage in economic interactions. State actors want to establish rights that further their own interests: an economic interest in revenues and a political interest in maintaining a level of aggregate growth sufficient to satisfy those social actors necessary to maintain power. The rights that satisfy the most powerful resource owners may differ from those preferred by the state. As long as the economic actors must rely on the state for external enforcement of these rights, the final structure of those rights will to some degree reflect the economic and political interests of the state actors.

The standard conclusion drawn from North's analysis is that the introduction of the state's interests increases the inefficiency of social institutions. And in fact, there are many situations in which the interests of the state would result in the creation of institutional rules that are more inefficient than those desired by private actors. But one of the interesting implications of my account is that the state might also enhance the social efficiency of many social institutions. If state actors prefer a formal rule that is more socially efficient than the one preferred by the more powerful private actors, the new law may be more efficient than the existing informal rule.

There are two cases in which the state may prefer a more socially efficient institution. First, it may prefer it if state actors are directly affected by the consequences of the rule and if they will benefit materially from a more socially efficient rule. Examples of such a case are the collective-bargaining procedures governing labor–management relations in many societies: The state may prefer the greater revenues derived from continuous production, whereas the private actors may prefer rules that would make it easier for them to stop production as a bargaining tactic.

Second, the state may prefer a more socially efficient institution if state actors are indirectly affected by the rule through its effect on their ability to stay in power and they will benefit politically from a more socially beneficial rule. Consider the following scenario: If state actors are concerned primarily about remaining in power, they will look to all potential sources of political support. In the process of creating formal institutions, they can consider the interests of all of the members of the society and not just those directly affected by the proposed rule. Those people who are not directly affected by a particular rule will have no particular distributional interest in the form that the rule takes. They might therefore prefer a socially efficient rule to one that gives distributional advantage to a particular actor. If these disinterested actors are an important source of political support for state actors, their preferences for a socially efficient rule may outweigh the distributional preferences of those directly affected and, therefore, significantly influence the substance of the formal institution.[9]

9 A potential objection to this scenario is that narrowly self-interested actors would not expend resources to affect state decision making if they would not be directly affected by the new rule. If so, these disinterested actors would not be a source of political support,

Institutions and social conflict

In all of these cases the changes in the structure of bargaining over so-cial institutions introduce the importance of new bargainers. When strategic actors ask the state to reinforce their distributional interests, they often must face the conflicting interests of state actors. If social actors cannot achieve distributional advantage without the state's assistance, the interests of these new bargainers will alter the substantive nature of formal institutions.

Effects on the actors' bargaining power

The introduction of the state into the distributional conflict over social institutions changes the manner in which bargaining power affects the institutional outcome. In the case of evolutionary emergence, the relevant power is grounded in the alternatives available to actors if a successful social interaction is not achieved. In the case of creation by decree, the relevant power is grounded in the resources that actors can provide to the state authority. In the case of political competition regarding state decision making, the relevant power is grounded in the resources that aid them in organizing and participating in that competition.

The introduction of new forms of bargaining power into the conflict over formal institutions raises a number of implications for our under-standing of the relationship between informal and formal change. What is especially interesting here is that the introduction of the state can alter the relative bargaining power among the different groups in a society. Whether or not it actually does so depends on the relative magnitude of the countervailing effects of the state's presence in the bargaining over formal institutions.

The importance of the accumulation of resources for efforts to influ-ence state decision making reveals another way in which formal rules are built on the foundation of informal institutions. The distributional con-sequences of informal conventions and norms translate into asymmetries in resources that in part determine political competition. In this sense the informal institutions reinforce a society's basic asymmetries and allow them to influence the creation of formal institutions.

However, the introduction of the state also can enhance the bargaining power of those disfavored by informal rules. First, state actors can im-prove the relative bargaining position of those disfavored by the status

and the state would be influenced in formal rule making only by those directly affected by the rule. This objection is analogous to the "rent-seeking" theory of state regulation proposed by Stigler (1975) among others. I admit that the proposed scenario does require some willingness on the part of people to influence state policy in areas in which they are not directly affected.

quo, by serving as a coalition partner in a bargaining game vis-à-vis those favored by the rules. If the interests of weak social actors coincide with the interests of the state in a conflict over formal institutions, this can increase the likelihood that the final form of the new institution will manifest the interests of those weak actors.

Second, the existence of a centralized process for institutional change can simplify the collective-action problems of such change. The previous analysis of evolutionary change illustrated the difficulty of changing social expectations through a decentralized mechanism. The logistics and costs of coordinating the individual strategies of enough actors to reorient a community's expectations are sizable. Hardin (1982) suggests that one of the conditions under which collective-action problems can be resolved involves the existence of an external source from which the group seeks a collective good. This external source provides a focal point for organizing the group and can lower the costs of achieving the group's goal. In the case of formal institutional change, the state can serve as the focal point for groups seeking change, thereby enhancing their chances of success.

We can see these last two effects in the twentieth-century social movements for changes in race and gender relations. The movements are oriented toward reforming long-standing networks of informal conventions and norms. These informal rules have structured race and gender relations in such a way as to disproportionately favor certain segments of society. Although the movements have tried to change the existing rules through both decentralized and centralized mechanisms, the primary focus has been on enacting legal proscriptions against behavior consistent with the informal rules. The existence of a state mechanism for institutional change has reduced the collective-action problems associated with these reforms and has hastened the rate of formal change. The fact that these legal changes have not succeeded in transforming much of the behavior associated with the enduring informal rules offers further evidence of the difficulty of changing enduring social expectations and of the stability of informal rules.

Additional sources of conflict

Once the state becomes the focal point for the conflict over institutional change, the institutions of the state become a new source of conflict. As with other forms of social institutions, the rules by which political competition is structured influence the distribution of influence over state decision making. This new source of conflict can significantly complicate the underlying bargaining over institutional change. The problem for social actors is that the conflict over formal institutional change depends in

part on the conflict over political institutions. Here the problem of uncertainty about the future can significantly affect the pursuit of institutional advantage in the political arena. If political uncertainty is high,
strategic actors will be confronted with two choices: either to design institutional arrangements that minimize the expected distributional effects or to design institutions that can easily be changed.[10]

Although there are counterexamples, such as the complex procedures
for change found in the United States Constitution, history suggests
that political actors more often choose to deal with this uncertainty by
establishing distributionally favorable procedures that can easily be
changed. Consider, for example, the conflict over electoral institutions in
democratic societies. Some of the earliest evidence of manipulation of
electoral institutions can be found in the assemblies of Rome in the
fourth century B.C. (Staveley, 1972). Because voting and representation were organized along tribal lines in these assemblies, the outcomes
could be manipulated by redrafting the eligibility requirements for tribal
membership. In 312 B.C., when Appius Claudius wanted to provide
greater influence to the emerging commercial interests in the urban
areas, he tried to reform the election laws by allowing residents of the
four urban districts to register as voters in the tribes of their choice.
This early effort at redistricting lasted a scant eight years before the
eligibility requirements were redrafted to restrict urban voters to the
original four districts. Those who sought to retain the basic agrarian
nature of Roman society prevailed for a time by manipulating this electoral institution.

From this early instance of institutional change onward, the history of
political conflict is replete with examples of leaders of government using
electoral institutions. One of the more recent and explicit examples of
such use was the electoral reform implemented by President François
Mitterrand in anticipation of the 1986 French parliamentary elections.
Faced with public opinion polls that predicted that his Socialist party
and its leftist coalition partners would suffer a serious defeat at the
hands of the moderate-right coalition, Mitterrand, in an effort to reduce
his potential losses, changed the existing double-ballot system of parliamentary election to a proportional-representation one. In doing so he
was able to reduce an anticipated fifty-seat moderate-right coalition tri-
umph to a single-seat parliamentary majority. This manipulation of the
system was far from an aberration; the party in power has amended the
electoral procedures to suit its own interests in every French parliamentary election since 1789 (Campbell, 1965).

---

10 Tsebelis (1990) focuses on some aspects of this trade-off in his discussion of the balance
between efficient and redistributive political institutions.

Stability and change

THE STRATEGIC CHOICE OF INSTITUTIONS: A COMPARISON OF EFFECTS

As this analysis suggests, the efficacy of a social institution depends on conditions pertaining to the structure of the interaction and the context in which it occurs. In most circumstances, when social actors intentionally create such institutions, these conditions restrict their choice of informal versus formal rules. However, there are some instances in social life in which the conditions are such that the actors have some flexibility over institutional form: when, given the proper information conditions, both informal and formal rules would be stable. In such instances the strategic choice of an institutional rule includes the choice of an enforcement mechanism.

In this section I analyze an example of a social interaction in which the choice of enforcement mechanism is often part of the strategic calculation: the bargaining between labor and management over wages and working conditions. I do so by comparing the types of institutional arrangements that have been established in various advanced industrial societies to structure workplace bargaining. This analysis shows the interplay of social institutions: the effects of institutions on both the power of strategic actors and the nature of social outcomes. It gives us an opportunity to assess the role of institutional rules as a strategic resource in distributional conflicts. In doing so it allows me to summarize the effects of different enforcement mechanisms on the underlying logic of intentional institutional design: When will social actors rely on informal rules, and when will they turn to the state to reinforce their interests?

The nature of the interaction

Bargaining among workers and employers involves numerous issues: wages, fringe benefits, working conditions, job security, methods of organizing production, participatory decision making, plant relocation, investment decisions, and so forth. Although each of these issues reflects the particular interests and concerns of the actors involved, all are related to questions of who will control the revenues of the firm's production process and how they will be distributed. Although this link may be explicit in bargaining over wage terms or implicit in conflicts over participatory issues such as investment and organization of work, each issue broadly affects the way in which the benefits of work and production are distributed.[11]

---

11 I can anticipate many objections to an exclusive focus on the conflict over the distribution of revenues. Workers have increasingly argued that they have a right to influence decisions that have traditionally been considered in advanced capitalist societies to

Within this bargaining over revenues is embedded a different, but related, conflict – the conflict over organizing collective actors. In its purest free-market form, bargaining at the individual workplace is a conflict between a group of disaggregated workers and a unified management. In an effort to enhance their bargaining power, workers enter into collective associations at the plant level. In addition, they may extend their efforts beyond the individual workplace and organize with similarly situated workers in other plants. At the same time, employers seek greater power by organizing employers' associations. Given the importance of relative bargaining power for determining the final distribution of revenues, there is a strong possibility of conflict over the scope and nature of these collective associations. To analyze the outcomes of economic conflict between workers and employers, we must look at both types of conflict: (1) conflict over the organization of collective actors and (2) bargaining over the revenues of production.

The key to understanding the preferences of economic actors regarding the different enforcement mechanisms is the effect of these institutional arrangements on these two conflicts. If we use the criterion of enforcement when defining institutional arrangements, we can distinguish three institutional forms that have been used to structure collective bargaining.

The first is the formal legal institution externally enforced by the state. Violations of these institutional arrangements usually result in the immediate enforcement of penalties by state officials. Examples are the institutions of the National Labor Relations Board in the United States and the state compulsory arbitration system in Australia.

The second institutional form is the informal set of conventions and norms that is established by an initial agreement between workers and employers and that continues to be recognized by later groups of actors as the framework for collective bargaining. These institutions are self-enforcing; they are not backed by the official sanction of the state (although they may have the state's informal support), and they rely on

---

be under the exclusive control of the firm's management, for example, investment decisions, plant relocations, and other decisions gathered under the rubric of "participatory" issues (see IDE, 1981, for a comparative review of the importance of participatory issues in union bargaining demands in European collective bargaining). Management, on the other hand, has generally resisted such claims and fought any efforts to expand collective bargaining into areas of exclusive "management prerogative." An exclusive focus on the distribution of revenues might be seen as an unrealistic simplification that ignores many issues crucial to the demands and power of workers. In defense of this focus I point out that it is sufficient for my purpose of investigating institutional effects. In the subsequent analysis I do address the effect of introducing participatory issues in the bargaining process on the conflict over revenues. This is an indirect way of considering the importance of these issues for the relative bargaining power of workers and firms.

information provision and the informal sanctions of the parties in the bargaining process. Examples are the Basic Agreements that can be found in Scandinavia and other European countries. The third institutional form is the legal contract establishing an institutional framework under which bargaining takes place for the duration of the contract period. The institutional enforcement depends on the specific terms of the contract, because the parties are often entitled to set their own enforcement procedures. The exact legal status of the contract varies across countries, but as a general rule the parties can seek external enforcement by the state. However, unlike the legal institutions of the state, which often include bureaucratic officials whose task it is to monitor compliance, the remedy of external enforcement results only from the express effort of one of the parties to exercise those rights.[12]

The organization of collective actors

Consider first the conflict over the organization of individual actors. A fundamental task for workers in the market is to resolve the collective-action problem vis-à-vis firms. The relative bargaining power of workers and employers depends directly on the workers' ability to organize and act collectively. There are two ways in which institutions can affect this process. The first encompasses the effects on the workers' ability to organize unions. The major institutional features to which we should look for these effects are (1) the extent of the state's involvement in institutions structuring the union's organization and recognition and (2) the existence of union security procedures (i.e., the legality of closed or union shop arrangements). The second type of institutional effect involves the union leaders' ability to maintain discipline and unity within their membership. This ability is affected by the extent of the state's involvement in the unions' internal affairs.[13]

12 The data on collective bargaining systems that are used throughout this section were compiled from several sources. The main focus was on advanced industrial societies in Europe, North America, Japan, and Australia. The most important of these sources include Blanpain, 1985; Clegg, 1976; Hanami and Blanpain, 1984; IDE, 1981; ILO, 1981; and OECD, 1979.
13 A third category of effects concentrates on the ability of individual firms to cooperate in their relations with unions. Many advanced industrial societies allow for a significant degree of cooperation among firms through national or regional employers' associations. In some countries the institutional framework actually encourages such cooperation. Other countries, most notably the United States, have created institutional barriers to such cooperation, through antitrust laws or similar legislation. However, the formal institutional distinctions across countries have been vitiated in part in the last several years by the rise in the number of mergers and acquisitions in the United States (Atleson, 1985; Getman, 1986; Oberer, 1986). Although this multifirm cooperation is

197

Consider the effects on union organizing, by reflecting on the logic of union growth.[14] Unions want greater union membership in order to enhance their bargaining power vis-à-vis employers. Their success in achieving greater growth depends on their ability to attract new workers and to withstand the employers' opposition to growth. Workers are more inclined to join unions when their chances of losing their jobs from membership are low and their chances of gaining benefits are high. Employers, on the other hand, resist union growth less when their demand for labor is high and when their potential losses from greater union power are less severe.[15]

In a comparative econometric analysis of union growth, Bain and Elsheik (1976) found a positive relationship between favorable changes in labor laws and the growth in union membership. This positive relationship can be explained by the institutional effects on the efforts of union leaders to attract new workers. The state's involvement in organizing and recognizing unions can have an important effect on the union leaders' efforts. The state may be involved to different degrees. First, some countries rely merely on a general constitutional or statutory protection for the "free association" of workers, avoiding more direct intervention in the organization process. This long was the case in Great Britain, Belgium, and the Scandinavian countries.

Second, some countries supplement their general protection of free association with established procedures for recognizing the bargaining rights of unions that satisfy certain criteria of representation. Such procedures now exist in Austria, Italy, France, and Germany. Representative of the necessary criteria for a union to receive official state recognition are those conditions laid down by French law: membership of a certain share of the relevant labor market, independence from management control, demonstrated financial strength, prior history of worker representation, and proof of patriotic allegiance during World War II (IDE, 1981).

---

a significant source of employer bargaining power, I have chosen not to discuss the institutional effects on this form of cooperation, except to the extent that national employers' associations enter into the analysis of bargaining with national or industrial unions.

14 This simple logic is drawn from several models of union growth: Ashenfelter and Penceval, 1969; Bain and Elsheik, 1976; and Dunlop, 1949. See Przeworski, 1984, for a comprehensive analysis of the findings of the various empirical studies of union growth.

15 This simplified model assumes that rational firms are opposed to unionization. Such an assumption may be appropriate as a means of understanding the task faced by union leaders, but as an empirical fact the degree of opposition to unions has varied among employers in industrial societies. This variation cannot be explained by a consistently high level of labor demand or by the lack of costs incurred by firms as a result of powerful unions. Instead, we must look to other factors relating to efforts by employers to reach accommodations with unions in exchange for strategic restraint by workers.

Third, some countries establish and enforce elaborate recognition procedures that result in substantial involvement in the organization of workers. Countries that have adopted such procedures include Japan, Canada, Australia, and the United States. The degree of state intervention of such procedures is exemplified by the National Labor Relations Board (NLRB) election procedures in the United States. These procedures control everything from the methods used by unorganized workers to initiate the unionization process through the strategies used by both union leaders and employers during the organizing campaign to the final election and recognition of the union representatives. Although this level of state control can be used to repress unions, as is demonstrated by the prohibitions against unionization in certain sectors of the labor market in several developing countries (Blanpain, 1985), state intervention has generally benefited union organizing efforts.

This direct state intervention affects the union growth dynamic in several ways. First, it lowers the cost to union leaders of organizing, by establishing an explicit standard for union recognition. This provides important information for both workers and union organizers; it designates the types of behavior constituting legitimate and binding union representation. The NLRB election system in the United States is an example of such an institutional procedure. When workers in a firm seek unionization, the NLRB calls an election of those workers in the relevant bargaining unit. The main purpose of the election is to determine whether a majority of the workers can agree on a particular union bargaining representative. Once a union wins this election it is guaranteed exclusive representative status for at least one year. During this period the employer is legally required to bargain with the victorious union and no others.

Compare this with the less stringent union recognition procedures in France and with the lack of institutional guarantees in Belgium. In both of these countries workers are represented by several different unions in the same workplace. In France each union must satisfy the recognition criteria, and although they all are allowed to compete among themselves for new members, they are encouraged to coordinate their bargaining efforts. In Belgium the lack of official procedures allows for multiple union bargaining with no explicit requirement of bargaining coordination. Unless these competing unions can reach some internal solution to the collective-action problems inherent in this multiunion setup, union leaders will be forced to expend additional resources to sustain their organizing efforts. On the other hand, in addition to providing an explicit standard – which, when satisfied, serves to legitimize the union – these U.S. procedures, with the exclusivity provision and the duty to bargain, relieves the union of continuously having to expend resources in an effort to maintain its status during the bargaining period. The value of these procedures for union organizing efforts have been documented in studies of aggregate union growth (Freeman, 1985) and of individual union elections (Prosten, 1979; Saltzman, 1985).

A second effect of state intervention is to lower the costs to union leaders by restricting employers' antiunion organizing strategies. The procedures provide for formal sanctions against the employment of certain antiunion strategies. Several countries have prohibitions against employers' establishing their own unions to compete with those created by workers. In addition, some countries have procedures that seriously restrict the ability of firms to prevent unionization. The NLRB procedures prevent employers from using several types of intimidating tactics against union leaders and workers.[16] However, as employers have learned to manipulate the NLRB procedures and avoid sanctions, they have become more sophisticated in their antiunion activities. Several recent studies of NLRB elections have discovered that employer manipulation of the duration of the election campaign (Heineman and Sandiver, 1983; Serber and Cooke, 1983) and of the definition of the union bargaining unit (Kochan, McKensie, and Chalykoff, 1986) has successfully defeated union organizing efforts.

Greater state involvement also lowers the costs of unionization for workers, by increasing the protections for individual organizing activities. Several countries have enacted explicit provisions protecting union organizing activities on the work site and during the workday. Employers are prohibited from firing or disciplining workers for participating in such activities. Here again formal sanctions are incurred by firms when they punish individual workers. Because individual workers are less likely to join a union when the costs of this decision are high, institutional procedures that decrease these costs enhance the likelihood of union growth.

These effects on the costs to workers are related to the effects on union growth brought about by union security provisions. These provisions create closed or union shops in the workplace, requiring workers either to join the union or at least to pay a fee equivalent to union dues as a prerequisite to employment. The advantages of a closed shop to union leaders are obvious: It greatly lowers the costs to leaders of organizing workers and maintaining their representative status in the workplace. At the same time, it simplifies the workers' decision of whether or not to

16 Note that these restrictions often fail to have the anticipated deterrent effect. Dickens (1983) and Weiler (1983, 1984) analyzed the circumstances in which employers have used illegal tactics in NLRB representational elections and in initial contract bargaining. They found that antiunion strategies were still employed, even though many of these tactics were deemed illegal by the NLRB.

join the union. The positive effects of such provisions on the outcomes of union organizing efforts have been confirmed by studies comparing the outcomes of union organizing efforts in states with union security laws and those without such laws (Cooke, 1983).

The practical importance of these effects is obviated somewhat by the fact that strong union security provisions are rare in most industrial societies. Australia and Sweden allow unions and employers to contract for a closed or a union ship in regard to new hiring. Great Britain has, for a long time, allowed closed shops as a matter of fact, but recent efforts by the Conservative party to reform labor procedures have included a prohibition of such practices. Because union shops are a matter of state law in the United States, there are various union security provisions, with nineteen states prohibiting any restrictions on the rights of individual workers to choose not to join a union.

The overall result of these different institutional effects on the costs of union leaders and workers is to enhance union growth. In situations in which there are established, externally enforced union organizing procedures and union security provisions, a union strategy of greater growth is more successful. In addition to the formal sanctions deterring antiunion strategies, the total set of institutional rules gives workers important information about the actions of other workers. As the collective-action literature shows, even those actors willing to participate in a union will be deterred from doing so if the prospects of success appear small (Hardin, 1982). This judgment is based on a worker's expectations about the future actions of other workers. These externally enforced procedures should reassure workers that others are willing to participate, thereby altering their expectations about the value of union membership. If, for example, workers view the union organizing effort not as a Prisoner's Dilemma problem but, rather, as an assurance game, the information about the actions of other workers becomes crucial to the union's success (Runge, 1984).

But from this discussion it does not follow that the highest levels of union membership are in those countries in which the state is most extensively involved. In fact, in comparing levels of union membership in most industrialized countries, we find that three of the four countries with the most extensive institutional arrangements (United States, Canada, and Japan) have some of the lowest levels of union membership (Bain and Price, 1980; Wallerstein, 1988). Much of this apparent contradiction can be explained by the third component of the union growth model – the level of employer opposition. Those countries with high levels of union membership are those in which employer opposition to unionization has been less pronounced. Although the initial opposition historically was high, employers eventually came to accept unions as an inevitable part of the bargaining process. Their strategy then shifted to one of seeking accommodation and restraint from union leaders. The ability of union leaders to adopt such a cooperative strategy is thus contingent on the degree of unity and discipline that they can maintain within their membership.

Consider next the effects of institutional rules on the union's internal affairs. The problems of unity and discipline are related to questions of free riding and collective action. The problem of free riding exists at various levels in the union movement. Individual workers prefer to receive the benefits of unionization without having to pay any of the costs of following a common union strategy. Individual unions prefer to reap the benefits of coordinating with other unions while retaining their ability to arrange a separate deal with their local employers. This tendency toward free riding reduces the unity and discipline that leaders need among their individual members, and this lack of discipline undercuts the effectiveness of certain strategies. Because many of these strategies require control of the labor supply, free riding decreases that control, thereby diminishing the unions' bargaining power in the negotiations over revenues.

Union leadership is crucial to resolving the free-riding problem. The leaders' ability to initiate decisions and coordinate their enactment makes it easier to implement strategies for the whole membership. The autonomy of union leadership is often the key to union discipline, but state involvement in a union's internal affairs can undercut this discipline. In most countries the state has generally avoided significant direct involvement in the internal affairs of national and local unions. But this laissez-faire approach has not prevailed in those countries in which the state has become directly involved in the organization and recognition process (Japan, Australia, Canada, and the United States).

Such state intervention in the union's internal affairs inhibits leadership efforts to discipline its membership by constraining the autonomy of union leaders. Several NLRB procedures require leaders to obtain the workers' approval of contract demands, strike decisions, and the like. Other regulations establish NLRB oversight of leadership activities, relations with other unions, and, most important, connections with political parties and candidates. Although one could argue that such constraints serve to protect the rights of individual workers, it is clear that such institutional constraints also inhibit the unity and discipline of the union movement.[17]

17 I do not want to be understood here as arguing against the possible significant abuse of workers' interests by unconstrained union leadership. There are important arguments to the effect that such institutional constraints further the interests of the individual worker. For example, Hyde (1984) presents a detailed argument supporting these NLRB provisions, on the grounds that they advance workplace democracy.

Stability and change

This analysis of institutional effects on the conflict over the organization of collective actors suggests that institutional arrangements can have a positive effect on the efforts of union leaders to build and maintain effective collective organizations. The best combination of institutional features from the workers' perspective consists of those institutions that further growth and those that enhance the unity and discipline of the membership. The workers' ability to control the local labor supply is strengthened by greater unionization. The loss of nonunion labor is also the loss of an important source of revenue for firms in the event of extended bargaining. Overall, this heightens the workers' relative bargaining power.

These conclusions are confirmed by the strategic choices of economic actors in the various nations being considered. In those countries in which workers were weak and poorly organized, they turned to the state for formal protection of their organizing efforts. This is why we see the most extensive formal rules in those states in which union membership is lowest. The effect of these protections was to enhance the workers' relative bargaining power. Yet in those states with better-organized working classes, unions originally chose more informal rules for structuring organizing activities. By turning to the effects of state involvement on bargaining strategies, we can see why powerful workers chose not to request the protection of the state.

Bargaining over wages and conditions

Workers and employers exercise their bargaining power through the strategies available to them. They use these strategies to force concessions from those with whom they are bargaining. Their ability to gain concessions is contingent on the losses that they can inflict on the other party (Bachrach and Lawler, 1981; Chamberlain and Kuhn, 1986). It is not necessary for them actually to carry out these strategies in order to force these concessions; often the mere expectation of incurring costs is sufficient to cause the actors to reduce some of their demands. But if these strategies are not available to the actors, their ability to inflict losses, and therefore their bargaining power, will be diminished. Of all the strategies available to workers and employers, those affecting the labor market are the most valuable for collective bargaining. The manipulation of available labor and job opportunities can inflict substantial costs on the parties. In fact, it is the high costs that these strategies can inflict that have been used to justify efforts to limit their use.[18]

18 Several countries have legal constraints on other types of strategies. I have previously discussed constraints on employer opposition to union organizing, for example, the independence requirement for union recognition, prohibitions against undue threats, and

Constraints on strikes and lockouts can be described according to two variables. The first variable distinguishes constraints according to whether they are established by state law or by some agreement (formal or informal) between the parties. The second separates conflicts over interests and conflicts over rights. The former are conflicts arising in the initial bargaining process, conflicts over the distribution of wages and profits and other contract terms. The latter are conflicts over rights granted in the contract and over contract interpretation and enforcement. The constraints on strategies can apply to either or both of these types of conflict.

In general these strategic constraints are established in most industrial societies by explicit contract between the parties. The constraints apply for the duration of the contract to all conflicts over rights. This reduces the available strategies for resolving contract disputes to either legal enforcement procedures or any private resolution mechanisms created by the contract. Several countries have additional restrictions established by law that apply to specific circumstances or sectors of the economy. Strikes are often prohibited for conflicts of interests when a work stoppage would seriously injure the "public good" (e.g., United States, Canada) or when it involves public employees. Australia prohibits both strikes and lockouts when the parties reject use of the state mediation and arbitration procedures. Only in France, Italy, and Great Britain are there no explicit constraints on using these strategies.

Consider first the effects of strategic constraints on conflicts over interests. This can be readily illustrated with an example of constraints on strike activity. If a well-organized work force is highly unionized, it should be able to (1) establish a fund that can partially offset lost wages during a strike and (2) exert influence over the local labor supply. This combination leads to a higher equilibrium wage. If an institutional constraint on strike activity is imposed, the union's ability to lower the firm's bargaining power will be diminished. In this way the workers' bargaining power is adversely affected by the institutional constraint.

Faced with such constraints, workers retain the option of violating them and pursuing the prohibited strategy, but they can expect to suffer the costs of sanctions for doing so. If the constraints are externally

the coercion of employees. There also are constraints against various union strategies, for example, picketing and demonstrations, and secondary boycotts. For example, in the United States, decisions by the Supreme Court and the NLRB have substantially curtailed the circumstances under which workers can publicly demonstrate against their employers (Kennedy, 1981; Klare, 1978; Stone, 1981). Secondary boycotts are deemed unacceptable in most countries, but they are explicitly illegal only in Great Britain and the United States (Blanpain, 1985). The effects of these latter constraints can be analyzed in the same way as I do here for constraints on strikes and lockouts.

enforced by law, workers may suffer heavy fines that can exhaust the resources on which they can rely in the event of prolonged negotiations. These penalties can be imposed by state officials as a matter of course. On the other hand, if the constraints are established by contract, the certainty of their imposition may be less sure. Such constraints can be enforced only through the explicit actions of the opposing parties. In the case of a strike, the firm must take into consideration its own costs of enforcement, which suggests that the anticipated costs of violating the constraint may not be as great in the former case. In either case, however, the costs of violating the constraints will lower the union's ability to survive extended negotiations and will lower the resulting equilibrium wage.

When we consider constraints in conflicts over rights, their effects on the conflict over revenues are less straightforward. One point of view argues that these are trade-offs that workers freely make in exchange for other benefits (Epstein, 1983; Posner, 1984). According to this view it would be inappropriate to consider the promise to refrain from striking as a constraint that may be detrimental to the parties. Others question to what extent a commitment to refrain from striking constitutes a freely given promise, given the asymmetry of the employment relationship (Atleson, 1985; Klare, 1985). In either case, the existence of a constraint on the strategies to be used in contract enforcement can enter the analysis of the original bargaining process only as an effect on the parties' future expectations. The rules provide information about the actions of others during the contract period. Here such constraints seem to work to the benefit of employers. By assuring employers that workers will be unable to choose to strike during the contract period, the constraint diminishes the workers' overall bargaining power.

Because control of the labor market is the principal source of power for workers in a system of private property, the effects of the constraints on these strategies will work to the detriment of the workers. Although a constraint on the use of lockouts will weaken the effect that employers can have on the labor market, this effect plays a far less significant role in their strategic calculations. Workers rely much more on the costs that strikes can inflict on employers. As we would expect, the historical record reflects efforts by unions to prevent the state from interfering in the creation of the rules governing workplace bargaining strategies.

Discussion

Given these various institutional effects, what forms of institutional arrangements will workers and employers seek to create as a framework for structuring bargaining over wages and working conditions? The relevant comparison is between bargaining in an unconstrained free market and bargaining within an institutionalized framework. In a free market, workers face a serious collective-action problem. Lacking organization and unity, individual workers are in a weak bargaining position vis-à-vis the firm. The basic question is whether the existence of a formal institutional framework for collective bargaining significantly alters the workers' weak bargaining position.

This analysis demonstrates that the formal institutional arrangements in advanced industrial societies produce countervailing effects on the workers' prospects. The differences arise between the effects on the organization of collective actors and the effects on the conflict over revenues. The first set of effects generally benefits workers by raising the possibility that they will resolve their collective-action problem and therefore improve their relative bargaining power. The second set of effects on balance works against the workers' interests.

This conclusion rests on the disproportionate constraints imposed on workers under these arrangements, which are the result of the interaction of collective-bargaining institutions with other social institutions, specifically the institutional protection of private property. The existence of the protections for private property skew bargaining power in the direction of the employers. Although these protections give employers a wide array of potential bargaining strategies, workers are forced to rely mainly on their ability to control the labor market. Because most of the institutional effects on the conflict over revenues restrict the exercise of strategies in the labor market, these effects hamper the workers' efforts to exercise their power.

This seems to imply that to workers the value of the formal institutionalization of economic conflict depends on their ability to resolve collective-action problems. In countries with a weakly organized working class where the collective-action problem has not been resolved without institutional protections, institutionalization is beneficial vis-à-vis the unconstrained market, because the increase in bargaining power through unionization is more significant than are the constraints on that power. In countries with a strong and unified working class where the collective-action problem has been resolved without formal institutional protections, such institutionalization is a hindrance to workers because the loss vis-à-vis the unconstrained market can be great.

But a consideration of the effects produced by different types of institutional enforcement shows that this might underestimate the importance of institutionalization for the fortunes of workers in an advanced capitalist society. The key here lies in the level of enforcement underlying the institutional structure. Consider again the workers' collective-action problems. Workers face a peculiarly difficult problem of organizing.

They have not only the usual problems of free riding but also the problem of an antagonist in their employer who can actively seek to thwart their efforts.

In those countries in which workers were able to organize without the aid of an externally enforced institutional framework, they overcame employer antagonism and eventually established an informal institutional framework that was intended to perpetuate their existence. These informal institutional rules emphasized information provision and informal sanctions as a way of structuring the bargaining process. Both unions and firms used these rules to formulate their future expectations of bargaining behavior. In these ways the rules limited the alternatives available to the parties and stabilized future relations.

Because the parties were engaged in an ongoing production relationship, there were sufficient incentives for the parties to invoke informal sanctions against isolated violations of the rules. This informal framework had the following effect on future generations of collective bargaining: As long as both sides continued to benefit from the arrangement, neither side violated the constraints on their strategies. But the framework did not establish significant costs and penalties for such violations, and so problems arose as circumstances changed in such a way as to threaten the efficacy of these rules.

As workers in various European countries began to use their power to incorporate participatory issues into the bargaining agenda, employers found it in their self-interest to violate the informal constraints against interfering in union organizing activities. They could do so, furthermore, without substantial penalty. In response to these new employer strategies, unions have sought greater state involvement in institutional protections for their activities, because the externally enforced institutional framework imposes greater costs for violating its constraints.

In a system of property relations that weights the bargaining process against workers, their unity is their principal source of power. Given the significant collective-action problems they face, the institutionalization of labor–management relations through externally enforced institutions offers significant benefits. But like a two-edged sword, the institutions that best protect their developing power are also those that can most effectively constrain its use. Here the interests of the state for continued production and stability in the workplace can conflict with the unconstrained institutional preferences of either workers or firms.

Such are the potential problems inherent in relying on externally enforced institutions. The establishment of a third-party enforcer forces social actors to give up a degree of control over their own actions. When those enforcers have interests and an agenda of their own (as is the case with state involvement in wage bargaining), the ultimate effects of those institutions depend in part on those interests. This illustrates the ongoing tension between the pursuit of distributional advantage and the costs of reliance on the state to ensure that advantage.

Strategic actors face a trade-off between distributional gain and the costs of external sanctions. Given the choice between a stable informal rule that provides a smaller distributional advantage and the pursuit of a potentially more beneficial formal rule with the requisite costs of external sanctions, those actors may choose to rely on the informal convention and to forgo recourse to the power of the state. For the weak, it is a mixed blessing; for the strong, it is a last resort.

7

Conclusion

What are the implications of a distributive conception of institutional emergence and change for the ways in which we think about social institutions? In the remaining pages I want to consider this question as a way of summarizing my analysis and arguments.

We started out with a set of questions about the social institutions in our everyday lives. Why do we have so many of them? Why does their basic structure differ across communities and societies? How do they develop and change? These questions are important for many reasons, but two are central here. First, their answers are crucial to our understanding of what happens in social life. And second, they are crucial to our assessments of what kinds of institutions we ought to have and whether or not our institutions manifest the goals and benefits by which we justify them. These are issues of explanation and justification, issues at the heart of our debates over the nature of the society in which we live.

EXPLANATION

Social institutions affect social life in many ways. Without them we would be unable to enjoy most of the benefits that we gain from acting in concert with others. They structure social life so as to produce collective benefits, variously characterized as gains from cooperation, coordination, and trade; functional and systemic needs; and so on. They enable complex interactions by providing information that can resolve uncertainty and stabilize strategic expectations. And social institutions influence the distribution of the benefits that they help produce.

Because social institutions have so many different effects, we are left with the question of how best to explain them. The explanations in this book are grounded in the relationship between institutions and human action. Social action can be based on a range of motivations. In my analysis I used the assumptions of rational-choice theory. People choose those strategies that maximize their expected utility. Institutions affect social outcomes through their effects on this expected-utility calculus. The key here is the capacity of social institutions to stabilize social expectations. Through the twin mechanisms of information provision and sanctions, institutions stabilize expectations and structure social action in the direction of equilibrium outcomes.

If we want to explain social institutions (their development, maintenance, and changes) in terms of the rationality of social actors, we commit ourselves to explaining them in terms of their preferences for these institutions. The principal conclusion of this book is that social institutions are best explained in terms of their distributional consequences. There are both theoretical and empirical grounds for giving priority to distributional benefits. Theoretically, an emphasis on distribution is consistent with the assumptions of strategic rationality on which the theory of rational choice is based. Empirically, this emphasis best captures what distinguishes the wide range of institutions we have observed throughout history.

The emphasis on distribution leads to the following explanations: Development and change are functions of the distributional conflict over substantive social outcomes; maintenance and stability are functions of the continuing ability of institutional rules to provide distributional advantages. Such explanations, which apply to both informal and formal institutions, conceptualize social interactions as bargaining problems and invoke the asymmetries of power in a society as a primary source of explanation.

These arguments have implications for different social-scientific approaches to the study of social institutions. For the rational-choice account, the main question is, What is the mechanism by which individual interactions are aggregated to the level of socially shared institutional rules? If we start from self-interested behavior at the level of the individual interaction, the pursuit of distributional advantage will drive the emergence of social institutions. The bargaining approach to spontaneous emergence relies on a mechanism of commitment and learning in which the commitments that resolve individual bargaining problems emerge as the socially shared solutions to those problems.

Explanations that stress collective benefits need to elaborate a mechanism to explain why collective benefits override distributional conflict. The failure to provide such a mechanism reduces an intentional explanation to a mere functionalist one: We *need* institutions, and therefore we *have* them. According to the standard economic analysis from which this approach is drawn, most rational-choice explanations adopt the mechanism of market competition. In analyzing the various theories of

210

spontaneous emergence, I argued that the theory of exchange and market competition is a special case of the more general bargaining theory.

When the empirical conditions defining market competition are found to hold, the market-competition theory adequately explains the emergence of social institutions. But these conditions define only one of many contexts in which institutional change occurs. The bargaining theory of spontaneous emergence allows us to vary the context in which social institutions emerge, and by doing so we can explain empirical events such as redistributive change, which the contemporary rational-choice explanations cannot cover. One implication of this argument for the rational-choice approach is that, as opposed to treating distributive questions as a residual category, they are in fact the basic issue on which institutional analysis is based.

For nonrational-choice approaches, either micro-level explanations, such as the norm-based account, or macro-level theories, some of which have concentrated on questions of distributional consequences, the theory of distributional conflict offers important lessons. Norm-based explanations can show how social actors maintain social rules, but they cannot offer an adequate micro-level explanation of emergence and change. They generally fall back on functionalist reasoning, explaining the emergence of norms in terms of the inevitable evolution of necessary rules. Although the distributive theory cannot explain how norms come to have a nonconsequentialist effect on social action (something that the norm-based explanation also fails to explain), it can offer a micro-level explanation of the emergence of the rules that come to have normative force in a community in terms of their distributional consequences.

Macro-level accounts of social institutions can find in the distributive theory those microfoundations that capture their underlying ideas. Not only does it capture the discriminating effects of social structure that are at the heart of their accounts, but it also allows us to incorporate important features of social interactions, which macro-level critics argue are not available to analyses of the rationality of social institutions. Here the distributive account demonstrates that rational-choice theory is capable of treating issues such as power, social context, and community.

One last point should be mentioned about the explanations offered in this book. The discussion of institutions as a product of bargaining may leave the impression that those who can commit to a future course of action unilaterally dictate institutional design. But asymmetries in power do not imply that those who cannot successfully assert their will have no influence. In cases of spontaneous emergence, the final institutional form is the by-product of repeated conflicts among actors with varying capacities. In cases of political competition, legal institutions are a function of

211

the various competitors' relative bargaining power. These mechanisms produce social institutions that have distributional effects, but generally not ones that exclusively favor any particular group of actors. The fact that the development of social institutions is the product of a bargaining game among social actors raises some questions about the theory's status.

Unfortunately, the present state of our bargaining theories can at best suggest what factors must be examined in seeking to understand the outcome of particular interactions. Thus, this distributive theory can provide only a general framework within which to analyze particular cases of institutional development. This may be discomforting to those who desire predictive rigor in their theories, but it is important to note that all theories of the rationality of institutional development and change contain some ambiguity. Advocates of the evolutionary and contractarian theories suffer significant and, as I have argued, more damaging ambiguity. Once we recognize that inevitable movements to Pareto-superior alternatives are inconsistent with strategic rationality, the seeming rigor of the other approaches evaporates.

JUSTIFICATION

Our justifications of social institutions are also affected by their distributional consequences. Both our normative beliefs about how institutions ought to be designed and our critical judgments about how well they manifest the goals by which they are justified must be grounded in our empirical understanding of how institutions work. There is nothing in this analysis that, in principle, prevents a normative argument favoring a particular institution on grounds of the collective benefits it provides. Rather, the implication is that the provision of the collective benefits must be justified on empirical grounds, not assumed because of some theoretical construct such as market competition.

For example, the old debate about efficiency versus distributional equality is generally couched in either/or terms: Either you construct an institution based on efficiency, or you construct one based on a criterion of equality. Another implication of this analysis is that when we are engaged in normative debates about real social institutions, the efficiency–distribution trade-off is more complicated than is the way in which this choice is generally posed. There may be a number of ways of satisfying the collective goals; each has different distributional effects. Because of this, normative arguments invoking collective goals to support a particular institution must take account of its distributive consequences.

The importance of empirical evidence also applies to our critical judgments about the degree to which our institutions satisfy the goals that justify their continued maintenance. A standard argument in the study of property rights and forms of economic organization is that an institutional rule established by decentralized emergence is more socially efficient than is one established by the state, because the latter is subject to political manipulation and the influence of distributive interests. Implicit in this claim is that a decentralized process is neutral and thus not subject to the effects of distributional conflict.

The arguments here have several implications for this standard assessment. First, a decentralized mechanism unaffected by distributional conflict is the exception and not the rule. Second, many Pareto-improving changes are redistributive. When the change works against the interests of the more powerful members of the community, it requires at the very least some form of state intervention to guarantee the compensation necessary to achieve the change. Third, contrary to the reasoning of many models of market competition, decentralized change is a slow and cumbersome process. This suggests that socially efficient changes may be more quickly accomplished by state intervention.

Now I admit that each of these implications is subject to the appropriate empirical conditions, but that is the underlying point that I want to emphasize. The standard argument for the superiority of the decentralized process is also subject to empirical conditions that should be justified in our critical assessments. We cannot resolve critical debates about real social institutions at the level of abstract constructs; we can do so only through our actual understanding of how these institutions affect social life.

Finally, the existence of distributional effects leads to two other implications for efforts toward intentional change in the name of reform. First, reform efforts in the name of the collective good will be resisted if the distributive effects tend to diminish the benefits of significant segments of the community. Second, the difficulty in achieving reform is not limited to resistance grounded in distributional conflict. The difficulty in changing enduring expectations brought about by cognitive and ideological factors exacerbates the problems of social reform. These conclusions are not intended to discourage reform, just to remind those who attempt it that it is a time-consuming and costly project.

RESEARCH AGENDA

The distributive conception of social institutions requires a reconceptualization of the research agenda for the rationality of social institutions. Analysis of maintenance and distribution should be structured by the conflicts of interest arising from the distributive effects of these institutions. Rather than focus on the collective-action problems of the collectivity in the process of institutionalization, we should concentrate on the interactions among the groups who benefit from institutional rules and those who are hampered by them.

Institutional maintenance involves a continuing conflict over the constraints produced by institutional rules. This conflict leads to research questions about the continuing efficacy of such constraints (e.g., do the rules remain the best means of providing distributional benefits?) and about the nature and costs of enforcement (e.g., do greater distributional asymmetries require a greater expenditure of resources on enforcement?). It should also be noted with interest that from this question of the costs of enforcement arise new questions about the relationship between equality and efficiency (e.g., do the greater costs of enforcement required by distributional differences produce greater inefficiency, in terms of increased expenditures and the introduction of the enforcers' interests?).

Because institutional development and change are products of an ongoing bargaining game among differing groups, the analytical focus should be on changes in the asymmetries in power (in this case, resources) and changes in the institutional rules: Do changes in asymmetries alter the credibility of the commitments necessary to establish institutional constraints? The process of institutional change implies that the emphasis on collective-action problems should be *within* the differing social groups: Can the members of groups, who want either to maintain the existing rules or to change them, resolve the collective-action problems in achieving their distributive goals?

These are the types of questions required by an emphasis on distribution. And it is in research questions such as these that our understanding of the effects of institutions on social life will be found.

Bibliography

Alchian, Armen A. 1950. "Uncertainty, Evolution and Economic Theory." *Journal of Political Economy* 58: 211–21.

Alston, Lee H., and Morton Owen Schapiro. 1984. "Inheritance Laws Across Colonies: Causes and Consequences." *Journal of Economic History* 44: 277–87.

Anton, Felix Lopez. 1985. "Creditor's Rights Under Spanish Law." *American Journal of Comparative Law* 33: 259–82.

Arkes, Hal R., and Kenneth R. Hammond, eds. 1986. *Judgement and Decision Making: An Interdisciplinary Reader.* Cambridge: Cambridge University Press.

Arrow, Kenneth. 1951. *Social Choice and Individual Values.* New Haven, CT: Yale University Press.

Ashenfelter, Orley, and J. H. Penceval. 1969. "American Trade Union Growth: 1900–1960." *Quarterly Journal of Economics* 83: 434–48.

Atiyah, P. S. 1981. *An Introduction to the Law of Contract.* Oxford: Clarendon Press.

Atleson, James B. 1985. "Reflections on Labor, Power and Society." *Maryland Law Review* 44: 841–72.

Auerbach, Jerold S. 1983. *Justice Without Law?* New York: Oxford University Press.

Aumann, Robert J. 1987. "Correlated Equilibrium as an Expression of Bayesian Rationality." *Econometrica* 55: 1–18.

Aumann, Robert J., and Michael Meschler. 1985. "Game Theoretic Analysis of a Bankruptcy Problem from the Talmud." *Journal of Economic Theory* 36: 195–213.

Axelrod, Robert. 1984. *The Evolution of Cooperation.* New York: Basic Books.
1986. "An Evolutionary Approach to Norms." *American Political Science Review* 80: 1095–112.

Bachrach, Samuel B., and Edward J. Lawler. 1981. *Bargaining: Power, Tactics and Outcomes.* San Francisco: Jossey-Bass.

Bain, George Sayers, and Farouk Elsheik. 1976. *Union Growth and the Business Cycle: An Econometric Analysis.* Oxford: Oxford University Press.

Bain, George Sayers, and Robert Price. 1980. *Profiles of Union Growth: A Comparative Statistical Portrait of Eight Countries.* Oxford: Basil Blackwell.

Barclay, Thomas. 1891. "The Definition of General Average." *Law Quarterly Review* 25: 22–42.

Bibliography

Barry, Brian. 1978. *Sociologists, Economists and Democracy*. Chicago: University of Chicago Press.

1982. "Is Democracy Special?" In Brian Barry and Russell Hardin, eds., *Rational Man and Irrational Society*. Beverly Hills, CA: Sage.

Barzel, Yoram. 1989. *Economic Analysis of Property Rights*. Cambridge: Cambridge University Press.

Bates, Robert H. 1985. *Essays on the Political Economy of Rural Africa*. Berkeley and Los Angeles: University of California Press.

1988. "Contra Contractarianism: Some Reflections on the New Institutionalism." *Politics and Society* 16: 387–401.

1989. *Beyond the Miracle of the Market: The Political Economy of Agrarian Development in Kenya*. Cambridge: Cambridge University Press.

1990. "Capital, Kinship, and Conflict: The Structuring Influence of Capital in Kinship Societies." *Canadian Journal of African Studies* 24: 151–64.

Becker, Gary. 1973. "A Theory of Marriage, Part I." *Journal of Political Economy* 81: 813–46.

1974. "A Theory of Marriage, Part II." *Journal of Political Economy* 82: 511–26.

Berkner, Lutz K. 1976. "Inheritance, Land Tenure and Peasant Family Structure: A German Regional Comparison." In Jack Goody, Joan Thirsk, and E. P. Thompson, eds., *Family and Inheritance: Rural Society in Western Europe, 1200–1800*. Cambridge: Cambridge University Press.

Berkner, Lutz K., and Franklin F. Mendels. 1978. "Inheritance Systems, Family Structure, and Demographic Patterns in Western Europe, 1700–1900." In Charles Tilly, ed., *Historical Studies of Changing Fertility*. Princeton, NJ: Princeton University Press.

Bernheim, B. D. 1984. "Rationalizable Strategic Behavior." *Econometrica* 52: 1007–28.

Bicchieri, Cristina. 1988. "Common Knowledge and Backward Induction: A Solution to the Paradox." In M. Vardi, ed., *Theoretical Aspects of Reasoning About Knowledge*. Los Altos, CA: Morgan Kaufmann.

Binmore, Kenneth. 1987. "Modeling Rational Players, Part I." *Economics and Philosophy* 3: 179–214.

Black, Duncan. 1958. *Theory of Committees and Elections*. Cambridge: Cambridge University Press.

Blanpain, Roger. 1985. *Comparative Labour Law and Industrial Relations*. Deventer, Netherlands: Kluver Law and Taxation Publishers.

Blinder, Alan S. 1973. "A Model of Inherited Wealth." *Quarterly Journal of Economics* 87: 608–26.

Boshkoff, Douglass G. 1982. "Limited, Conditional and Suspended Discharges in Anglo-American Bankruptcy Proceedings." *University of Pennsylvania Law Review* 131: 69–118.

Boudon, Raymond. 1981. *The Logic of Social Action: An Introduction to Sociological Analysis*. London: Routledge & Kegan Paul.

1982. *The Unintended Consequences of Social Action*. New York: St. Martin's Press.

1989. *The Analysis of Ideology*. Chicago: University of Chicago Press.

Bowman, John. 1989. "Transaction Costs and Politics." *European Journal of Sociology* 30: 150–68.

Boyd, Robert, and Peter J. Richerson. 1985. *Culture and the Evolutionary Process*. Chicago: University of Chicago Press.

Bibliography

Brennan, Geoffrey, and James Buchanan. 1985. *The Reason of Rule*. Cambridge: Cambridge University Press.

Buchanan, Allen. 1985. *Ethics, Efficiency and the Market*. Totowa, NJ: Rowman and Allanheld.

Buchanan, James, and Gordon Tullock. 1962. *The Calculus of Consent*. Ann Arbor: University of Michigan Press.

Buckley, F. H. 1986. "The Bankruptcy Priority Puzzle." *Virginia Law Review* 72: 1393–470.

Calvert, Randall. 1991. "Elements of a Theory of Society Among Rational Actors." Paper presented at the Public Choice Society annual meeting, New Orleans.

Campbell, Peter. 1965. *French Electoral Systems and Elections Since 1789*. Hamden, CT: Archon Books.

Carr, Lois Green, and Lorena S. Walsh. 1977. "The Planter's Wife: The Experience of White Women in Seventeenth-Century Maryland." *William and Mary Quarterly* 34: 542–71.

Censer, Jane. 1984. *North Carolina Planters and Their Children, 1800–1860*. Baton Rouge: Louisiana State University Press.

Chamberlain, Neil W., and James W. Kuhn. 1986. *Collective Bargaining*. New York: McGraw-Hill.

Clarke, E. H. 1971. "Multipart Pricing of Public Goods." *Public Choice* 2: 17–33.

Clegg, Hugh. 1976. *Trade Unionism Under Collective Bargaining*. Oxford: Oxford University Press.

Coase, R. H. 1960. "The Problem of Social Cost." *Journal of Law and Economics* 3: 1–44.

Cohen, G. A. 1978. *Karl Marx's Theory of History: A Defence*. Oxford: Oxford University Press.

1982a. "Functional Explanation, Consequence Explanation and Marxism." *Inquiry* 25: 27–56.

1982b. "Reply to Elster, 'Marxism, Functionalism and Game Theory'." *Theory and Society* 11: 483–96.

Coker, G. B. A. 1958. *Family Property Among the Yorubas*. London: Sweet and Maxwell.

Coleman, James S. 1990. *The Foundations of Social Theory*. Cambridge, MA: Harvard University Press.

Coleman, Jules. 1984. "Economics and the Law: A Critical Review of the Foundations of the Economic Approach to Law." *Ethics* 94: 649–79.

1988. *Markets, Morals and the Law*. Cambridge: Cambridge University Press.

Coleman, Jules, and Ellen Frankel Paul. 1984. *Philosophy and Law*. Oxford: Basil Blackwell.

Comaroff, John L., and Simon Roberts. 1981. *Rules and Processes: The Cultural Logic of Dispute in an African Context*. Chicago: University of Chicago Press.

Cooke, William. 1983. "Determinants of the Outcomes of Union Certification Elections." *Industrial and Labor Relations Review* 36: 402–14.

Coons, John E. 1964. "Approaches to Court Imposed Compromises – The Uses of Doubt and Reason." *Northwestern University Law Review* 58: 750–94.

1980. "Compromise as Precise Justice." *California Law Review* 68: 250–62.

Cooper, J. P. 1976. "Patterns of Inheritance and Settlement by Great Landowners from the Fifteenth to the Eighteenth Centuries." In Jack Goody, Joan Thirsk, and E. P. Thompson, eds., *Family and Inheritance: Rural Society in Western Europe, 1200–1800*. Cambridge: Cambridge University Press.

Countryman, Vern. 1976. "A History of American Bankruptcy Law." *Commercial Law Journal* 81: 226–33.

Crawford, Vincent. 1985. "Dynamic Games and Dynamic Contract Theory." *Journal of Conflict Resolution* 29: 195–224.

Crowley, John E. 1984. "Family Relations and Inheritance in Early South Carolina." *Social History* 17: 35–57.

Dahl, Robert, and Edward Tufte. 1973. *Size and Democracy*. Stanford, CA: Stanford University Press.

Dalhuisen, J. H. 1968. *Compositions in Bankruptcy: A Comparative Study of the Laws of the E.E.C. Countries, England and the U.S.A.* Leyden: Sijthoff.

Davidson, Donald. 1980. *Essays on Actions and Events*. Oxford: Clarendon Press.

Dickens, William T. 1983. "The Effect of Company Campaigns on Certification Elections: Law and Reality Once Again." *Industrial and Labor Relations Review* 36: 560–75.

Ditz, Toby L. 1986. *Property and Kinship*. Princeton, NJ: Princeton University Press.

Dunlop, John T. 1949. "The Development of Labor Organization: A Theoretical Framework." In R. A. Lerster and Joseph Shister, eds., *Insights into Labor Issues*. New York: Macmillan.

Dworkin, Ronald, ed. 1977. *The Philosophy of Law*. Oxford: Oxford University Press.

1985. *A Matter of Principle*. Cambridge, MA: Harvard University Press.

Eggertsson, Thráinn. 1990. *Economic Institutions and Behavior*. Cambridge: Cambridge University Press.

Eisenberg, Melvin A. 1976. "Private Ordering Through Negotiation: Dispute Settlement and Rulemaking." *Harvard Law Review* 89: 637–81.

Ellickson, Robert. 1991. *Order Without Law*. Cambridge, MA: Harvard University Press.

Elster, Jon. 1978. *Logic and Society*. New York: Wiley.

1980. "Review of G. A. Cohen's *Karl Marx's Theory of History.*" *Political Studies* 28: 121–8.

1982. "Marxism, Functionalism and Game Theory." *Theory and Society* 11: 453–82.

1985. *Making Sense of Marx*. Cambridge: Cambridge University Press.

1986. *Rational Choice*. New York: New York University Press.

1989a. *The Cement of Society*. Cambridge: Cambridge University Press.

1989b. "Social Norms and Economic Theory." *Journal of Economic Perspectives* 3: 99–117.

Elster, Jon, and Karl Moene. 1988. *Alternatives to Capitalism*. Cambridge: Cambridge Universtiy Press.

Enelow, James, and Melvin Hinich. 1984. *A Spatial Theory of Voting*. Cambridge: Cambridge University Press.

Ensminger, Jean. 1992. *Making a Market: The Institutional Transformation of an African Society*. Cambridge: Cambridge University Press.

Epstein, Richard A. 1983. "A Common Law for Labor Relations: A Critique of the New Deal Labor Legislation." *Yale Law Journal* 92: 1357–408.

Evans, Peter, Daniel Rueschemeyer, and Theda Skocpol. 1985. *Bringing the State Back In*. Cambridge: Cambridge University Press.

Faia, Michael. 1986. *Dynamic Functionalism: Strategy and Tactics.* Cambridge: Cambridge University Press.

Fama, E., and M. Miller. 1972. *The Theory of Finance.* New York: Holt, Rinehart and Winston.

Felde, Leon S. 1953. "General Average and the York–Antwerp Rules." *Tulane Law Review* 27: 406–56.

Freeman, Richard B. 1985. "Why Are Unions Fairing Poorly in NLRB Representation Elections?" In Thomas Kochan, ed., *Challenges and Choices Facing American Labor.* Cambridge, MA: MIT Press.

Friedman, James W. 1986. *Game Theory with Applications to Economics.* New York: Oxford University Press.

Fuller, Lon. 1969. *The Morality of Law.* New Haven, CT: Yale University Press.

Gardenfors, Peter, and Nils-Eric Sahlin. 1988. *Decision, Probability and Utility.* Cambridge: Cambridge University Press.

Gardner, Richard N. 1980. *Sterling-Dollar Diplomacy in Current Perspective: The Origins and the Prospects of Our International Economic Order.* New York: Columbia University Press.

Gauthier, David. 1986. *Morals by Agreement.* Oxford: Clarendon Press.

Geertz. Clifford. 1964. "Ideology as a Cultural System." In David Apter, ed., *Ideology and Discontent.* Glencoe, IL: Free Press.

   1982. *Local Knowledge: Further Essays in Interpretive Anthropology.* New York: Basic Books.

Gellner, Ernest. 1956. "Explanations in History." *Proceedings of the Aristotelian Society* 30: 157–76.

Gessner, Vollemer, Barbara Rhode, Gerhard Strate, and Klaus A. Ziegert. 1978. "Three Functions of Bankruptcy Law: The West German Case." *Law and Society* 12: 499–544.

Getman, Julius G. 1986. "Ruminations on Union Organizing in the Private Sector." *University of Chicago Law Review* 53: 45–77.

Gilmore, Grant, and Charles L. Black, Jr. 1958. *The Law of Admiralty.* Brooklyn: Foundation Press.

Goldberg, Victor. 1981. "Bridges over Contested Terrain: Exploring the Radical Account of the Employment Relationship." In Gunter Dlugos and Klaus Weiermair, eds., *Management Under Differing Value Systems.* New York: Walter de Gruyter.

Goody, Jack. 1983. *The Development of the Family and Marriage in Europe.* Cambridge: Cambridge University Press.

Goody, Jack, Joan Thirsk, and E. P. Thompson. 1976. *Family and Inheritance: Rural Society in Western Europe, 1200–1800.* Cambridge: Cambridge University Press.

Gordon, Robert W. 1984. "The Critical Legal Histories." *Stanford Law Review* 36: 57–125.

Grafstein, Robert. 1988. "The Problem of Institutional Constraint." *Journal of Politics* 50: 577–99.

Gray, John. 1984. *Hayek on Liberty.* 2nd ed. Oxford: Basil Blackwell.

Groves, Theodore, and M. Loeb. 1975. "Incentives and Public Inputs." *Journal of Public Economics* 4: 211–26.

Habakkuk, H. J. 1955. "Family Structure and Economic Change in Nineteenth Century Europe." *Journal of Economic History* 15: 1–12.

Hanami, Tadashi, and Roger Blanpain. 1984. *Industrial Conflict Resolution in Market Economies: A Study of Australia, the Federal Republic of Germany,*

Italy, Japan and the U.S.A. Deventer, Netherlands: Kluwer Law and Taxation Publishers.

Hardin, Russell. 1980. "Rationality, Irrationality and Functional Explanation." *Social Science Information* 19: 755–72.

———. 1982. *Collective Action.* Baltimore: Johns Hopkins University Press.

———. 1984. "Difficulties in the Notion of Economic Rationality." *Social Science Information* 23: 453–67.

———. 1987. "Why a Constitution?" Unpublished manuscript, University of Chicago.

———. 1988. "Contractarianism: Wistful Thinking?" Paper presented at the American Political Science Association meeting, Washington, DC.

Harsanyi, John. 1977. *Rational Behavior and Bargaining Equilibrium in Games and Social Situations.* Cambridge: Cambridge University Press.

Hart, H. L. A. 1961. *The Concept of Law.* Oxford: Clarendon Press.

Hayek, F. A. 1967. "Notes on the Evolution of Systems of Rules of Conduct." In *Studies in Philosophy, Politics, and Economics.* Chicago: University of Chicago Press.

———. 1973. *Law, Legislation and Liberty. Vol. 1: Rules and Order.* Chicago: Univeristy of Chicago Press.

———. 1978. *Law, Legislation and Liberty. Vol. 3: The Political Order of a Free People.* Chicago: University of Chicago Press.

———. 1988. *The Fatal Conceit.* Chicago: University of Chicago Press.

Heckathorn, Douglas D., and Steven M. Maser. 1987. "Bargaining and Constitutional Contracts." *American Journal of Political Science* 31: 142–68.

Hechter, Michael, Karl-Dieter Opp, and Reinhard Wippler, eds. 1990. *Social Institutions: Their Emergence, Maintenance, and Effects.* New York: Walter de Gruyter.

Heineman, Herbert, and Marcus Sandiver. 1983. "Predicting the Outcome of Union Certification Elections: A Review of the Literature." *Industrial and Labor Relations Review* 36: 537–59.

Hirshleifer, Jack. 1977. "Economics from a Biological Viewpoint." *Journal of Law and Economics* 20: 1–52.

Hobbes, Thomas. 1963. *Leviathan.* New York: Meridian Books.

Hodder, B. W., and U. I. Ukwu. 1969. *Markets in West Africa.* Ibadan, Nigeria: Ibadan University Press.

Hoebel, E. Adamson. 1954. *The Law of Primitive Man.* Cambridge, MA: Harvard University Press.

Hollis, Martin. 1987. *The Cunning of Reason.* Cambridge: Cambridge University Press.

Honoré, Tony. 1981. *Emperors and Lawyers.* New York: St. Martin's Press.

Hooker, M. B. 1975. *Legal Pluralism: An Introduction to Colonial and Neo-Colonial Laws.* Oxford: Oxford University Press.

Howell. C. 1976. "Peasant Inheritance Customs in the Midlands, 1280–1700." In Jack Goody, Joan Thirsk, and E. P. Thompson, eds., *Family and Inheritance: Rural Society in Western Europe, 1200–1800.* Cambridge: Cambridge University Press.

Hume, David. 1978. *A Treatise of Human Nature.* 2nd ed. Oxford: Oxford University Press.

Hyde, Alan. 1984. "Democracy in Collective Bargaining." *Yale Law Journal* 93: 793–856.

IDE (Industrial Democracy in Europe). 1981. *European Industrial Relations.* Oxford: Clarendon Press.

ILO (International Labor Organization). 1981. *Collective Bargaining in*

Bibliography

Industrialized Market Economies. Geneva: International Labour Office.

Ingram, Peter. 1985. "Maintaining the Rule of Law." *Philosophical Quarterly* 35: 359–81.

Jackson, Thomas H., and Anthony Kronman. 1976. "Voidable Preferences and Protection of the Expectation Interest." *Minnesota Law Review* 60: 971–1010.

Jeffrey, Richard C. 1983. *The Logic of Decision.* 2nd ed. Chicago: University of Chicago Press.

Johnson, James. 1991. "Symbol and Strategy." Ph.D. diss., University of Chicago.

Jones, W. J. 1979. *The Foundations of English Bankruptcy.* Philadelphia: American Philosophical Society.

Kahneman, Daniel, Paul Slovic, and Amos Tversky, eds. 1982. *Judgment Under Uncertainty: Heuristics and Biases.* Cambridge: Cambridge University Press.

Kairys, David. 1982. *The Politics of Law: A Progressive Critique.* New York: Pantheon.

Katz, Stanley N. 1977. "Republicans and the Law of Inheritance in the American Revolutionary Era." *Michigan Law Review* 76: 1–29.

Katzenstein, Peter. 1978. *Beyond Power and Plenty: Foreign Economic Policies in Advanced Industrial Societies.* Ithaca, NY: Cornell University Press.

Kennedy, Duncan. 1981. "Cost Reduction Theory as Legitimation." *Yale Law Journal* 90: 1275–83.

Klare, Karl. 1978. "Judicial Deradicalization of the Wagner Act and the Origins of Modern Legal Consciousness, 1937–1941." *Minnesota Law Review* 62: 265.

——— 1985. "Traditional Labor Law Scholarship and the Crisis of Collective Bargaining Law: A Reply to Professor Finkin." *Maryland Law Review* 44: 731–840.

Kochan, Thomas A., Robert B. McKensie, and John Chalykoff. 1986. "The Effects of Corporate Strategy and Workplace Innovations on Union Representation." *Industrial and Labor Relations Review* 39: 487–501.

Krehbiel, Keith. 1988. "Spatial Models of Legislative Choice." *Legislative Studies Quarterly* 13: 259–319.

Kreps, David M. 1990. *A Course in Microeconomic Theory.* Princeton, NJ: Princeton University Press.

Kronman, Anthony, and Richard A. Posner. 1979. *The Economics of Contract Law.* Boston: Little, Brown.

Kukathas, Chandran. 1989. *Hayek and Modern Liberalism.* Oxford: Clarendon Press.

Kula, Witold. 1986. *Measure and Man.* Trans. R. Szreter. Princeton, NJ: Princeton University Press.

Kuran, Timur. 1988. "The Tenacious Past: Theories of Personal and Collective Conservatism." *Journal of Economic Behavior and Organization* 10: 143–71.

Ladurie, E. LeRoy. 1976. "Family Structures and Inheritance Customs in Sixteenth Century France." In Jack Goody, Joan Thirsk, and E. P. Thompson, eds., *Family and Inheritance: Rural Society in Western Europe, 1200–1800.* Cambridge: Cambridge University Press.

Landes, William M., and Richard A. Posner. 1987. *The Economic Structure of Tort Law.* Cambridge, MA: Harvard University Press.

Langlois, Richard N. 1985. *Economics as a Process.* Cambridge: Cambridge University Press.

Bibliography

Langton, John. 1982. "The Behavioural Theory of Evolution and the Weber Thesis." *Sociology* 16: 341–58.

Levi, Margaret. 1988. *Of Rules and Revenue*. Berkeley and Los Angeles: University of California Press.

Levinthal, Louis Edward. 1919. "The Early History of Bankruptcy Law." *University of Pennsylvania Law Review* 66: 223–50.

Levy, David M. 1985. "The Impossibility of a Complete Methodological Individualist: Reduction When Knowledge Is Imperfect." *Economics and Philosophy* 1: 101–8.

Lewis, David. 1969. *Convention*. Cambridge, MA: Harvard University Press.

Libecap, Gary D. 1989. *Contracting for Property Rights*. Cambridge University Press.

Lijphart, Arend. 1984. *Democracies*. New Haven, CT: Yale Universtiy Press.

Livadas, Christopher. 1983. *The Winding-Up of Insolvent Companies in England and France*. Deventer, Netherlands: Kluwer Law and Taxation Publishers.

Lloyd, Eyre. 1877. *The Succession Laws of Christian Countries with Special Reference to the Law of Primogeniture as It Exists in England*. London: Stevens and Haynes Law Publishers.

Lowndes, Richard, and George Rupert Rudolf. 1975. *The Law of General Average and the York–Antwerp Rules*. London: Stevens.

Luce, R. D., and Howard Raiffa. 1957. *Games and Decisions*. New York: Wiley.

Lukes, Steven. 1968. "Methodological Individualism Reconsidered." *British Journal of Sociology* 19: 119–29.

1974. *Power: A Radical View*. London: Macmillan.

Macauley, Stewart. 1963. "Non-Contractual Relations in Business." *American Sociological Review* 28: 55–67.

MacNeil, Ian. 1967. *Bankruptcy Law in East Africa*. Nairobi: Legal Publications.

1980. *The New Social Contract*. New Haven, CT: Yale University Press.

Maine, Henry. 1986. *Ancient Law*. Tucson: University of Arizona Press.

Makdisi, John. 1984. "Fixed Shares in Intestate Distribution: A Comparative Analysis of Islamic and American Law." *Brigham Young University Law Review* 1984: 267–304.

Mandelbaum, Maurice. 1955. "Societal Facts." *British Journal of Sociology* 6: 305–17.

Mannheim, Karl. 1954. *Ideology and Utopia*. London: Routledge & Kegan Paul.

Manser, Marilyn, and Murry Brown. 1980. "Marriage and Household Decision Making: A Bargaining Analysis." *International Economic Review* 21: 31–44.

March, James G., and Johan P. Olsen. 1989. *Rediscovering Institutions: The Organizational Basis of Politics*. New York: Free Press.

March, James G., and Herbert Simon. 1958. *Organizations*. New York: Wiley.

Marcus, George E. 1981. "Litigation, Interpersonal Conflict and Noble Succession Disputes in the Friendly Islands." In M. Cappelletti, ed., *Access to Justice*. Vol. 4. Alphen aan den Rijn: Sijthoff.

Marglin, Stephen. 1974. "What Do Bosses Do? The Origins and Functions of Hierarchy in Capitalist Production." *Review of Radical Political Economics* (pt. 1) 6: 60–112 and (pt. 2) 7: 20–37.

Marshall, Geoffrey. 1983. "The Role of Rules." In David Miller and Larry Siedentop, eds., *The Nature of Political Theory*. Oxford: Oxford University Press.

Bibliography

Martin, Andrew, and George Ross. 1980. "European Trade Unions and the Economic Crisis: Perceptions and Strategies." *West European Politics* 3: 33–67.

Marx, Karl. 1970. *The German Ideology. Collected Works.* London: Lawrence and Wishart.

——— 1986. "A Preface to a Critique of Political Economy." In Jon Elster, ed., *Karl Marx: A Reader.* Cambridge: Cambridge University Press.

Matthews, R. C. O. 1986. "The Economics of Institutions and the Sources of Growth." *Economic Journal* 96: 903–10.

Maynard-Smith, John. 1982. *Evolution and the Theory of Games.* Cambridge: Cambridge University Press.

——— 1987. "How to Model Evolution." In John Dupre, ed., *The Latest on the Best: Essays on Evolution and Optimality.* Cambridge, MA: MIT Press.

McCoid, John C. 1981. "Bankruptcy, Preferences and Efficiency: An Expression of Doubt." *Virginia Law Review* 67: 249–73.

McElroy, Majorie B., and Mary Jean Horney. 1981. "Nash-bargained Household Decisions: Toward a Generalization of the Theory of Demand." *International Economic Review* 22: 333–49.

McKelvey, Richard D., and Peter Ordeshook. 1984. "An Experimental Study of the Effects of Procedural Rules on Committee Behavior." *Journal of Politics* 46: 182–205.

Meillassoux, Claude. 1971. *The Development of Indigenous Trade and Markets in West Africa.* Oxford: Oxford University Press.

Menchik, Paul L. 1980. "Primogeniture, Equal Sharing and the U.S. Distribution of Wealth." *Quarterly Journal of Economics* 94: 299–316.

Menger, Carl. 1963. *Problems of Economics and Sociology.* Urbana: University of Illinois Press.

Merton, Robert. 1968. *Social Theory and Social Structure.* 3rd ed. New York: Free Press.

Milgrom, Paul, and John Roberts. 1991. "Adaptive and Sophisticated Learning in Normal Form Games." *Games and Economic Behavior* 3: 82–100.

Miller, J. Gareth. 1977. *The Machinery of Succession.* Oxford: Professional Books.

Montesquieu, Charles de Secondat. 1989. *The Spirit of the Laws.* Trans. Anne Cohler, Basia Miller, and Harold Stone. Cambridge: Cambridge University Press.

Moore, Sally F. 1989. "History and the Redefinition of Custom in Kilimanjaro." In June Starr and Jane Collier, eds., *History and Power in the Study of Law.* Ithaca, NY: Cornell University Press.

Morriss, Peter. 1987. *Power: A Philosophical Analysis.* New York: St. Martin's Press.

Moulin, Herve. 1981. *Game Theory for the Social Sciences.* New York: New York University Press.

Nader, Laura. 1969. *Law in Culture and Society.* Chicago: Aldine.

——— 1989. "The Crown, the Colonists, and the Course of Zapotec." In June Starr and Jane F. Collier, eds., *History and Power in the Study of Law.* Ithaca, NY: Cornell University Press.

Nash, June. 1989. "A Redistributive Model for Analyzing Government Mediation and Law in Family, Community, and Industry in a New England Industrial City." In June Starr and Jane Collier, eds., *History and Power in the Study of Law.* Ithaca, NY: Cornell University Press.

Nelson, Richard R., and Sidney G. Winter. 1982. *An Evolutionary Theory of Economic Change.* Cambridge, MA: Harvard University Press.

223

Bibliography

Nordlinger, Eric. 1981. *On the Autonomy of the Democratic State*. Cambridge, MA: Harvard University Press.

North, Douglass C. 1981. *Structure and Change in Economic History*. New York: Norton.

1990. *Institutions, Institutional Change and Economic Performance*. Cambridge: Cambridge University Press.

Oberer, Walter E. 1986. "The Regulation of Union Economic Power." *Utah Law Review* 1986: 267–95.

Oberschall, Anthony, and Eric M. Leifer. 1986. "Efficiency and Social Institutions: Uses and Misuses of Economic Reasoning in Sociology." *American Review of Sociology* 12: 233–53.

OECD (Organization for Economic Cooperation and Development). 1979. *Collective Bargaining and Government Policies in Ten OECD Countries*. Paris: OECD.

Okin, Susan Moller. 1989. *Justice, Gender, and the Family*. New York: Basic Books.

Olson, Mancur. 1965. *The Logic of Collective Action*. Cambridge, MA: Harvard University Press.

Ordeshook, Peter. 1986. *Game Theory and Political Theory*. Cambridge: Cambridge University Press.

Osborne, Martin J., and Ariel Rubenstein. 1990. *Bargaining and Markets*. San Diego: Academic Press.

Ostrom, Elinor. 1986. "An Agenda for the Study of Institutions." *Public Choice* 48: 3–25.

1990. *Governing the Commons*. Cambridge: Cambridge University Press.

Oxford English Dictionary. 1971. Oxford: Oxford University Press.

Papenak, Hanna. 1990. "To Each Less Than She Needs, from Each More Than She Can Do: Allocations, Entitlements, and Value." In Irene Tinker, ed., *Persistent Inequalities: Women and World Development*. New York: Oxford University Press.

Parsons, Talcott. 1945. "The Problem of Controlled Institutional Change." In Talcott Parsons, ed., *Essays in Sociological Change*. New York: Free Press.

Patterson, Orlando. 1982. *Slavery and Social Death*. Cambridge, MA: Harvard University Press.

Paulsen, Gordon W. 1983. "An Historical Overview of the Development of Uniformity in International Maritime Law." *Tulane Law Review* 57: 1065–87.

Peltzer, Martin. 1975. *German Insolvency Laws*. Cologne: Verlag Dr. Otto Schmidt.

Posner, Richard A. 1980. "A Theory of Primitive Society, with Special Reference to Law." *Journal of Law and Economics* 23: 1–53.

1984. "Some Economics of Labor Law." *University of Chicago Law Review* 51: 988–1011.

1986. *Economic Analysis of Law*. Boston: Little, Brown.

1987. "The Law and Economics Movement." *American Economic Review* 77: 1–13.

Prosten, Richard. 1979. "The Longest Season: Union Organizing in the Last Decade." *Industrial Relations Research Association: Proceedings of the Thirty-First Annual Meeting, August 29–31, 1978, in Chicago*. Madison, WI: IRRA.

Pryor, Frederic L. 1973. "Simulation of the Impact of Social and Economic Institutions on the Size Distribution of Income and Wealth." *American Economic Review* 63: 50–72.

Bibliography

Przeworski, Adam. 1984. "Union Growth: A Literature Review." Unpublished manuscript, University of Chicago.

1986. "Marxism and Rational Choice." *Politics and Society* 14: 379–410.

1990. *The State and the Economy Under Capitalism.* New York: Hardwood Academic Publishers.

Radin, Max. 1940. "The Nature of Bankruptcy." *University of Pennsylvania Law Review* 89: 1–9.

Rae, Douglas. 1967. *The Political Consequences of Electoral Laws.* New Haven, CT: Yale University Press.

Raiffa, Howard. 1982. *The Art and Science of Negotiation.* Cambridge, MA: Harvard University Press.

Rapoport, Anatol. 1966. *Two-Person Game Theory: The Essential Issues.* Ann Arbor: University of Michigan Press.

Rapoport, Anatol, and Melvin Guyer. 1966. "A Taxonomy of 2 × 2 Games." *General Systems* 11: 203–14.

Rawls, John. 1955. "Two Concepts of Rules." *Philosophical Review* 64: 3–32.

1971. *A Theory of Justice.* Cambridge, MA: Harvard University Press.

Rhode, Deborah. 1989. *Justice and Gender.* Cambridge, MA: Harvard University Press.

Richerson, Peter J., and Robert Boyd. 1987. "Simple Models of Complex Phenomena: The Case of Cultural Evolution." In John Dupre, ed., *The Latest on the Best: Essays on Evolution and Optimality.* Cambridge, MA: MIT Press.

Rifkin, Jeremy. 1987. *Time Wars: The Primary Conflict in Human History.* New York: Henry Holt.

Riker, William. 1980. "Implications from the Disequilibrium of Majority Rule for the Study of Institutions." *American Political Science Review* 76: 753–66.

1982. *Liberalism Against Populism.* San Francisco: Freeman.

1988. "The Place of Political Science in Public Choice." *Public Choice* 57: 247–57.

Rothstein, Bo. 1990. "Marxism, Institutional Analysis, and Working-Class Power: The Swedish Case." *Politics and Society* 16: 317–45.

Rubinstein, Ariel. 1982. "Perfect Equilibrium in a Bargaining Model." *Econometrica* 50: 97–109.

1988. "Comments on the Interpretation of Game Theory." London: ICERD Discussion Paper no. TE/88/181.

Runge, Carlisle Ford. 1984. "Institutions and the Free Rider: The Assurance Problem in Collective Action." *Journal of Politics* 46: 154–81.

Salmon, Marylynn. 1986. *Women and the Law of Property in Early America.* Chapel Hill: University of North Carolina Press.

Saltzman, Gregory. 1985. "Bargaining Laws as a Cause and Consequence of the Growth of Teacher Unionism." *Industrial and Labor Relations Review* 38: 335–51.

Saltzman, Michael. 1981. "Indigenous Law Among the Kipsigis of Southwestern Kenya." In Mauro Cappelletti, ed., *Access to Justice.* Vol. 3. Alphen aan den Rijn: Sijthoff.

Schelling, Thomas C. 1960. *The Strategy of Conflict.* Cambridge, MA: Harvard University Press.

Schotter, Andrew. 1981. *The Economic Theory of Social Institutions.* Cambridge: Cambridge University Press.

1986. "The Evolution of Social Institutions." In Richard Langlois, ed., *Economics in Process.* Cambridge: Cambridge University Press.

Bibliography

Schwartz, Alan. 1981. "Security Interests and Bankruptcy Priorities: A Review of Current Theories." *Journal of Legal Studies* 10: 1–37.

Schwartz, Thomas. 1986. "The Meaning of Instability." Unpublished manuscript, University of Texas.

Scitovsky, Tibor. 1971. *Welfare and Competition.* Homewood, IL: Irwin.

Searle, John. 1969. *Speech Acts.* Cambridge: Cambridge University Press.

Selmer, Knut S. 1958. *The Survival of General Average: A Necessity or an Anachronism?* Oslo: Oslo University Press.

Selten, Robert. 1980. "A Note on Evolutionary Stable Strategies in Asymmetric Animal Conflicts." *Journal of Theoretical Biology* 84: 93–101.

Sen, Amartya K. 1990. "Gender and Cooperative Conflicts." In Irene Tinker, ed., *Persistent Inequalities: Women and World Development.* New York: Oxford University Press.

Sened, Itai. 1990. "A Political Theory of the Evolution of Rights." Working paper no. 152, Department of Political Science, Washington University in St. Louis.

Serber, Ronald L., and William N. Cooke. 1983. "The Decline in Union Success in NLRB Representation Elections." *Industrial Relations* 22: 33–44.

Shaked, Avner, and John Sutton. 1984. "Involuntary Unemployment as a Perfect Equilibrium in a Bargaining Model." *Econometrica* 52: 1351–64.

Shammas, Carole. 1987. "English Inheritance Law and Its Transfer to the Colonies." *American Journal of Legal History* 31: 145–63.

Shammas, Carole, Marylynn Salmon, and U. N. Dahlin. 1987. *Inheritance in America from Colonial Times to Present.* New Brunswick, NJ: Rutgers University Press.

Shepsle, Kenneth. 1979. "Institutional Arrangements and Equilibrium in Multidimensional Voting Models." *American Journal of Political Science* 23: 27–59.

    1986. "The Positive Theory of Legislative Institutions: An Enrichment of Social Choice and Spatial Models." *Public Choice* 50: 135–78.

    1989. "Studying Institutions: Some Lessons from the Rational Choice Approach." *Journal of Theoretical Politics* 1: 131–47.

Shepsle, Kenneth, and Peter Ordeshook. 1982. *Political Equilibrium.* Boston: Kluwer-Nijhoff.

Skocpol, Theda. 1985. *States and Social Revolutions: A Comparative Analysis of France, Russia and China.* Cambridge: Cambridge University Press.

Skowronek, Stephen. 1982. *Building a New American State.* Cambridge: Cambridge University Press.

Smith, Adam. 1969. *The Theory of Moral Sentiments.* Indianapolis: Liberty Classics.

    1976. *An Inquiry into the Nature and Causes of the Wealth of Nations.* Indianapolis: Liberty Classics.

Snidal, Duncan. 1985. "Coordination Versus Prisoners' Dilemma: Implications for International Cooperation and Regimes." *American Political Science Review* 79: 923–42.

Sober, Elliott. 1987. "What Is Adaptationism?" In John Dupre, ed., *The Latest on the Best: Essays on Evolution and Optimality.* Cambridge, MA: MIT Press.

Spencer, Herbert. 1969. *Principles of Sociology.* Hamden, CT: Archon Books.

Starr, June. 1978. "Turkish Village Disputing Behavior." In Laura Nader and Harry F. Todd, Jr., eds., *The Disputing Process and Law in Ten Societies.* New York: Columbia University Press.

226

1989. "The 'Invention' of Early Legal Ideas: Sir Henry Maine and the Perpetual Tutelage of Women." In June Starr and Jane F. Collier, eds., *History and Power in the Study of Law*. Ithaca, NY: Cornell University Press.

Starr, June, and Jane F. Collier. 1989. *History and Power in the Study of Law*. Ithaca, NY: Cornell University Press.

Staveley, E. S. 1972. *Greek and Roman Voting and Elections*. Ithaca, NY: Cornell University Press.

Stigler, George. 1975. *The Citizen and the State: Essays on Regulation*. Chicago: University of Chicago Press.

Stiglitz, J. E. 1969. "Distribution of Income and Wealth Among Individuals." *Econometrica* 37: 382–97.

Stockard, Janice E. 1989. *Daughters of the Canton Delta: Marriage Patterns and Economic Strategies in South China, 1860–1930*. Stanford, CA: Stanford University Press.

Stone, Katherine. 1974. "The Origins of Job Structures in the Steel Industry." *Review of Radical Political Economics* 6: 61–97.

1981. "The Post-War Paradigm in American Labor Law." *Yale Law Journal* 90: 1509–80.

Sturmthal, Adolf. 1943. *The Tragedy of European Labor 1918–1939*. New York: Columbia University Press.

1972. *Comparative Labor Movements: Ideological Roots and Industrial Development*. Belmont, CA: Wadsworth.

Sugden, Robert. 1986. *The Economics of Rights, Cooperation and Welfare*. London: Basil Blackwell.

1989. "Spontaneous Order." *Journal of Economic Perspectives* 3: 85–97.

Sydenham, P. H. 1979. *Measuring Instruments: Tools of Knowledge and Control*. Stevenage: Peter Peregrinus.

Taylor, Michael. 1982. *Community, Anarchy and Liberty*. Cambridge: Cambridge University Press.

1987. *The Possibility of Cooperation*. Cambridge: Cambridge University Press.

1989. "Structure, Culture, and Action in the Explanation of Social Change." *Politics and Society* 17: 115–62.

Telser, Lester G. 1980. "A Theory of Self-Enforcing Agreements." *Journal of Business* 53: 27–44.

Thirsk, Joan. 1976. "The European Debate on Custom and Inheritance, 1500–1700." In Jack Goody, Joan Thirsk, and E. P. Thompson, eds., *Family and Inheritance: Rural Society in Western Europe, 1200–1800*. Cambridge: Cambridge University Press.

Thompson, E. P. 1967. "Time, Work-Discipline, and Industrial Capitalism." *Past and Present* 38: 56–97.

Thompson, James W. 1928. *An Economic and Social History of the Middle Ages*. New York: Century.

Thompson, Leonard. 1990. *A History of South Africa*. New Haven, CT: Yale University Press.

Tinker, Irene, ed. 1990. *Persistent Inequalities: Women and World Development*. New York: Oxford University Press.

Tocqueville, Alexis de. 1969. *Democracy in America*. New York: Anchor Books.

Tsebelis, George. 1990. *Nested Games*. Berkeley and Los Angeles: University of California Press.

Ullman-Margalit, Edna. 1978. *The Emergence of Norms*. Oxford: Oxford University Press.

Bibliography

Van Parijs, Phillippe. 1981. *Evolutionary Explanation in the Social Sciences.* London: Tavistock.

——— 1982. "Perverse Effects and Social Contradictions: Analytical Vindication of Dialectics?" *British Journal of Sociology* 33: 589–603.

Wade. M. J. 1978. "A Critical Review of the Models of Group Selection." In Alan Ryan, ed., *The Philosophy of Social Explanation.* Oxford: Oxford University Press.

Wallerstein, Michael. 1988. "Union Growth from the Union's Perspective: Why Smaller Countries Are More Highly Organized." Unpublished manuscript, University of California at Los Angeles.

Watkins, J. W. N. 1957. "Historical Explanations in the Social Sciences." *British Journal for the Philosophy of Science* 9: 104–17.

Watson, Alan. 1971. *The Law of Succession in the Later Roman Republic.* Oxford: Clarendon Press.

Weber, Max. 1952. *Ancient Judaism.* Trans. and ed. Hans H. Gerth and Don Martindale. Glencoe, IL: Free Press.

——— 1978. *Economy and Society.* Berkeley and Los Angeles: University of California Press.

——— 1989. *The Protestant Ethic and the Spirit of Capitalism.* London: Unwin Hyman.

Weiler, Paul. 1983. "Promises to Keep: Securing Workers' Rights to Self-Organization Under the NLRA." *Harvard Law Review* 96: 1769.

——— 1984. "Striking a New Balance: Freedom of Contract and the Prospects for Union Representation." *Harvard Law Review* 98: 351–420.

Weingast, Barry R., and William J. Marshall. 1988. "The Industrial Organization of Congress: Or, Why Legislatures, Like Firms, Are Not Organized as Markets." *Journal of Political Economy* 96: 132–63.

Weisberg, Robert. 1986. "Commercial Morality, the Merchant Character and the History of the Voidable Preference." *Stanford Law Review* 39: 3–138.

White, Michelle J. 1980. "Public Policy Toward Bankruptcy: Me-First and Other Priority Rules." *Bell Journal of Economics* 11: 550–64.

Whitrow, G. J. 1988. *Time in History.* Oxford: Oxford University Press.

Williams, G. C. 1966. *Adaptation and Natural Selection.* Princeton, NJ: Princeton University Press.

Williamson, Oliver. 1975. *Markets and Hierarchies.* New York: Free Press.

——— 1985. *The Economic Institutions of Capitalism.* New York: Free Press.

——— 1986. "The Economics of Governance: Framework and Implications." In Richard N. Langlois, ed., *Economics as a Process: Essays in the New Institutional Economics.* Cambridge: Cambridge University Press.

Wilson, David S. 1983. "The Group Selection Controversy: History and Current Status." *Annual Review of Ecological Systems* 14: 159–88.

——— 1989. "Levels of Selection: An Alternative to Individualism in Biology and the Human Sciences." *Social Networks* 11: 257–72.

Wilson, David S., and Elliott Sober. 1989. "Reviving the Superorganism." *Journal of Theoretical Biology* 136: 337–56.

Wilson, Robert. 1985. "Reputation in Games and Markets." In Alvin Roth, ed., *Game-Theoretic Models of Bargaining.* Cambridge: Cambridge University Press.

Yasgoor, Stuart Jay. 1977. "Comparative Negligence Sails the High Seas: Have the Recovery Rights of Cargo Owners Been Jeopardized?" *California Western International Law Journal* 7: 179–202.

Bibliography

Zald, Mayer N. 1987. "Review Essay: The New Institutional Economics." *American Journal of Sociology* 93: 701–8.

Zerubavel, Eviatar. 1981. *Hidden Rhythms: Schedules and Calendars in Social Life.* Chicago: University of Chicago Press.

1985. *The Seven Day Circle: The History and Meaning of the Week.* New York: Free Press.

Index

Alchian, Armen, 12, 39, 90, 115, 118–19
altruism, 91–3
apartheid, 68, 73
Arrow, Kenneth, 10
Aumann, Robert, 161–2
Axelrod, Robert, 93, 174–5

Bain, George, 198
bankruptcy, 68, 157–64, 177–81
bargaining (*see also* institutional emergence and change; power): costs of, 134–5; games, 127–36, 147–51; and power asymmetry, 127, 131–6, 143–51; and resources, 131–3; and risk aversion, 129, 133–4, 135; and the state, 188–94; and time preferences, 135
Barry, Brian, 38
Barzel, Yoram, 111n
Bates, Robert, 41
Bayesian updating, 56, 144
Boudon, Raymond, 10, 15
Boyd, Robert, 88, 89

Coase, Ronald, 12, 111
Coase theorem, 31
Coleman, Jules, 33–4
collective action problems, 72–3, 147, 193, 197–202
collective bargaining, 70, 78, 79, 138–9, 144–5, 195–208
collective benefits, 5–8, 11–13, *see also* efficiency; Pareto optimality; social institutions; stability
Comaroff, John, 175–6
commitment: credibility of, 65, 129–36; recognition of, 139–45
common knowledge, 75
compensation, 114–15
competition: and bargaining power, 121–2, 132; requirements for market,

116, 118–22; as a selection mechanism, 115–21; and technical change, 119–20
Condorcet Paradox, 52–3
conflict: over distributional benefits, 19, 40–1, 64–6, 126–7; of interests, 8–9, 33–4; in mixed-motive games, 52, 107–8; resolution, 151; and the state, 188–94
contracts, 5, 77–8; of individual exchange, 109–15; and self-enforcement, 110–11; social institutions as, 108–9, 188
conventions: and coordination, 99–105; definition of, 97, 101; theory of, 97–108; *see also* informal institutions; norms
cooperation, 72n, 93, 128, 178–81; and informal institutions, 174–5
coordination, 50–2; classical accounts of, 4–7; and conventions, 99–105; and Pareto-superiority, 106–7; tacit, 100–1, 104

Dalhuisen, J. H., 159n
decision making: and expectations, 53–9; parametric, 17; strategic, 50–64, 117
dispute resolution procedures, 62
distribution (*see also* collective bargaining; property rights; social institutions): of alternative institutional forms, 117–18, 119–20, 121–2; and bargaining, 127–36; classical accounts of, 8–9; conflict over, 19, 40–1, 64–6, 123–4, 126–7; institutional effects on, 22–7, 136–9
Ditz, Toby, 169

efficiency: classical accounts of, 5–8; contemporary accounts of, 11–13; criti-

Index